POWER AND CONFLICT IN CONTINUING EDUCATION

Survival and Prosperity for All?

Sponsored by:
Wadsworth Publishing Company
and
The National University Extension Association

Wadsworth Publishing Company
Belmont, California
A Division of Wadsworth, Inc.

374.9
P887

The Wadsworth Series in Continuing Education
Philip E. Frandson, Consulting Editor
Dean of Extension, University of California, Los Angeles

Continuing Education Editor: Nancy Taylor
Production Editor: Jeanne Heise
Designer: Janet Wood

Printed in the United States of America

1 2 3 4 5 6 7 8 9 10—84 83 82 81 80

Library of Congress Cataloging in Publication Data
Main entry under title:

Power and conflict in continuing education.

   Proceedings of a symposium held Mar. 29–30, 1979 at Wadsworth, Belmont, Calif.
   1. Continuing education—United States—Congresses.
I. Alford, Harold J. II. Wadsworth Publishing Company.
III. National University Extension Association.
LC5251.P64   374'.973   79-27685
ISBN 0-534-00849-6

POWER AND CONFLICT IN CONTINUING EDUCATION:
Survival and Prosperity for All?

CONSULTING EDITOR:

Philip E. Frandson, Dean
University Extension
University of California, Los Angeles

AUTHORS:

Grover J. Andrews, Assistant Vice-Chancellor
for Extension and Public Service at North Carolina State University;
former Associate Executive Secretary
Southern Association of Colleges and Schools

John B. Ervin, Vice-President
The Danforth Foundation

Morton Gordon, Professor
Adult and Continuing Education
University of Michigan

William S. Griffith, Chairman
Department of Adult Education
University of British Columbia

Lillian Hohmann, Associate
Blessing/White, Inc.

Robert J. Kost, Director
Marketing Education Services
General Motors Corporation

Rosalind K. Loring, Dean
College of Continuing Education
University of Southern California

George H. Robertson, President
Mohawk Valley Community College

Milton R. Stern, Dean
University Extension
University of California, Berkeley

EDITED, WITH CHAPTER COMMENTARY BY:

Harold J. Alford, former Dean of Continuing Education
Rochester Institute of Technology

ASSISTED BY:

Patricia Niederpruem
College of Continuing Education
Rochester Institute of Technology

CONTENTS

PREFACE

This is a book about power and politics in education—more particularly, in continuing education. This book is not a survey of continuing education. It is not a comprehensive guidebook to continuing education. It is not a directory of services in continuing education. It is not a "how to" book in program planning for continuing education. Rather, it explores where the power lies in continuing education today. It explores the numerous political constituencies and the ways each major provider of continuing education attempts to prosper amidst the building threat of internal conflict, competition, and inflation.

Why this book? And why now? The yearly issue of new books on continuing education is already at an unprecedented level; why another? A meeting of minds agreed that none of the books grappled with the urgent and key issues in continuing education, the largest component of education in America today. Wadsworth Publishing Company and the board of directors of the National University Extension Association independently concluded that what was needed was a frank, face-to-face dialogue among the influential providers and shapers of continuing education, including the universities, the community colleges, business and industry, the professional associations, the accrediting councils, and the schools of adult education. Upon seeking out these institutions, Wadsworth and NUEA found, not surprisingly, that the issues of power and competition were of utmost concern. As a consulting editor for Wadsworth and as president of NUEA, I had the pleasant task of proposing a meeting of these organizations.

For Wadsworth Nancy Taylor undertook the market research of professional interest in such a book, and the NUEA Publications Committee was enlisted to deliberate on theme and content. (Four members of this committee should be specifically acknowledged for their extensive contributions: Harold Alford, Marjorie Farley, Helen Farlow, and Rodney Lane.) I met with Ms. Taylor and the Publications Committee to arrive at a final theme, to outline the content, and to select the leaders in continuing education who would be invited to participate.

Invitations were sent to national leaders in higher education throughout the United States and Canada—some NUEA members, others not—enclosing the outline of the book and asking each to address a specific issue. Drafts of all papers were circulated among the contributors, with the request that they be studied in advance of a three-day symposium to be held at Wadsworth in Belmont, California. The symposium took place on March 29–30, 1979. In addition to the authors, its participants included Harold Alford—selected by the NUEA Publications Committee to serve as editor—several members of the Wadsworth staff, and myself as moderator. Since all participants had received papers in advance, there was no need for formal presentations. The entire time was devoted to discussion, giving each participant the opportunity to contribute extensively and to enlarge upon the issues presented. Tape recordings were made of all sessions so that the editor might synthesize the discussion of each major topic.

This book is that symposium, in print. It includes the final revised version of the papers, highlights of the discussion, and transitional commentary by the editor, Harold Alford. The symposium-in-print is organized into three sections. The first section addresses the question "Who should provide what, for whom?" in the broad spectrum of continuing education. Although the authors do not purport to speak for their colleagues, each is an administrator of a major provider institution: a university, a major industry, a community college, and professional associations. The second section addresses the question "How should continuing education be evaluated, financed, organized, and staffed?" Each of these key issues is addressed by a professional educator with considerable experience in the area. The final section allows the participants time to speculate about the future of continuing education.

As moderator, I would like to comment on the unique character of this three-day meeting. It was special, first, in its format because of the total absence of "speeches," thanks to the advance circulation of what would normally have required "presenters." But it was special, too, in its combination of a high level of seriousness and knowledgeability with an informal atmosphere that permitted wit as well. This was a gathering of professionals uniquely willing to listen and with a true respect for the opinions of others. Finally, it brought forth an infusion into what otherwise might have been the "same old group" of a number of new voices, engendering freshness, new perspective, and new perceptions. I am grateful to have been a part of this exciting and valuable project.

Philip E. Frandson

About the Editor: Harold J. Alford

Harold Alford was the founding editor of *Continuum*, National University Extension Association's award winning quarterly (successor to the *Spectator*). He authored *Continuing Education in Action*, the story of the Kellogg Centers, and *The Proud Peoples: The History and Culture of the Spanish Speaking Peoples in the United States*. In addition, he wrote short stories and articles on continuing education for various national publications.

Alford served as director of the division of continuing education and professor of adult education at Kansas State University; as dean of instruction and director of programs of continuing education at Educational Testing Service; and as dean of the College of Continuing Education, professor of English, and professor of continuing education at Rochester Institute of Technology. Earlier he had been an administrator of evening classes, conferences and institutes, correspondence study, and special classes, as well as associate professor of English, during seventeen years of service at the University of Minnesota. Prior to that he was administrator of lectures and concerts and an associate in the English department at the University of Washington. At Washington he moderated a weekly radio program, and at the University of Minnesota he taught several courses on public television.

Alford received two degrees, with a major in English and a minor in music, from the University of Washington, and a Ph.D. in adult education from the University of Chicago. He served on the boards of directors and chaired several committees of both the National University Extension Association and the Adult Education Association of the U.S.A.

ONE

Continuing Education Providers

Who Should Provide What for Whom?

1 THE UNIVERSITIES

Paper by Milton R. Stern

BIOGRAPHY

 MILTON R. STERN is dean of University Extension at the University of California, Berkeley, a position he has held since 1971. After receiving two degrees from Columbia University and doing graduate work at Princeton, he began his continuing education career at New York University, where he served in a variety of administrative roles for twenty years. In 1966 he left his post as assistant dean of the Division of General Education and director of Liberal Arts in Education at NYU to become director of the University Center for Adult Education in Detroit, a joint appointment with the University of Michigan and Wayne State University.

Stern's teaching career began as *assistant d'anglais* at the Lycée de Bayonne in France in 1937. Subsequently he taught graduate-level adult education and English literature and semantics at NYU from 1947 to 1966. At the University of Michigan he was associate professor in the Graduate School of Education. He has also lectured at the universities of Edinburgh, Sheffield, Liverpool, and Keele.

A frequent speaker on continuing education before a wide variety of groups, Stern has served on the Executive Committee of the Adult Education Association of the USA, has chaired a number of committees of the National University Extension Association, including the Committee on Liaison for Accreditation and Standards in Continuing Education; has served as a consultant to the Fund for Adult Education, the Center for the Study of Liberal Education for Adults, and the Ford Foundation; and Exxon Educational Foundation. In addition, he is the author of *People, Programs and Persuasion: Promoting University Adult Education* (1960) and coeditor of *The First Years of College* (1966). A number of his articles have appeared in *Adult Leadership*, the *NUEA Spectator*, and *Adult Education*. He has been a contributing editor to the *Journal of Higher Education*.

INITIAL COMMENTARY

"Continuing education" has become an almost magical phrase. For many individuals, it promises a path to new skills, knowledge, and understanding—the things necessary for career changes and satisfaction, or just for coping with social change. For many institutions and organizations, desperately seeking new roles, new constituencies, or new sources of income, it promises opportunities for survival, prosperity, and growth. Yet as Milton Stern points out, "continuing education" has been around a long time; the only thing that is new is that it is being "discovered" both from within educational institutions—where in the past it was seen as peripheral, a frill, a marginal activity to be tolerated, or at best as "service" subordinate to "teaching" and "research"—and from without—in business and industry, in professional associations, and by profit-oriented entrepreneurs.

Stern explores the frontier antecedents of continuing education as well as the resort "learning-vacations" of the contemporary scene. He shows how continuing education has at once endorsed the stable practitioner, the philosopher, the zealot, the opportunist, and the charlatan; how it has dealt with the substantive, yet has accommodated the ephemeral; how it has created its own institutions, but has also been an adjunct activity of institutions only remotely linked to education. Writing from the point of view of the university, Stern shows how continuing education has seldom been seen as contributing materially to the central purposes of the university—scholarship and schooling. Yet over the years, continuing educators have extended the university in bits and pieces from the daytime into the night, from the campus to the hinterlands, from youth to adults, from a rigid calendar to flexible scheduling, from a fixed curriculum to need-oriented learning, from penury to plenty. And they have done this with a minimum of financial support, with little or no professional or academic recognition, and with little or no support from the faculty and the administration. And now ironically, having achieved so much, continuing educators find themselves again being bypassed as all those who have just discovered continuing education seek to take over the enterprise.

In this arena of intensified competition but also of great expectations, university continuing education stands embattled and at bay. Just where the power will eventually lie, and which programs will survive and prosper, no one can tell at this point. Indeed, continuing education may not be a magical phrase; rather, it may be a chimera or a tantalizing El Dorado—a vision of no substance, a place of no gold. But Stern argues that there is both substance and gold in continuing education, and that if the power conflict can be resolved in a rational, constructive way, the outcome will most certainly be survival and prosperity for all, including society as a whole.

Milton R. Stern

Universities in Continuing Education

From Barn Raising to Claim Jumping: The Social Ecology of Continuing Education

> *Old images never die; they have to be publicly broken. In the case of adult education, this is a matter of some urgency.*
> Raymond Williams,
> *New Statesman*, May 1959

A major change, with unclear implications, is taking place in continuing education; the field is in the process of accelerated but confused movement from cooperation to competition. The present period is one of mutation.

This change, essentially a consequence of post–World War II expansion, is intimately tied to the social, political, technological, and economic developments of the past generation. It amounts to an underlying change of climate that affects everyone in continuing education. Who would have predicted such a change when contemplating Ralph Waldo Emerson riding horseback through the snows of the Wisconsin woods to talk to a group of adults about self-reliance? Emerson and the Lyceum movement represent a romantic, if not a sentimental, image of the adult education of the nineteeth century. Chautauqua and "night school" carried right through World War I into the 1920s. And in the 1930s, community development was still a serious watchword of adult education as people struggled with the Great Depression.

Today? Today the image projected is significantly different. A recent advertisement in the leisure magazine *Ski Run* invites physicians to take an eastern Mediterranean cruise to study "Progress in Pediatric Cardiology, Pediatric Hematology and Pediatric Urology" and, presumably, to obtain category I credit from the American Medical Association even as their cruise ship sets them ashore in Alexandria or Istanbul. Just beneath that advertisement, and others headed "Medical and Dental Seminars at Sea," *Ski Run* lists a "Real Estate Tax Saving Seminar at Sun Valley, March 17–24."[1]

"Great spring skiing and continuing education credit for real

[1] *Ski Run* 8, no. 2 (February 1979), p. 12.

estate licensees and CPA's." This Sun Valley program was not offered by the University of Idaho or the University of California, or
by a national or state professional association; it was announced by
an individual who stated his credentials as "tax attorney, realtor and
college professor of the California Institute of Real Estate Education."
Relicensure credit was offered as acceptable by the California Department of Real Estate and the California Board of Accountancy, and the
tuition included six days' use of all ski lifts at Sun Valley—full information from a travel agency.

Such seductive and competitive advertising was not a crucial
part of continuing education before the turn of the century, but it was
nevertheless present. Indeed, even universities, as well as profit-
oriented proprietary and correspondence schools, promoted programs actively. Harvard University, for example, did not think
it demeaning to advertise its summer session in the pages of the
Atlantic Monthly in the 1890s. Nevertheless, without our being
overly wistful about the past, it is clear that the dominant image
of continuing or adult education for more than a century was one,
not of competition, but of cooperation. The very change of names,
from the rather drab, steady-state "adult education" to the forward-
sounding, developmental "continuing education," expresses the
new go-getter attitude.

In the past the providers of continuing education did not significantly intrude upon each other's work; they did not compete for
audiences. There was, in effect, an open market. Generally speaking,
most of the providers operated from a floor of Judeo-Christian moral-
ity and the sunnier side of the Protestant ethic, rather than from
expectation of financial gain. They were barn raisers, not claim
jumpers. The providers were missionaries. They were apostles of a
church militant in a war against ignorance and superstition. They
welcomed other laborers in the vineyard with hymns of praise. They
saluted and encouraged each other's good works. They were serious
about the ideas of fellowship, and they were, in solemn pact, members of the adult education *movement*. Perhaps, also, they shared the
field agreeably and happily with one another because there was just
not enough money to fight about in those early years and even
through the 1920s and 1930s. The present huge pool of monied
adults, already educated and needful of more, was not yet a reality,
although the adult education movement itself was helping to bring it
about. The theme of the 1920s was still "Americanization," Leo Ros-
ten's Hyman Kaplan being archetypal. The words "night school" told
a story of earnest endeavors to reach high school diplomas and
college degrees. Then, in the 1930s, economic, social, and political
concerns were major themes among people holding hands for
mutual comfort against the disasters of the Great Depression.

The adult education movement was a social movement in its goals and curriculum, and the improvement of the individual was regarded as part of a common good; even today, in developing countries the goals of continuing education are often linked to national purpose. In the United States, not until after World War II was there that runaway technological development that called upon new types of skills for the ordinary practice of professional and business life; it was then that "manpower development" goals took over as national policy. In the adult programs run by school districts in the 1920s and 1930s, typing was as far as technology took the students. Today the equivalent is complex and sophisticated instruction in computer, semiconductor, and laser technology, both in application and development. And this merely names the obvious.

We tend to overlook the most significant factor in enlarging the audience for continuing education: during this century the college-educated population has increased almost incalculably. At the beginning of the century, high school graduation was barely the rule, because the public high schools did not emerge as a considerable force until after World War I. The conception of formal education was quite different from today's. It was *expected* that the very few graduates of secondary ("prep") schools in the 1880s and 1890s would go on to college; there were so few secondary schools, in fact, that in 1890, only 3 percent of their graduates *failed* to go on to college!

There was a golden age of adult education: Chautauqua, university extension, labor unions, public schools, charitable organizations, settlement houses, YM(W)CAs, libraries, profit-oriented and university-based correspondence schools, business colleges, civic organizations, fraternal clubs, women's clubs—all of these, and more, were actively and cheerfully doing their own thing, without really competing at all. They could all subscribe to that moving line of novelist Dorothy Canfield Fisher, who, in her presidential address to the American Association for Adult Education in 1927, said, "I always have in the back of my mind the problem of educating everybody."

That noble goal remains unfulfilled: there remain millions of ill-educated and uneducated people in the United States. Adult basic education, as it is now called to avoid the stigma of "remediation," remains important. To some degree, such basic education lies outside the arena of competition, save as publishers and providers of audiovisual materials compete for the business of organizations trying to reach this audience. But the main concern of providers today is elsewhere.

The More Things Change . . . ?

Changes now taking place may even be classifiable as organic, revolutionary. Twenty years ago, one observer said:

> *We are living at the end of the Neolithic Age. The changes taking place in the world today are not merely changes from one form of society, one form of technology, to another. They are so wide-sweeping that they are taking us from one major epoch of human history into another. This is an order of change which is completely different from anything our ancestors ever knew—unless we go back about 10,000 years, when man invented property, when they invented ownership, when they invented work, and mechanics based on the wheel.*[2]

Now in 1980 this seems less extravagant than when it was uttered. True, they are the words of a technologically-oriented scholar, not technically a humanist, but they must be considered as a backdrop for the relatively short-run changes we are considering in the field of continuing education. Against such a conception, what does it matter that there are new providers, new dispensations of fees, new curricula, and so forth? They are all part of something richer and stranger that will carry us . . . where? To keep ourselves steadily on course, we must look at a shorter span—the century past and the next thirty years. That will perhaps be enough change for the human nervous system to cope with. Let us examine, then, where we are now in continuing education and, by cautious extrapolation, where we may be going. *Perhaps* the kind of changes we are talking of will not be regarded as earthshaking, *sub specie aeternitatis*. What will it matter 100 years from now, for example, if professional societies replace universities as providers of professional education?

Still, it would be valuable to be aware of the circumstances in which we practice and to learn more about our own profession. The major providers have changed in many parts of the field, and where they have remained constant to their goals, the content of instruction is likely to have changed considerably. In other instances providers have both wittingly and unwittingly changed goals, curriculum —everything. Let us trace briefly some social changes that have affected the provision of continuing education.

It is self-evident that both World War I and World War II gave impetus to the education of mature people. In both wars millions of adults had to be trained for precise tasks in a great variety of skills new to them and, indeed, new to the world. This level of training activity abated somewhat in the 1920s following World War I, but the opposite happened following World War II, when billions of federal dollars supported the GI Bill, not only for veterans enrolled in universities but also for those in proprietary schools and other types of institutions.

[2]Bernard J. Muller-Thym, as quoted by Milton R. Stern, "The Neanderthal Spaceman," *Adult Education*, Autumn 1963, p. 4.

The new money bred a host of new providers, who soon began to replace the old; for during the 1950s many of the old providers were declining or allowing their programs to lapse. Many social institutions, some even consciously, were going through reassessments of organizational purpose. Just as in the 1950s and 1960s railroads were effectively and permanently bypassed by the airlines in the competition for passenger travel, so, in the same period, many organizations that had been major providers of continuing education were bypassed by others.

The changing nature of society contributed to the replacement of the established providers by new ones. New technologies and mass communication reduced the continuing education activity of churches, labor organizations, and many of the charitable providers. The work of libraries diminished. The providers who have maintained their place through 1980 include public schools (although these have diminished in importance as community colleges have taken over tasks from them) and universities (primarily through university extension and agricultural extension). Some parts of society, particularly business and industry, have considerably increased their share of the market. Independent proprietary schools survive and flourish, the most successful ones training for business, new technologies, and service functions. A few providers, patterned after the more altruistic groupings of the past—for example, the League of Women Voters—have remained effective and have held their own, usually through more intensive collaborative efforts with other organizations.

What is the reality today of cooperation and competition? There is extraordinarily little documentation or statistical data, thus explanations must be drawn from direct observation by participants in the field and from their naturally self-interested reports. Some parts of the mosaic of continuing education have been described; for example, the Conference Board on Education in Industry has figures limited to business activities. But no scholars have attempted organized surveys of the entire sprawling field. The professors of adult education either do not think this worthy of their efforts or have given up in despair at the scope of the task of data collection. (Conceptually, the field has been difficult to define. Pragmatically described—and the providers, at least, are nothing if not pragmatic—it overlaps all earlier elementary, secondary, and higher education at the same time it has developed a post-tertiary, postgraduate, post-degree arena of activity that is all its own.) The National Center for Educational Statistics has not brought together figures in any orchestrated way to explore the relative level of, or mixture of, competition or cooperation. From the universities, or at least from those that provide centralized instruction through an extension arm in continuing education, there is little evidence and little concern. In effect, the absence of data allows a conventional wisdom to persist —namely, that there is ample room for everyone in this field.

This view may be what motivates the sponsors of a program advertised recently in the *Chronicle of Higher Education*: "How Your University or College Can Capitalize on the 30 Billion Dollar Continuing Education Market." When queried, the sponsors were uncertain about the statistics cited in bold headline. The dollars represented may be $30 billion—or $20 billion—or $40 billion. But the generosity of spirit activating the sponsors in helping their colleagues may be more an instance of feeding off a kill of the pride than of belief in an unlimited food supply. In fact, there are no comprehensive figures to suggest the scope of the market. Cautiously, one can say that it is not as generally imagined. The advertisement is sound in suggesting new audiences for universities, but it does not begin to tell the story. Nor can we do more, in the absence of data, than suggest some lines of useful research.

It is possible to assert that there is brisk, if not fierce, competition for the continuing education dollar. This fact is obscured by the absence of qualified information, and disguised by the large number of providers, the large number of subfields in which they work, and the relative absence of competition for dollars by many of them, particularly those employed by higher education institutions and professional associations. The latter count continuing education income incrementally to their basic functions and other productive activities. Thus a professional organization may well regard its primary function as service to members and regard as only incidental the continuing education programs mounted at annual meetings. These may be an attractive source of additional income, but they are not regarded as a major necessity. As such organizations get used to a higher standard of living—and they do—they may take a new look. Universities, also, have regarded continuing education as adjunct to their basic purpose. Even in land grant institutions the last thirty years have seen an erosion of the sense of high purpose represented by the phrase "public service." And even public universities continue to slight continuing education and to ignore the competitive threat from outside the campus. That threat comes from private entrepreneurs and the professional associations who function nicely by using the faculty resource (capital) of universities without paying the universities. (True, they pay the professors, who are pleased with that.)

The universities do not regard the professional associations as competitive. The professionals in the university are at one and the same time faculty members and members of professional associations. They are primarily dedicated to the advancement of their

profession, and by and large they think of the university as a convenient site providentially available for the practice or teaching of that
profession. That is a usual attitude of professionals and therefore
induces them—mindful, too, of their own consultant income—to
favor their associations as a logical recipient of whatever monies may
be obtained through continuing education. This circumstance will be
generally true in large, complex institutions, whether public or private. Furthermore, the permissive tradition of university faculties
allows a college or department to function as it will, provided it leaves
others to do as they will.

There remains a free market in continuing education, despite the
developing bureaucratization through the compulsory requirements
of relicensing laws in many states. But this free market is "naturally"
divided among professional groups. As it affects professional education, we now see the development on a national scale of tacit agreements among professional groups that they leave each other alone as
each generates continuing education programs in its own discrete
area. The only intrusion upon this development will be the consumer movement if, as it begins to understand the situation, it
chooses guerilla war upon the little empires growing up in the
professional groups. These empires will be national, with satrapies
in the several states. The consumer movement, of course, is ham-
pered by its leaders' tendency to be professionals themselves. At
the same time that such professionals in their consumer persona
are vigorously trying to control others, they are unconsciously inclined to protect their own constituencies. The competition among
providers favors professional associations. The trend is there and
will probably continue. A gloomy scenario would hold that "live-
and-let-live" is the optimum possibility; that the professional
groupings will allow one another to exercise their own hegemony,
government intrusion being held at a minimum by the interlocking directorates of professionals, who move back and forth from
their roles in professional associations, to university faculty appoint-
ment, to licensing board, to private entrepreneur. Seen this way,
the situation may best be likened to a murky tank full of guppies,
some larger, some smaller, all darting around, feeding sometimes
in a frenzy of happy plenty, sometimes ganging up on a bigger fish,
sometimes doing away with smaller fish, sometimes parasitic or
piloting a big fish or school.

The untidy little universe we are describing must be termed a
mutation. We are at an undefined, transitional stage in the social
ecology of continuing education. Cooperation blends indefinably
with competition, as competitive units get together to cooperate in
competing with others. As much as we can extract order from Chaos
and Old Night, in an absence of statistical data, with a poverty of

concept and a vacuum of policy, here is—not a taxonomy—but an enforcedly anecdotal treatment of what seems to be going on.

The Declining Traditional Providers

The traditional providers, those that have been traditional for at least half a century, include several large categories that have not maintained their previously vigorous level of activity, such as the churches, the public schools, libraries, and labor unions. The explanations are various. The churches have suffered a crisis of identity and by and large, apart from occasional forays into human relations workshops and the like, have limited themselves to quite traditional adult Sunday school instruction. The libraries, victims of fiscal starvation in a thirty-year period of inflation, have been reduced to being providers of space for other providers, involved occasionally in co-sponsorship, but essentially limited in their own original instructional programs. Furthermore, they have up to now been culturally by-passed, as have the churches, by the movement to secular, materialist interests. Will this pattern change in the next generation? It is difficult to predict, although one can probably say that we have come to an end of the narcissist cycle in popular interests, and that may signal a shift to social concerns, which do relate to the interests of churches and libraries.

The public schools, still a large force in continuing education, have lost a great deal of their audience to the community colleges. In the more chic suburban areas around the great cities, where imaginative energy may be deployed for a sophisticated audience, there are frequent examples of humanities and arts programming, competitive, indeed, with the continuing education activity of local universities, and certainly with that of community colleges.

The museums, particularly the great urban art museums, are an exception to the rule of decline among the traditional providers. The great growth of museum-going in the United States, the energetic promotion of large exhibitions, the improvement of gallery display, and the collateral growth of museum education programs have combined to create a large new continuing education activity. The museums, which ten years ago were generally content, if not grateful, to undertake programs in concert with the art history departments of neighboring universities, freely providing visitor and donor lists, have now assumed a decisively independent posture. They have learned rapidly that it is just as easy (and cheaper) to hire a professor as an individual as it is to undertake institutional cooperative activity with university departments or extension units. The museums, after all, now have thriving memberships, and mailing lists they no longer give away, but sell. They have their own logistical, printing, and mailing provisions and space—lovely space—for instruction. Indeed, they have come into their own as a force to be reckoned with and have learned to charge a great deal when they are asked to share in any continuing education effort. They are likely to develop an even larger share of the market in the foreseeable future.

The continuing education of labor unions, and the in-service further education provisions of large industrial firms, have tended to be self-contained and isolated. Both maintain their own instructional and staff provisions, supplemented by ad hoc personnel from colleges, universities, and other providers, steer their own course, and only occasionally collaborate with other providers, although frequently enough by union contract with each other. Recently, for the first time in many years, there has been some collaborative effort with higher education, beyond the cautious adventures of industrial and labor institutes in some of our universities. Working with Wayne State University's Weekend College, the United Automobile Workers has stimulated part-time degree activity among its members, as has the United Electrical Workers. There are echoes of the day-release schemes of some English universities, by arrangement with unions and management, and the program has apparently had an encouraging response from union members. As for the universities, the already declining enrollment in conventional programs makes it the more probable that many will adapt to part-time degree work on a large scale. Still, as a group, unions must be declared to be quiescent in continuing education.

Erosion of the University Extension Base

No longer may centralized extension units be equated exclusively with university continuing education, much as their continuing education deans and directors may polemically claim they are, or more candidly deplore they are not. The traditional pattern of extension has been subjected to take-overs—decentralization by policy and design, or through inadvertence and inanition. The major erosion of the centralized provision has come from professional schools, although frequently not for their own benefit so much as for the reward of individual professors and the professional associations. The chief threat to the continuance of university extension units —and to universities for that matter—comes from these cartel-like combinations.

To speak first of other impingements, alumni associations have offered increased numbers of continuing education programs as they have come to understand that their members are less and less interested in fun and games. Sometimes these are given exclusively by the association, sometimes in concert with extension units, or with a specialized professional school alumni group.

Meanwhile, the faculty entrepreneur, who has learned all about teaching adults from extension assignments, is much in demand by providers at *other* campuses. He or she may go off to teach in a corporate in-service program or become a faculty member of Moonlight University—that is, go circuit-riding by jet—for an institution specializing in off-campus work. The faculty entrepreneur comes from an honorable line; after all, making both ends meet by extra work has been part of the teaching tradition since Socrates. Today's faculty entrepreneur, however, needs more sophisticated bookkeeping. Ingenious avoidance of the income tax has been developed. Professor Professor may say, "Please make my honorarium check payable to John Q. Professor, Ph.D., P.C. (Professional Corporation)." To be sure, all disciplines are not equal in their need or ability to take advantage of this procedure; professors of classics do not find it as useful to become a professional corporation as do medical doctors or professors of management.

In the last generation another threat to the universities has been the amazingly rapid development of community colleges. For several years, in the 1960s, they were being established one a week like the mechanics institutes 150 years ago in Britain and America. The mechanics institutes have seen their day, but the community colleges have continued right up to this decade and have responded directly, as the institutes had, to society's needs. They provide part-time lower-division work available for transfer, they provide terminal instruction in many skilled occupations and service fields, and they also are providers in the broader area of noncredit continuing education. In many places community colleges have been and still are competitive with university extension programs. The relation between the community college and upper-division undergraduate provisions in many states remains unsettled, as does the matter of territorial rights in several areas of post-degree (continuing) instruction. Community colleges in many states have asserted their right to offer courses in professional areas not only for paraprofessionals but also for nurses, teachers, pharmacists, and other licensed professionals. But it is difficult to legislate academic turf, and when denied a mandate because this level of instruction exceeds their faculty's competence, skilled community college administrators have discovered ways to circumvent regulation.

In California, of course, an additional frustration to community colleges has been Proposition 13. In fact, both in California and in other states, as similar legislation and subsequent fiscal cuts are ordained, community colleges, lacking public money, may become more restricted in their competition with universities. But that is by no means certain. In the jurisdictional dark ages that are upon us, the contrary is also possible—an even more assertive competitive stance. There would appear to be no statewide master plan in force that can inhibit a vital organism like the community college from growing, even to the extent of permanently changing the larger body social, higher education as a whole.

Community colleges and universities live in an uneasy relationship with each other and with their competitors. The literature tends to scant the issues of conflict: The scholars of the community college touch lightly on the matter of competition, as do their colleagues in the other specialized fields of higher education, such as graduate education, fiscal policy, and continuing education.

"In my Father's house are many mansions." So John quotes Jesus. It is noteworthy that the Episcopal Book of Common Prayer uses this generous and compassionate expression as a familiar funeral text. So be it with higher education? Yet how can one deny the great vitality of such competition in higher education? It would be difficult at this time to say whether regulation to inhibit changes potentially helpful to adult students might or might not be premature. The issue is clear, even though the answer is obscure: Is the established organization of higher education, with clear jurisdictional divisions among providers, compatible with the best interests of students or only with the special interests of some providers?

Let us deal, for example, with what might be called "the Doctrine of the Distributed University," meaning off-campus education. This was invented by Thomas Aquinas and the Dominicans who taught in the houses of their order and in universities throughout Christendom in the Middle Ages. The idea of teaching off-campus has moved rapidly in the last few years. Following certain adventures after World War I, many institutions have had study centers in Europe for decades. Vigorous exploitation of the off-campus idea came first from energetic private universities, followed, particularly in the last five to eight years, by public universities. This activity has gone past the post–World War II phenomenon of instruction on military bases. Instruction is now given in factories and plants around the country in collaboration with corporate enterprise. Some universities offer classes in twenty or thirty states. Both graduate and undergraduate programs are given. These colleges and universities occasionally call upon their own faculty, but the economics of the situation are improved when they can co-opt the faculty of local universities. This tends to create hostility from these institutions, who increasingly are petitioning not only the regional accrediting bodies but also departments of education and other appropriate licensing boards within their states to limit and police such "invasions."

The conventional arguments given are typically and piously academic: that a matter of quality is at issue, that universities offering instruction from outside the state cannot be as good as those inside. The developments so far do not uniformly bear this out. The issue of quality is, however, an early step in an inevitable conflict. Fairly soon it will be clear that *polity*, not quality, is a central question for higher education as it contemplates what to do about the spread of off-campus education. In five or six states registration and quality evaluation are now being established for out-of-state providers who offer ad hoc programs within the borders of a given state. Political politics appear to be taking over from academic politics in the vacuum of academic self-regulation. There are probably no dispassionate observers of this phenomenon in higher education today. The issues must work themselves out in practice, not in thought or reasoned judgment. Competition will result in the survival of the fittest—probably not the academic fittest, but those with the most managerial, promotional, and political acumen. It may be that competition itself will regulate the commerce better than regulation, and we will probably have the opportunity to find out.

Recently, another set of enterprising providers (if they may be called providers in a substantive sense) have added themselves to the mix. These are jobbers, entrepreneurial organizations, sometimes spun out of the large conglomerates that discovered the "knowledge industry" in the 1960s in the wake of Camelot, but more frequently smaller-scale operators who relate more efficiently not only to extension units but also to the professional schools of universities. They deal most frequently in management and technology. Sometimes they find it convenient to play off one professional school against an extension unit in a given institution. And they do represent, for a school, an opportunity for incremental income (whether above or below the counter).

The jobbers relate to, and represent, several important universities in the United States, and they work in various ways. A favorite activity is to export successful programs of a given institution, particularly one with a reputation, to one or other of the great convention cities of the country. There are fifteen to twenty cities in the United States which are favorites of the jobber community. The jobbers do valuable chores for universities like efficient promotion of programs, mass development of mailing lists, and logistical on-site support. They obtain benefits, too: they use the institution's mailing privileges; they may use university faculty; and above all, they use the university's name. Accordingly, the managerial and technological communities of such cities as Los Angeles, Atlanta, and Dallas have become accustomed to receiving jobber announcements, probably without being aware of the jobber involvement—advertising programs in the name of, for example, the University of Chicago School of Business, New York University, the Wharton School of the University of Pennsylvania, or Columbia University.

In a typical arrangement the universities receive a percentage of the gross income for very little work, and they seem to be content with what they receive. Another pattern, of course, is that of a jobber who will divide net income with an institution and will join with it in devising programs to be given locally in the university's own city or within a close radius of the institution. This is particularly attractive to professional schools of universities whose extension units may be weak. In effect, this is a contractual arrangement, perfectly legal, and unexceptionable from the point of view of institutional financial practice.

The important question is that of polity—of relations among peers in higher education. The issue of quality is not so relevant. It may be that some programs are poor, but that question must be subordinated to an overarching consideration of the meaning of programmatic sprawl across state lines, across hitherto accepted "independent" territories. The issue of "turf" as it applies to continuing education is going to be a most important question for many universities in the next decade.

Naturally, the phenomenon of mandated continuing education for state relicensure of professionals has contributed to the growth of interest. The entrepreneurial community ranks this kind of compulsory adult education with the voucher system as a likely source of profit. Relicensure of professionals in the United States is only at its beginning. We may expect that as patterns emerge in the near future, all professionals in all states will be more closely regulated, presumably in the public interest (and more probably in the professionals' own interest) in ways that are not even foreseen today. There will be conventions established and agreements arrived at among national professional associations, their state bodies, state licensing boards, and eventually, federal bureaus. The Federal Trade Commission has already become interested in continuing education, but not to anything like the extent that it and other federal agencies will be involved by the year 2000. We can safely predict ample employment opportunities in federal and state regulatory bodies governing higher and continuing education in the next twenty to thirty years.

Television and other media instruction appear to have seen their day, at least for the present. They have proved much too costly and cannot be undertaken without private-foundation or public funding. PBS instructional programming cannot be sustained by local institutions or even by the ingenious national franchise developed by University Extension at the University of California, San Diego. Of course, programs in community colleges and universities can benefit from media backing; and without question, video discs and videotape, or whatever technology the industry settles on, will be useful as an adjunct to instruction, but it will likely be conventional classroom instruction. There are few opportunities for private entrepreneurs or for universities to do much directly in media instruction. Audiotape, for example, for doctors or lawyers in transit in their automobiles, is sometimes said to be a useful development, and it may well be; but it is not a major line of continuing education for the future—and definitely not cost-effective for providers.

New colleges and universities keep being born all the time. "Nontraditional" has been the watchword for a decade. There are "nontraditional students"; "nontraditional experimental learning"; "nontraditional part-time, off-campus programs." There may even be activities so different as to be *non*-nontraditional. Be that as it may, it would appear that the nontraditional has been around long enough to become traditional. Yet some formations *are* in fact new: (1) the establishment of the International Correspondence School of Scranton, Pennsylvania, as a credit-giving institution from its proprietary correspondence base—ICS is now accredited to offer an associate degree by the Middle States Association of Schools and Colleges and will probably seek status to provide the bachelor's and graduate degrees; (2) the establishing of an M.B.A., also with appropriate accreditation, by the American Management Association, which has, for over forty years, provided instruction to the management community, using practitioners for the most part but occasionally members of the professoriate as well; and (3) the phenomenon of hospitals' offering the M.D. degree—already two hospitals, Rush Hospital in Chicago and Mt. Sinai Hospital in New York City, offer a qualified medical degree. Will hospitals replace university-based medical schools as loci of instruction? The subject is already being discussed by continuing educators in the health sciences. A conference coordinator in health sciences at a large university wrote recently:

> Medical schools never have controlled their residency programs. Those have always been structured and organized by hospitals. Is there any reason why hospitals shouldn't be the institutions accredited to do all continuing medical education? And if they can do that, why not let the hospitals do the training of the medical student and so on. Most laboratory training programs also benefit from association with the hospital directly. In a way it is rather stimulating to follow the thesis through to its projected conclusion. It forecasts a picture of health education quite different to our present concepts. What I am seeing now across the country is an effort by the academic health centers to pull continuing medical education back into the control of the teaching institution. It may very well be too little and too late.[3]

Another change in the university atmosphere of continuing edu-

[3]Personal letter to the author. Excerpt is used with permission.

cation, one that signifies cooperation rather than competition, has resulted from the American Council on Education's developing an Office of Educational Credit (OEC). The OEC is responsible for evaluating programs undertaken by noncollegiate providers: the military, in-service in industry, private entrepreneurs, government agencies, and the like, who wish to establish appropriate credit status for the instruction they offer. This function is also helpful as a short-cut for colleges and universities that have established policies for giving equivalent credit or advanced standing on admission to applicants who have such programs in their background. It is now a large undertaking. The OEC publishes *The National Guide to Credit Recommendations for Noncollegiate Courses*, which is valuable not only to established institutions but also to nontraditional programs like the Regents' external degree program in New York State. Such useful activity is likely to remain a voluntary function unless there is a major intrusion into evaluation and accreditation by the federal or state government.

The Rise of the Professional Associations

Professionals, defined broadly, as they must be, are the most important group to be considered in this discussion. Professional associations have been mentioned before, intertwined with other elements. As we consider continuing education, professionals are not only the most important group; they represent a growing proportion of the population. An industrial, technological society needs not only doctors, lawyers, and clergy (the student body of the medieval university) but also engineers, teachers, and (more recently) foresters, managers, and public relations and real estate people —all the new groups represented by the complexities of contemporary culture. Even farming is now a profession; agriculture is high technology. Many of the new professions are suppliers of abstract goods and symbolic services—banking, insurance, communications; in the United States, people in the finance sector alone outnumber farmers.

In place of the agricultural peasantry of the past we have now a society of professional peasants. The line between workers and professionals becomes ever cloudier. University faculties, frustrated by the job market, now welcome unions and collective bargaining, a method previously relegated to "workers." The idea of what constitutes a professional becomes ambiguous when we see doctors and teachers strike, and even judges organize.

The cultural change in self-image from that of the medieval guild to that of the contemporary professional may be seen in these statements of organizational purpose:

thirteenth century, the Drapers Company: "to the honour of God and continuance of brotherly love."

1660, the Royal Society: to discover "the Sciences of natural things and of useful arts to the Glory of God the creator, and the advantages of the human race."

1818, the Institution of Civil Engineers: "To direct the great resources of Power in nature for the use and convenience of man."

1918, the Institute of Physics: "For the advancement and diffusion of a knowledge of pure and applied Physics and for the elevation of the profession of Physicist."[4]

The professions represent the ongoing quality, the basic skeletal structure, of human culture. Whether the dominant power has been religious, military, or business, the professions have been a constant. From the time of the priesthood of Egypt with its scribes and functionaries in the Houses of Life and Death, the professionals have carried on the traditions and knowledge that enabled human societies to move forward with a minimum of interruption. Conventional wisdom may allege that only government bureaucracies survive changes in power structure, but it is the independent professions and guilds that have maintained themselves in society and government as well. The captains and the kings depart and leave the world to lawyers, doctors, and shamans, now disguised as computer technologists.

In a way there is a quality of helplessness about this vast new population of "educated" professionals in society. Outside his or her own field, every professional is a consumer of everyone else's service. It is this paradoxical quality of individual skill and knowledge, simultaneously coupled with almost awesome dependence upon others, that gives most meaning to the discussion of continuing education. To some extent this quality explains the passion that inspires the consumer movement, which has its immediate effect in the area of relicensure. Its implications in politics—what new groupings may emerge, what changes take place in present party structure—are still incalculable. This is an anxious, exciting, humbling, and exalting time in which to live. And to be in the field of continuing education today is to be riding the ninth wave in to the shores of a new world.

Such a conception makes clear why the university provisions both for professional education and for continuing professional education are changing, no matter what policies may be expressed. It

[4]National Institute of Adult Education, *Liberal Education in a Technical Age* (London: Max Parrish & Co., 1955), pp. 17–18.

explains why the relation of professional societies and associations to universities, to each other, and to state and federal government is changing. Ironically, for all the brisk policy making, the changes are unplanned and messy. Changes of organization, of coalition, represent the usual mixed package of rationality, greed, and power play that makes up politics.

Those professions, like accountancy, that provide discrete and clear-cut services have predictably organized themselves, through their professional societies, in clear-cut ways; less so those, like medicine (which has already gone through the sea of change into renaming—the health sciences), whose services have been less clear-cut. It is not surprising that the American Institute of Certified Public Accountants (AICPA) has organized a neat and tidy package, and has contracted not only with state accounting associations, but also presently with some twenty-eight state accounting (licensing) boards, to codify AICPA's provision of continuing education. In their arrangement, the Institute has considered only a limited role for university providers and even less for private entrepreneurs, the predominant role being that of the professional associations. The national office of the AICPA has a continuing education branch which budgeted $7 million for its activity in 1979. Some of this is for seminars and workshops throughout the country, but most is for the provision of materials, books, programmed instruction, and so forth, to be used to a limited extent by individual accountants, and more broadly by the state association for classroom instruction throughout the country. The accountants do not seem at present to be concerned about other rival interests, as is, for instance, the medical profession.

Medicine, the health sciences, is a volatile field. A whole profession in human services is regrouping in response to new technology, growing population, new demands from the public, and newly established folkways of semi-public-supported health insurance. In the prevailing climate it is unlikely that medical doctors will maintain their hegemony over the field indefinitely. Inevitably, as more paraprofessionals are enlisted for various functions, as subprofessions become more active, as diagnosis is computerized, as laboratory work becomes more detailed and complex, the political result of interaction among these forces will be to modify the current power structure of the health sciences. Inevitably there will also be pervasive, if incalculable, changes in the provision of continuing education for the field, which deserve the most careful prophetic scrutiny. Although the Delphic computer tools of modern futurologists seem no more effective in arriving at a firm conclusion than did the astrological tables of the Middle Ages, we can be sure that there will be change. We can reasonably suppose that education and continuing education in the health sciences will be restructured, that the ancient role of the practitioner-physician will become still more specialized, and that concomitant changes will occur in nursing, pharmacy, and the subspecializations in the health field. A new professional will probably emerge, the broadly trained health manager. One hopes that the new people at the top will be animated by as compassionate a world view as was Hippocrates of Cos.

If the health sciences are viewed in this way, does it matter which part of the university—or if a university at all—has its share of the continuing education market? Larger questions are stirring than whether the medical school faculty maintains full control over continuing education in the health sciences. The broad changes in health, intermingled with social and technological change, will eventually dictate the organization of continuing education. At present, watchful waiting is the appropriate role.

Each profession presents a different set of issues to the observer who seeks to estimate the appropriate continuing education role for the several categories of providers. Without question, the professions themselves will have the most influence. The obvious channel for such influence must be professional associations, and where the associations interlock with licensing boards and with specialized university faculties, there is little probability of dispassion, fresh outlook, or a broad-gauged philosophic awareness of society's needs.

The continuing education of lawyers is much less well developed as a field than that of the health sciences. Law is much less complicated in its relations with other professions; it is only now beginning to develop subspecializations requiring additional study. It has had extremely beneficial relations with universities in the provision of legal education; its special relation to government has always made it less respectful of authority than any other profession. As a community, lawyers have been immunized by thousands of years of lay hostility from feeling that they need more than they *themselves* determine to be necessary for training in the profession. Continuing legal education has had no major overview save from lawyers. The universities' provision of that education has been closely supervised by the profession, through the bar association or the law school faculty. Thus the program in Continuing Education of the Bar (CEB) of the University of California is jointly sponsored with the State Bar Association. In similar programs elsewhere the legal profession may not play so direct a role, but more than any other group, including medicine, it is automatically saluted by the administration of American universities. But notwithstanding its special characteristics, today even the legal profession is beginning to develop, through state-based relicensure requirements, the same set of compulsory requirements in continuing education that have become general throughout the United States.

Some professions are more sparsely represented in continuing education than others by university departments and schools. There are relatively few schools of social work, optometry, public health, or veterinary medicine, for example, engaged in formal continuing education. In such instances, centralized extension units have been the significant providers, typically in collaboration with local or state associations. But there are no set regulations or even accepted folkways to determine who shall collaborate on such instruction or how it may be organized. More uniform programs will undoubtedly emerge as the state licensing authorities compare notes and determine general patterns that seem to work better than others. By no means, however, will such programs always be considered from the point of view of the consuming public; the politics of continuing professional education will still give preeminence to professional authority.

The variety of professional continuing education makes it difficult to summarize, but the rapidly growing interest from the professional associations promises to divert funds, as well as audiences, from the university provision, even in those instances where the professional schools are deeply involved. The fundamental attitude of professionals, almost without exception, is to expect that, like the basic professional degree, continuing education will be provided at public expense. This has the force of tradition, save to a limited extent in engineering and in business, where basic payment for instruction comes from the employer, not the student.

Consider a bleak prediction for the relation between universities and professions: Thirty years from now, several important universities will lose their law schools, medical schools, and other professional schools. The reasons?

The university as an institution has no independent policy and no independent set of practical guidelines in continuing professional education. It has consented to be led by professional societies, by faculty members representing the professions who are, in turn, members of interlocking directorates—of licensing boards, and of the high command of professional societies and professional faculties. In the typically anarchic way in which most universities operate, we have allowed departments and professional groups to run things, expecting that out of such activity we get the best of all possible worlds.

A failure of leadership in this area will result in the weakening of the complex comprehensive university in our country and in its atomization into constituent elements. If the university does not (or cannot) provide continuing education to professionals under its own auspices, it will find that the associations will willingly take over. Once, however, the associations have done that, it will soon occur to them that, either at their own expense or, by lobbying the legislature, at public expense, they could readily offer the first professional degree as well. While professional leaders may view this scenario with equanimity, it is surprising that higher education leaders are not concerned. The loss to society implicit in the ever-narrowing education of professionals should not be viewed with complacency. Yet that seems to be the wave of the future.

To be sure, there may well be an increased call for humanistic education if earlier training is limited and technical in nature. So, in the long run, an adjustment might be made; but it would probably be made at the expense of universities as they are now organized.

The 1980s

What conclusions can be drawn about the provision of continuing education in the future? What will the role of universities be? How will they relate to other providers in that part of the field which is postsecondary?

The fundamental part of prediction is reliable information, but in its absence, conclusions may be drawn from observation, experience, and intuition. Several generalizations, in no particular order, may be suggested about the decade of the 1980s:

1. The next ten years will be a period of uncertainty for all providers.

2. The combinations, coalitions, and agreements that develop will be of short duration, expedient, and ad hoc.

3. Competition will reduce the numbers of private entrepreneurs.

4. The jobbing provision for universities will flare out like a meteorite.

5. Off-campus part-time degree programs will grow for the next few years; then they will be sharply regulated and reduced, possibly supervised by a national authority.

6. "Nontraditional" programs will lose their separate identities, and their strength will be absorbed into orthodox programs.

7. Universities will be proportionately reduced as providers of continuing professional education; the gainers will be the professional associations.

8. Continuing professional education will become articulated, under federal regulation, as a post-tertiary part of education.

9. Universities will markedly increase their continuing education offerings in the humanities, arts, and general culture.

10. Large-scale entrepreneurs will lobby for the voucher system. If successful, they will move into proprietary education at the subcollegiate level and at the postsecondary level.

11. The community colleges' provision of noncredit continuing education, for professionals and in other areas, will be limited.

12. Voluntary accreditation will be subordinated to state and fed-

eral licensing and relicensing, in ways which will be confusing for several years. At the end of a decade we will see new standards developed for continuing education, conceived both as degree education and as post-tertiary professional education.

13. Perhaps by 1990 a unified policy on continuing education will be developed by the university leadership of the United States.

DISCUSSION

"My point of view," *Milton Stern* says, "is that in the social ecology of continuing education, we're at an indeterminate, very confused place. Everything else I've said, the various lines I've followed, merely comment on that sense of where we are."

"Certainly," *Rosalind Loring* adds, "the number and kind of organizations who believe they have the expertise to provide continuing education is multiplying, and it's a fascinating process to observe. And it's also sometimes threatening to participate with them or to be the recipient of their 'assistance' or 'collaboration.'"

"I agree," *Grover Andrews* says. "Nearly every type of institution—the small private liberal arts college, in particular, which has never even thought of continuing education before—is asking, 'Shouldn't we get into continuing education, community-based education?' I have a whole backlog of dates to go to that kind of institution for the first time in their lives—and some of them are 150 years old. We're doing the best we can to help, from the role of the accrediting association; but the profession itself has a very heavy responsibility—and they don't know what it is they're doing! That's where the danger is for the established institutions. In addition to the legitimate but inappropriate colleges, entrepreneurs with the wrong characteristics—charlatan characteristics—are moving in, and many institutions are getting burned by these folks, and many adults are getting taken in by them."

"You're talking about turf," *Morton Gordon* says, "and one way to look at turf is that 'they' are moving in on me—and I'm sure as hell they are! And another way of looking at turf is that 'they' are all out there like sharks, and like sharks 'they' are everywhere. But I guess I don't really care how big sharks they are, because we're the biggest sharks of all!"

"I'd like to make another point about turf," *Lillian Hohmann* says. "Turfs are like apparitions or mirages or something. They're there, and you see them, and sometimes you can reach out and touch them. But they come and go depending apparently on resources and other factors. And it seems to me strange that we sit around and worry about turf in a nation where you can see infant mortality seventeenth highest in the world—and yet the continuing education of physicians doesn't address that issue very much. I think that puts into some kind of perspective what it's all about."

Mort Gordon sums up: "We're saying that there are a lot of places that worry about competition all the time—and it's true, they should! But at the same time, I don't think they rely on the comparative advantages they have. They worry a great deal about competition in general, but they don't pay enough attention to the places where they're strong. And I can hardly give you a better example of that than the fact that now that Harvard University has discovered continuing education, it won't be long before they'll discover also that they've invented it! It doesn't become knowledge until they find it out! Before that it's hearsay, and it's interesting, and God knows what it is. But when *they* discover it, it finally exists! And they have an enormous competitive advantage!"

The university is a national resource . . .

Milt Stern says: "There's something I think is assumed tacitly, unconsciously in all of this. We—and that's everyone, here and everywhere else—assume that the university is a national resource, a milk cow! The staff is a national resource, the professors are a national resource, the expertise developed is a national resource, the whole system is a national resource to be drawn on by anybody. The American university system provides the workers, and they're ants, because by and large they don't get that much out of it! The public won't support them; industry doesn't pay; private entrepreneurs don't pay. I get indignant at the very visible examples of rip-off. But in the long run I don't stay indignant, because of the social good. And I think it would be wise for us here to look at how those university resources can be best organized, not in the interests of the university, but in the interests of society."

John Ervin shakes his head. "The whole thing is just the opposite of what you've implied! The fact is that the resource is too narrowly distributed. The great segment of society goes right along, not affected by it one bit! The thing that upsets me as a black American and an educator is that the ones who come out at the other end of your pipeline look just like the ones that have been going through it all the time! If it's changing at all, it's changing, not because of the creativity of continuing educators, but because of the push for access from outside by minorities who are saying: 'We want a piece of the action! And it's clearly demonstrated to us that the way to get a piece of the action is to go through these mechanisms that you have provided, that have been the great selectors of those who get through the doors of salvation!' It's just the opposite of what you've implied!"

"What I've been saying," *Milt* replies, "is that the university has this capacity and it's being misused! What I'm saying is that if we allow an unrestricted use of the university faculty by anybody who comes down the pike with a buck to pay them—and they usually sell out for a pittance—we're misusing a national resource!"

"That being the case," says *Robert Kost,* "why does it appear that in periods in which the main objective of the universities is diminished, they tend to prostitute themselves and become service stations? Why is it that universities become increasingly interested in continuing education only when there is a diminution of funds from either eighteen-year-olds or other sources?"

All universities are not the same . . .

George Robertson breaks in: "We're not really getting to the point. All universities are not the same! Berkeley isn't Blockhead Community College; Dartmouth isn't Georgia Tech! The fact is that some institutions in American higher education have a prime and overriding purpose to advance knowledge and operate at the postgraduate level. What's wrong with a degree of specialization? Let's ask a kind of in-house question: How is your institution going about the provision of appropriate kinds of service? That really is a question that can be answered if you know what your job is. If you accept the concept of specialization, you shouldn't worry whether Flathead Community College or General Motors steals some help from you!"

It's simply market economics . . .

William Griffith says, "I think it's possible to overlook—quite understandably—the demographic shift and to assume that there have been philosophical changes when there have simply been changes in supply and demand. We shouldn't lose sight of the fact that even within the institution of higher education the supply-demand market continues to operate to restrict what people are able to do. It would mean that some are doing things which they are not eager to do. It isn't a philosophy that's guiding them; it's simply market economics."

"I've been out of this for two years," *John Ervin* says, "but I've been ten years the trustee of a foundation that's had an interest in higher education for more than fifty years and has been really concerned about what a university is.

"There are some who feel that the universities are only interested in making money and that they don't take a thoughtful look at the whole of society and their responsibility to it. That's not true.

"Let me go back to what I think is true. It is in many ways inappropriate to define the university as society's servant, to feel that it sits there with the idea of going out to solve society's problems. Universities weren't designed for that. The best universities don't see that as essential to their mission, and I think they ought not to. The other piece is that the face of higher education is changing, and from my point of view it's changing more rapidly in other parts of the institution than in continuing education. To take my very narrow little indication of progress—minority participation. Since I've been in higher education, continuing education, I've been appalled that I could be *the only* black dean in continuing education. Go to the major universities and you'll find minority persons everywhere else. You'll see black deans of education, social work, business—and provosts —everywhere.

"When you talk about the response to American business, one of the most important institutions on the Washington University campus is a Center for the Study of American Business, which came directly in response to that institution's conception of the importance of business. The School of Business of that institution is responding to the needs of business. The problem is that that university does not see its responsibility for responding to the workers, and so they're not going out looking at how you improve the lot of the worker except as it becomes a part of course work in the sociology department, psychology, and other kinds of disciplines. But the university, as I see it, *is* sensitive to what is going on and responding to it.

Self-support forces conservatism . . .

"I think that the reason continuing education operations don't respond to what's out there any more than they do is the self-support mandate under which continuing education in all of our institutions has to operate. When you describe self-support in some institutions, it's different. At Washington University when we talk about self-support, what we're talking about is the direct costs of the program, plus the costs of those who participate in it, plus the costs of the unit within which it develops, plus a contribution to the university. Now some institutions talk about self-support and all they're talking about is returning the *direct* costs. It's still a self-support mandate, however, which forces that part of the institution to be conservative, so that the creative edge is the perception of perceived trends and the ability to get into them early enough to get maximum return from them and stay in them and get out of them before it's all milked dry. I would maintain that instead of being the most creative and risk-taking part of the institution, continuing education is forced into a conservative position, more conservative than some others."

"I guess," *Mort Gordon* says, "this is the time to take slight issue with the idea of tracing the conservatism of continuing education —which I don't deny completely—to the mandate of self-support. I'd like to take issue at least to the extent that someday I'd like to find a tame Ph.D. student and propose the following dissertation

(I'm being quite serious—I haven't found one yet): 'By reputational analysis, identify the ten best university extension programs in the country; and then identify the ten most financially lavish continuing education units.'

"My hypothesis is that the University of Wisconsin would be on both lists, and it would be the only one. None of the other lavishly supported ones would be on the list of the *best* ten. I'm not arguing that it's better to be poor than rich; I'm just saying that, for some, the mandate of self-support still leaves some room to maneuver, still leaves some grease in the system, still leaves some qualities to emerge, including the ability to get up after you fall down. (Others can't find their way to the bathroom unless they get a grant or unless they call the president's office.)

"Two years ago, in one of our distinguished professional schools, it was announced that the federal government had decided to cut all the students' stipends. The place became a lunatic asylum. They thought they were going to have to close down the school. It never occurred to them for just a minute that there were other schools throughout the campus where students were paying tuition. It absolutely never occurred to them! And fortunately, Washington reconsidered and reinstituted the stipends, because otherwise this famous school would have gone out the window.

"So—a lot of people go on like this: 'If only we had money we would walk on water!' It's not true."

"You haven't said anything I don't know as a dean," *John Ervin* says. "I take from Peter to pay Paul. And I am able to do the kinds of things I want to do only because I have something else that will subsidize them. All of us are able to keep or maintain the creative edge only because we have something else that *is* a money-maker that would permit experimentation."

Some things we may not wish to think about . . .

Bill Griffith changes the subject: "Let's move beyond money for a little bit and perhaps get into some other things that we may or may not wish to think about. It seems to me that here—and elsewhere —there has been kind of a passive acceptance of the notion that what the university is about is simply trying to change human behavior and that there is no longer any question that Benjamin Bloom, with his taxonomies of education, and Robert Mager, with his behavioral objectives, are the gurus that everyone should follow without exception. I would simply like to say: Do you really believe that there is only one philosophy that should guide all of our work in education? And if you do, what, pray tell, do you use for evidence?

"The second kind of concern that I have is: How compatible are the objectives of universities with those of business? As university extension divisions move more and more toward the business model, will they not at the same time move farther and farther from the university? And are they prepared to do that?

"I think, further, that before we get too enthusiastic about the free enterprise system within the university, within higher education, we had better look very carefully at the number of automobile manufacturers in the United States and generalize with some caution. Do we really want only one correspondence instruction university in the United States? Do we really want only one institution running all the adult education? I believe we need to think about it.

Universities appear chaotic and confused . . .

"Universities appear to anyone who understands business to be chaotic, fragmented, and confused. That is certainly an accurate perception. That does not make them bad, however. To assume that a university can be a university and also be neat and tidy is, I think, a foolish assumption. To assume that one has monolithic goals for a university indicates one has not paid much attention to universities over the last several hundred years. The president may have a set of goals, and so may the trustees, and so may the deans. And *you* may be able to exert some little bit of control over individual faculty members about what they can do, when, and under what circumstances. But that has little to do with a set of goals. And that doesn't suggest that if the university had a set of monolithic goals, that would make it a better place. It is, in fact, because the university does *not* mirror society exactly that it is able to make unique contributions to society. To the extent that the university takes society as its model, it becomes less capable of criticizing, which is, of course, one of its major functions.

"It has been suggested that anything the university is capable of doing, somehow it ought to do—which I regard as utter nonsense. If the university is worth anything at all, then surely as soon as it can get anyone else to take over routine functions which it initiated, it ought to be thankful that it can do so and move on, to roles that only it can play. The protection of turf by doing last year's work over and over again, I think, is not a dignified role for universities.

A history dominated by competition . . .

"The hypothesis that adult and continuing education is in the process of movement from cooperation to competition is also certainly quite interesting. I suggest it's in variance with the facts. I think an examination of the organization and programs within the whole field of adult education—not simply one tiny slice—provides persuasive evidence of a history dominated by competition and a growing awareness of the potential benefits of cooperation and collaboration.

"Within university extension circles, as you are aware, the first national meeting to foster cooperation was held in the early 1890s. It took more than twenty years before we could get universities to convene together again to think about what they had in common. But when they did meet—in 1915—the National University Extension Association was formed. Then, fifty years ago Kenyon Butterfield of Michigan State College threw the weight of his prestige and the power of the presidency behind the combining of cooperative and general extension at that university. It cost him his job. The man he named first director of the combined extension division became the first professor of adult education in the United States at Columbia University, because Michigan was not having a combined extension division. In fact, we had our first effective matchmaking in 1960 at the University of Missouri, engineered by Elmer Ellis and executed by Brice Ratchford, either of whom could testify to the political factions that such a proposed unification aroused.

"In 1969 we had our first Galaxy Conference of major national adult education associations in Washington, D.C., and although that cohabitation yielded only one handicapped offspring—the Coalition of Adult Education Organizations—the experience was productive in demonstrating just how great the problems of parochialism and territoriality are. Only recently have adult educators begun to coop- erate in their lobbying activities. In fact, cooperation is increasing precisely because the process of competition has failed to provide prosperity for all adult education."

Universities function in today's world . . .

John Ervin nods. "Let me say that what I think I perceive is a kind of recognition that colleges and universities have to function in to- day's world; and that means that the kinds of things they do, the kinds of constituencies they have that they have responded to in the past, can no longer, for them, be the only ones to which they re- spond. So when you say—as Grover has put it—that they are sud- denly interested in continuing education, I guess I would reply that what they have done is to recognize that they have to broaden the base of their relationships with all those people out there; I don't think that is *just* suddenly becoming interested in continuing education."

"And yet," says *Mort Gordon*, "don't you find something like this happening? I've been doing a little work as an individual entrepreneur . . ."

"Oh, there *are* good entrepreneurs," interjects *Grover Andrews*.

". . . with one of those colleges," *Mort* goes right on, "where, when you walk in the main building, there's a statue commemorating the fallen dead of the Civil War. And they want to do two things—in addition to staying alive, which is quite a problem in itself: they want to get into continuing education, but they don't want to change anything they're doing."

"Right!" *Grover* says. "Right! It's an added-on function."

"Whenever I'm talking to their new provost," *Mort* continues, "who would really like to do something, I'll suggest, 'Well, let's think about doing X'—nothing very revolutionary or brilliant—and he says, 'Well, but it wouldn't be *us*!' As one of my colleagues says, 'Institutions change only enough to keep from changing!'"

It all comes back to mission appropriateness . . .

"It all comes back to this business of mission-appropriateness," *Grover Andrews* says. "I've been looking at institutional purposes for eleven years—the good ones and the bad ones—and helping institutions to see that they're not at all like what their purpose says. They may have a good statement of their purpose, but any relationship to what they really are is purely accidental. For example, there's one we went in to look at—coeducational, graduate programs, several professional curricula including a school for business, and so forth—and the purpose still said it was a small, private liberal arts women's college. The statement was still as it had been written in 1835!"

"It's also a question of legitimacy," says *Roz Loring*. "What the field of continuing education started from was a set of convictions on the part of the people who brought the field to a place where everybody else could enter it. And if there is a resistance on the part of those people to accepting everybody else, it's because they come in with less than a sense of philosophy about the meaning of what they're doing. Somehow or other we might try to be old-fashioned for a moment and define why we do all these things. If it *is* the profit motive, we ought to say so clearly, so that the consumer can beware!"

"Your point is well taken," *Milt Stern* agrees. "I sent a draft of my paper to my opposite number at Oxford University in England, and the one point that he was sharply critical about was the fact that there was an absence of philosophic outlook."

What about the role of government?

"Let me ask you about another point," *Philip Frandson* suggests. "We have this mythology about the student's having an increasing role in decision making and so forth, but what about the role of government, the growing fears on the part of some that goverment is intruding in the field with considerable force?"

"We could say it the other way," *Roz Loring* replies. "I'm more concerned that there isn't enough government in it—including ac-creditation, by the way—but more in terms of support. The amount of dollars which the government provides now as incentives for all kinds of institutions to be providers is still painfully small when compared with other kinds of support."

"And there's also the way the support is doled out," *John Ervin* says. "Let me give you a specific example. When Title I—support for solving community problems—was begun, there was a 75:25 match, so that at Washington University, I could get into the market of community service, providing for the people in public housing in St. Louis—service! We hired someone from the Urban League to come to Washington University. We matched her with a law school profes-sor whose specialty was urban housing. We helped her understand enough about law to at least write housing codes, which made it possible for her to work with tenants in public housing to the extent that they could then deal with landlords, the city, etcetera. I could get my 25 percent match with all kinds of incoming contributions. But when Title I shifted to a 50 percent match, I couldn't generate it! What I had to do was give up that market. I could no longer be of use to them. I could no longer provide service. I had to shift to other kinds of populations who could pay."

"How much government and for what?" *Phil Frandson* says. "That would be the issue?"

"Exactly the point that Roz and John are making," *Milt Stern* says, "namely, how do you utilize these resources for maximum effect in terms of providers? Briefly in the sixties government was a provider of consequence. Government should be added again as a major provider—because unless you can make provision through a source which is cooperative (speaking about cooperation and competition), unless you can make provision acceptable to people through the one cooperative measure we have, which is government, it's not going to be made appropriately, in my view, under the present dictates of society."

If we could tie the pragmatic and philosophical together . . .

"And I think," *Roz Loring* says, "some note ought to be made of what we were saying before: we, in the real world, are living less philosophically and more and more practically. The interrelatedness of funding and turf, for example, is crucial. If we're doing something for profit, that's one thing. But if we're doing it for the kind of reasons that John did his project in the housing area, that's a very different thing, growing out of a very different philosophy! It's not cost-effective; you couldn't do a cost-benefit study; there's a whole array of things you can't do with his philosophy except to believe that what you're doing is contributing to a better world. So as we go through these next two days, if we could set some kind of foundation as we explain these different parts, if we could tie the pragmatic and the philosophical together, we may end up sick and tired of some of the subjects, but at least we will have explored why the wheels have to work together."

"I think," *Milt Stern* says, "that again we have to distinguish between colleges and universities of various kinds. Many institutions are still not interested in continuing education, and they're fools not to be—not because of the money, but because they are going to lose their birthright! In medieval Europe universities taught the technological cadres and the bureaucratic cadres of society. That isn't true of the American university. It became untrue to a certain extent for the English university; it remained true of continental universities. The point, it seems to me, is that the American university is now in a period of some kind of immobility, conceptually. Continuing education *has* become part of the basic mission. It *has* become so if you look at it in theory, because when you expand the function of a profession and expand the function of technology in society, if the university does not expand its functions to include regular training of the people whom it itself has graduated into the world, it has denied its own birthright. And that is what is in the process of happening today. And that is not happening only in selected places; it's happening generally. There are very, very few exceptions to this.

Where's the leadership . . . ?

"Yet I've heard very few words about the importance of continuing professional education from anybody in the high command of higher education in the United States. Where are they? Where are these voices? They're not around! Where's the leadership of higher education when it comes to this point? They don't see it! OK, they don't see it! If it's outside their conception, then, by God, they'll lose it!"

But *John Ervin* shakes his head. "That's not true either," he says. "When I was president of NUEA three years ago, Lee Metzger had been funded to do a rather extensive survey of external degree programs and other kinds of extensions of the university. Lee called together about eighty people in Washington to look at this and to indicate what the implications were for the universities. Now, the very significant thing for me was that there was nobody from a professional association for continuing education invited. Every other professional association was there. I happened to be there only because Cy Houle said John Ervin ought to be invited. And I was. But I kept saying, 'I'm president of NUEA!' I wanted NUEA as one of the official representatives because all of the other higher education organizations were. But there was not a single AEA, ACHE, or

NUEA official representative—nobody was there! They spent three days—the leaders of all those higher education associations, except extension associations—and whenever I'd bring it up, they said, 'Continuing education guys are just registrars! They're not important. All they do is function as credit keepers,' etcetera, etcetera.

"What I'm saying is, the face of higher education is changing! There's a dialogue going on out there, and there are voices that are speaking about us! What I'm saying is, the dialogue is going on, and the representatives of continuing education are not participating in the dialogue as the shape of higher education is changing! That's all I have to say."

"I think what you say, John, is very much to *my* point," *Milt Stern* responds. "The only way I would supplement it would be to emphasize a very important notion that hasn't been discussed so far, and that is the point that, on the issue of power, the matter of 'will' is paramount. From my point of view—if I adhere to my sense of the past and my own philosophic outlook, not only with regard to education but also with regard to everything else—life is something in which, if you have the will to do so, you can exercise some power! And deans of extension, or deans of schools of graduate study, or deans of professional schools, or chairpersons of philosophy departments *can* make some impact—if they make the effort! And what results as an observable phenomenon for researchers of the future is the result of *human effort!* It's not something that just happens as night succeeds day! And that's all *I* have to say."

FINAL COMMENTARY

Continuing education never was, and is not now, the exclusive prerogative of universities, although universities have always been major providers and will likely continue to be. In recent years, however, university continuing educators have become increasingly apprehensive about the entry of new providers into the field. Protection of "turf" has become a professional preoccupation. Continuing educators are concerned about university faculty's being employed by competitors, about departments' seeking to take over continuing education in their subject areas, and about the lack of fiscal support for continuing education as compared with other segments of the university. The self-support position of most programs has, in one sense, made many continuing educators conservative; it prompts them to look for the "sure thing" by following popular trends. Yet the fiscal flexibility of continuing education units—for example, where funds generated in one area can support another area—can encourage creativity and make public service possible. Fiscal anomaly and pragmatic idealism are reasonably accurate descriptions of the predicament and philosophy of university continuing educators.

Higher education as a whole is in transition, adjusting to changing constituencies and changes in mission, and continuing education is at a pivotal point in that transition. Whether or not a national policy for continuing education is achieved in the 1980s, the power to influence the direction of change and the formulation of policy lies with those who have the determination to become involved in the discussion.

2 Industry

Paper by Robert J. Kost

BIOGRAPHY

ROBERT J. KOST is director of Marketing Educational Services for General Motors Corporation. He attended Denison University in Ohio, and received his A.B. magna cum laude from the University of Pittsburgh in 1952. He completed his M.A. at Pittsburgh in 1956. Before he joined General Motors in 1957, his business experience included engineering and sales positions with the Westinghouse Airbrake Company.

Kost has served in a wide variety of positions since joining General Motors. In 1967 he was appointed director of Sales and Dealer Development Activities for General Motors Institute. In 1975 he was named director of General Motors Corporation Education and Training. In 1976, after serving for several months as director of Organizational Research and Development, he was appointed to his present position. With a staff of nearly sixty professionals, Kost is responsible for providing management training and consulting services throughout the world to General Motors sales departments and their affiliated dealer and distributor organizations. Affiliations include the American Society for Training and Development, American Marketing Association, and Conference Board. He is a member of the Commission of Education Credit for the American Council on Education. He is a frequent speaker on continuing education before industry and university groups.

INITIAL COMMENTARY

Industry spends on employee education more than six times the amount appropriated by all the states for all of higher education! If money is power, then industry occupies a power position in continuing education.

Industry is not only a major consumer of continuing education provided by others, it is also a major provider of continuing education, with large "in-house" training staffs and facilities. If competition is conflict, then industry is a source of conflict in continuing education, competing directly with other providers and pitting provider against provider as bidders for its continuing education dollars.

Robert Kost points out that industry's principal objective in continuing education is pragmatic: Continuing education should provide skills and knowledge that will improve employees' capabilities and be reflected in the quality of their performance and in their productivity. But industry is not so pragmatically profit-oriented that its concept of continuing education is totally restricted to task-related training; there is considerable support for Quality of Work Life programs, and the liberal arts as well as industrial arts.

Industry, Kost says, wants to cooperate with educational institutions, yet is not receiving the response it expects from academic sources, which is surprising in view of the widely-held assumption that such sources are struggling for economic survival. Now courses designed and taught by in-house instructional staffs are being marketed to other businesses and industries, are securing college-credit equivalents, and some programs are even securing degree-granting accreditation. As John Ervin said, the face of higher education *is* changing.

Robert J. Kost

Competition and Innovation in Continuing Education

An Industrial Point of View

In industry, continuing education is perhaps best defined as any technical or professional education and training that a person receives from the start of a career until retirement. Thus for industry, continuing education encompasses the very diverse formal and informal developmental experiences of a person's career, including experiences that are self-initiated as well as those initiated by the organization.

Continuing education has often been perceived as existing solely within the realm of academic institutions. This perception needs to be modified through an awareness of the extent of the continuing education provided by industrial, governmental, and private institutions. In major corporations, continuing education is an integral part of the business operation, a way of life for employees, and commonly available at all levels and for all disciplines within the organization. The objective of all continuing education for a company, regardless of its source, is to upgrade the personal, technical, and professional knowledge, the skills, and the competencies of both individuals and the work force as a whole.

To achieve this objective, most major corporations maintain sizable internal professional staffs as providers of both technical and professional continuing education. They also draw very heavily upon external sources, including academic institutions, consultants, and private educational agencies. Many thousands of smaller companies, with very limited internal staffs, lean almost exclusively upon external sources for their developmental needs.

In 1974 General Motors initiated a study of the educational and training activities in Fortune 500 companies, major trade associations, and government at all levels. In addition to other findings, the study revealed that the annual spending on internal and external continuing education was estimated at $30 billion in 1972 and projected to be $50 billion by 1980.

The figures are approximate largely because it is difficult to identify the relevant cost information from respondents in such studies and because their definition or perception of what constitutes continuing education varies significantly. It is clear, however, that industry and government make substantial investments in the continuing education of their personnel and represent an enormous market for providers of continuing education who can adapt to their needs.

It may be helpful to highlight the sources for continuing education in a single company such as General Motors. GM maintains several internal staffs to deliver continuous professional development and to forestall technical obsolescence. These professional staffs include—

1. *General Motors Institute,* which is a wholly owned subsidiary of the corporation and a degree-granting institution chartered in the State of Michigan and accredited by the North Central Association. With approximately 2,200 students, this Cooperative Engineering and Industrial Administration School is a major source of engineering and management talent in General Motors.

2. *GMI's Continuing Engineering Education Department,* which provides technical training programs aimed at upgrading and updating engineering and manufacturing personnel throughout the corporation. These courses are taught by the academic faculty of GMI.

3. The *GM Education and Training Department,* which provides a wide variety of management and nonmanagement continuing education programs for the staffs and operating units of General Motors.

4. *Division and plant personnel trainers,* who administer the work segments of the GMI program and those of other cooperative academic institutions, as well as the local apprenticeship programs and the employee tuition-refund program. They also conduct the programs developed by the Corporate Education and Training Department.

5. The *GM Marketing Education Department,* which provides continuing-management development and consulting services all over the world to the sales and service operations of General Motors and their franchised dealer organizations.

6. The *GM Dealer Marketing Development Department,* which provides sales and service training for nonmanagement retail dealers. These programs are conducted in thirty-one General Motors Training Centers in major cities across the United States.

7. The *GM School of Product Service,* which provides technical-product training for new and experienced retail technicians in the thirty-one training centers.

In addition to the nearly one thousand full-time professional education and training personnel on these staffs, many thousands of line supervisors and managers provide a variety of informal development activities for both salaried and hourly employees.

In meeting its continuing education needs, General Motors also cooperates with external sources. It participates, for example—

1. with more than 100 colleges and universities in formal cooperative education programs

2. with schools throughout the country and in many parts of the world where employees pursue degree and nondegree programs on the tuition-refund plan

3. with schools throughout the country and in many parts of the world where employees pursue the academic requirements of apprenticeship studies

4. with major universities in graduate fellowship programs for selected employees

5. with major universities in executive development for selected employees

6. with a host of individual educators, consultants, and private agencies who contract with the corporation, with individual operating units, or with both.

It is obvious that for General Motors, and for most other major corporations as well, continuing education is a high priority, and millions of dollars are spent on it annually. Most major corporations tend to view lifelong learning for their employees as a very practical business requirement and a very vital function in maintaining the competitive health of the business.

For this reason, the objective or bottom-line measure of virtually all industrial continuing education is its effectiveness in changing behavior, in improving job performance. Thus the educator must not only impart knowledge and concepts but also translate these into skills that the recipient can apply back on the job.

This requirement may be the greatest single obstacle to an increased role for campus sources in industrial continuing education. Campus sources have the capability to meet the needs of industry for application-oriented continuing education. To date, very few appear to be either interested or concerned about such needs.

It is possible that this situation exists simply because the objectives of industry for continuing education are incompatible with the objectives of many academic institutions. Regardless of the cause, industry represents a vast potential market for campus continuing education. Presently, internal company staffs continue to grow and provide by far the greater part of such continuing education. It is sound business, however, for industry to hold down the growth of internal staffs if viable delivery systems are available in the marketplace.

For those campus institutions that desire to become more substantial providers of continuing education for industry and government, the opportunities are unlimited. To take advantage of these opportunities, however, they must make some dramatic changes in their present philosophy and in the direction of many continuing education functions.

Competition versus Collaboration in Continuing Education

In industry we continue to believe firmly in the free enterprise system, holding that a free market flow of competitive goods and services is the best means for ensuring the quality of life most beneficial to American society as a whole. Such a position is not unusual coming from an industry advocate. Unfortunately, there are those who view this free enterprise position as simply another form of defense for the profit motive. Certainly profit is an important element, an absolute essential, in fact, if business is to continue to compete in a free system. More important, however, a free competitive system fosters innovation, and it is this innovation that produces the goods and services that consumers need and want and in a most cost-beneficial manner.

Similarly, competition or conflict among institutions in the delivery of continuing education has in the past fueled innovation in both the substance and form of such services and will do so increasingly in the future. Indeed, the community college system has been more than willing to enter the competitive arena of industrial continuing education.

Many major colleges and universities, however, appear to be extremely slow in responding to the needs of a very sizable and rapidly growing market, so that the pace of innovation in continuing education in many parts of the country has been painfully slow. Progress will continue to be slow until such institutions sense the need and opportunity in industrial continuing education and decide to enter the market in a thoughtful, aggressive, and substantive way. Without competition, many of the programs offered by academic institutions today miss the mark in qualifying as contributive adult education. This is particularly true in professional and business programs, more so than it is in the technical and vocational field.

Whether taught by a business practitioner or an academic professor, many programs are unresponsive to the changing needs of society and shifts in the business environment and practices. As a result, course curricula are often poorly planned and program content is frequently inappropriate. When an instructor who is unaware of basic learning theory and appropriate adult teaching methodologies is added to the scenario, the program results are disastrous.

Competition is needed to drive up the quality of such programs or to replace them in the marketplace. Competition is also needed to produce more innovative approaches in curriculum planning, program development, instruction, and program delivery.

If, indeed, there is a quality gap and an innovation lag in the continuing education supplied by academic institutions, and if competition is one key ingredient needed to reverse the situation, why is it not forthcoming in greater volume? We in industry can only speculate, but there appear to be at least three major causes.

First, the entire educational system appears to be geared to young people and not to adults, despite estimates that several million people over age thirty-five are enrolled in schools in degree, vocational, and continuing education programs. Buildings and services are oriented to the young, and most important, faculty-reward systems are generally geared to achievements in educating young people. Many of the faculty have little incentive to excel in adult education.

It is not uncommon for institutions to find new legitimacy for continuing education functions when the market for the eighteen-year-old shrinks. This is an understandable reaction but the wrong reason for expanding continuing education, whose direction should be determined by thoughtful research and a concern to meet educational needs.

Second, not only is the education system geared to the young, but many institutions also seem to view continuing education as simply an adjunct to the institution rather than as an integral part of education. To some it is simply a way of making existing facilities more productive and supplementing individual and institutional income.

As long as continuing education exists outside the academic core of an institution, it will be a secondary priority for that institution, and it will lack both the administrative and the academic support to respond effectively to the educational needs of society.

Third, there is a void in meaningful research on continuing education at both the national and the local levels. As a result, many institutions are unable to identify needs and opportunities for their services. Frequently, when markets are identified, the institution lacks the money and skills to merchandise its services successfully. The net result is that funds that would permit continuing education to remain vital, and to grow, are not generated.

Each year the Department of Health, Education, and Welfare collects extensive data on primary, secondary, undergraduate, and graduate education for use in decisions on the allocation of funds. Continuing education is included in this research in a cursory manner at best. As long as this information gap exists, continuing education will continue to be regarded as marginally important and the funds for its growth will be limited.

Private independent research in the field has also been sparse, despite the availability of governmental and foundation funds for such purposes. Some serious research has been done by individuals and institutions on questions of how adults learn and how to teach adults. Very little has been done to determine such key issues as the scope of the market for continuing education, the needs of various segments of society, the adequacy of existing delivery systems, and the dollars and methods required to achieve results.

Appropriate research in continuing education, coupled with a reordering of institutional priorities, would substantially increase the number of major institutions entering the competitive arena of industrial continuing education, and decrease business's dependence on internal staffs.

Competition among academic providers will tend to drive up the quality of services among all providers and force those who wish to survive to be more responsive to the educational needs of business and to meet its educational goals.

Those institutions that remain viable and responsive to the educational needs in their community or marketplace will increasingly need to seek cooperative means of staying vital and expanding their markets. The three most promising areas of collaboration seem to be those of information interchange, cooperative activities with industrial and other nonacademic continuing education sources, and academic-consortium approaches to the educational needs of larger markets.

Information interchange between academic and industrial institutions of continuing education should be accelerated and should focus on research efforts, educational needs, educational technologies, teaching methodologies, and environmental and societal trends that are likely to influence program content and teaching methods.

Cooperative activities between academic and industrial continuing education sources might usefully be extended from information interchange to include joint research, joint program development, and joint instruction. One very promising linking activity is carried on by the Commission on Educational Credit of the American Council on Education. The commission has made progress in putting the technical and professional education given by nontraditional sources such as industry and the military on an equal footing with that given by academic institutions. Most of the major management development and technical development programs within General Motors have been evaluated by academic teams and are recommended for college-level credits. These are described in the ACE Guide, which is distributed to academic institutions throughout the United States. The record thus far for the acceptance of these credit recommendations by academic institutions is reasonably good. Stated simply, the objective of this activity is to recognize educational attainments in programs conducted by nontraditional sources as a means of encouraging individuals to continue to pursue formal education.

Consortium approaches by academic continuing education sources are needed for industry. These often fail in local metropolitan markets and even in state markets because of lack of institutional interest. They also fail because of the academic sources' lack of innovation, creativity, and initiative.

When successful, the drive for consortium efforts invariably comes from sources outside the academic community such as the military, industry, foundations, and the like. The academic community appears to be generally reactive and critical rather than proactive as an initiator of cooperative efforts. Certainly institutions should deal individually with local chambers of commerce, associations, and companies to identify continuing education needs in their local communities. At the same time, institutions should exercise leadership in examining the basic needs for technical and professional development on a national scale, and they should consider the possibilities of educational consortia.

What can be accomplished nationally has been demonstrated by the military, which, with highly diverse locations and a highly mobile work force, has succeeded in providing certain kinds of basic education in conjunction with colleges across the country. The Community College of the Air Force is an outstanding example of the feasibility of integrating internal and academic sources on a national scale.

Earlier it was suggested that as consumers of continuing education, companies face make-or-buy decisions and would prefer to buy if the programming and instruction could meet their objectives and there were a viable delivery system. Now, there are certain continuing education needs that a single academic institution cannot meet on a national scale and, as a result, a company will address such needs with internal resources. Many such needs in both technical and professional areas are generic rather than unique to a particular company or industry. To cite a single example, every major company with offices and plants in several geographic locations has an important and continuing need to educate newly appointed supervisors in basic management with an emphasis on the behavioral sciences. Academic institutions are generally well equipped to offer such instruction. As yet, however, few enterprising institutions have researched the field with particular companies or industries and proposed meeting their needs nationally through a consortium of institutions located in the cities where such companies have major operations and therefore a continuing flow of students.

The opportunities for cooperative efforts are virtually unlimited. Industry must provide the commitment, but academia must provide the creative leadership and imaginative systems that will permit the efforts to succeed. In summary, a combination of increased competition and collaboration will bring new vitality to the continuing education provided by academic institutions.

Continuing Education's Response to Environmental and Societal Changes

The nature of development is such that it is future-oriented. We are teaching people today to function more effectively tomorrow, and the environment in which they will function is changing more rapidly than it has ever changed in the history of the world. Development efforts, whether internal to industry or obtained through the continuing education activities of academic institutions, must therefore be keyed to these changes, and indeed be anticipating them, if we are to prepare people to meet them.

The business person who will compete successfully in the marketplace of ideas, attitudes, and opinions must be conscious of the environment of the business, sensitive to the shifts in societal values, and thoroughly knowledgeable about socioeconomic and governmental trends that affect the business situation.

To paraphrase Peter Drucker, we are all in a race between obsolescence and retirement and the best we can hope for is a photo finish. Regardless of whether we can agree with his contention, it is clear that one major function of continuing education is to provide the knowledge and skills necessary to protect people from becoming technically and professionally obsolete in the environment in which they function. Continuing educators are well aware of changes in technology, and these commonly lead to a modification of existing technical programs or the initiation of new programs. Business and management education programs do not always demonstrate the same sensitivity to environmental trends and changes.

In General Motors four obvious trends in the business environment bear increasingly upon the way in which managers must manage, and therefore upon the concepts and content of management education.

First, the demand for products and services will continue to increase very substantially. Even though the gross national product may slow in the short term to perhaps 2 percent or less, the long-term average *real* growth rate in the United States is projected to be 4.5 percent a year. The gross world product is projected to be much higher. In the automotive business this trend has transformed the content of many educational programs. Managers must be prepared to cope with and manage larger sales volumes, larger facilities, sizable capital investments, higher fixed-cost ratios, an increased work force, and more sophisticated organizational structures and control systems.

Second, the combination of slower growth in North America and increasing opportunities in world markets is causing General Motors and other major companies to give increasing priority to international operations. To function effectively in these markets, managers will need to be educated in a variety of subjects; in particular they must receive a thorough understanding of world economics and an intimate knowledge of the social, economic, political, and cultural systems of many regions and countries of the world.

The third obvious trend is the ever-expanding role of government at all levels. Governmental agencies are here to stay as senior partners in the manufacturing and marketing process, and as a result, many traditional management concepts are becoming less and less valid. EPA, FTC, FEA, MVSS, DOT, CPA, EEO, Truth in Lending, Truth in Advertising—the list is endless and growing at both federal and state levels. The effect of government on the management of business is enormous, and few businesses have escaped attention. In both the sales and service ends of the business, certain classic marketing concepts are being eroded. Consumer wants and needs are increasingly conditioned by governmental wants and needs as articulated by legislatures, regulatory agencies, and judicial settlements. The free market flow of competitive products and services is increasingly challenged by governmental regulation. Consider for a moment the fact that the doctrine of *caveat emptor*, or "buyer beware," which has been applied since Roman times and for over 1,500 years has served our trading society well, today is unmistakably being replaced by a doctrine of "let the manufacturer and seller beware."

The examples of governmental intrusion into the manufacturing and marketing process are as endless as the list of agencies and regulations themselves. The pros and cons of this trend can be debated, but—while we should not cast aside proven concepts, strategies, and techniques—those of us in continuing education must bring to our instruction an awareness of governmental constraints.

The fourth and perhaps most important trend is the rapid escalation of the knowledge sophistication, and expectations, as well as the shifting values, of both employees and consumers. We put in hazard productivity and profit for business and the economy if we fail to teach managers and encourage organizations to modify traditional notions about how we structure an organization, how we manage people, and how we satisfy our customers. The manager or organization that insists upon clinging to traditional approaches with people and plays the same old game in the same old way will not survive in competition.

There are many other significant trends in the environment of all our businesses. It is imperative for continuing education that we constantly sense and anticipate change. If the development system of a company or academic institution is not sensitive to the environment, its program content will have little relevance, and its students will not be prepared to function effectively as responsible employees or citizens.

General Motors and Quality of Work Life

Whereas economic trends and increasing regulation by government are obvious conditions in themselves and in their effect upon decisions within a company, societal trends that touch people's knowledge, expectations, and values may be less obvious but more far-reaching in the long term. In General Motors an activity referred to as Quality of Work Life is having a profound effect on traditional approaches to running a segment of the company, and the company as a whole, in terms of human resources. Although in its infancy, the Quality of Work Life movement will undoubtedly influence the future content of many management and nonmanagement continuing education programs.

It is noteworthy that this particular company response to societal changes was in part sparked by a collaborative research effort with a major university. Such research is another example of the business-market opportunities for academic institutions. Rather than wait for the order, more institutions should seek out such opportunities for mutually beneficial research and experimentation.

Quality of Work Life, as an organizational philosophy, did not develop overnight. It originated in 1969, when General Motors suffered a series of sporadic and crippling strikes in car- and truck-assembly plants across the country. It was decided that the traditional adversarial relations between the union and management had to change and that management must find more effective ways to manage the human resources of the company.

Therefore, the then president of General Motors, Edward Cole, contracted with the Institute for Social Research at the University of Michigan to work with internal resources on experimental projects in four diverse plants. Organizational-development projects were initiated, their emphasis being employee involvement, information sharing, and training.

Quality of Work Life is not a package or a program. It is a process aimed at: increasing employees' involvement on the factory floor and in the office, improving interpersonal and organizational relations, maximizing decision making at the lowest possible level, furthering cooperation between union and management, developing more innovative and effective designs for jobs and organizations, and advancing the integration of people and technology.

In a speech in February 1979, a General Motors executive vice-president said:

> *Improving the quality of work life is a major priority in General Motors and for a very good reason. When we talk about "Quality of Work Life," we're also talking about the effectiveness and future success of our organization . . . its objective is not to make working fun, easy or undisciplined. Rather, its objective is to put some quality into human work, from the top to the bottom in a work organization.*

Some examples of the application of Quality of Work Life concepts are as follows:

☐ In one assembly plant, management and the union jointly initiated a three-day training program for all employees on team problem-solving skills and the interrelatedness of jobs in the plant. The program was completely voluntary and nearly half of the 3,600 employees participated during the year. The investment in the program was well over $1 million. The return to the people and the organization includes high employee morale, low absenteeism, a low number of grievances, and a much-improved quality of work life. It is presently one of the best-performing assembly plants in General Motors.

☐ Several plants have initiated involvement programs patterned after the Japanese Quality Control Circle concept. Participation is totally voluntary, and employees and supervisors are trained in problem-solving techniques. They meet regularly as teams, on company time, and the supervisor may or may not be the team leader. The teams work on problems they have identified, develop recommendations, and present these to a union-management committee.

☐ The objective in designing new plants and redesigning old plants is to create sociotechnical systems that are more responsive to people and more effective for business. The design develops from a "blank sheet" and an articulation of organizational philosophy and objectives. In several plants the layout, organizational structure, nature of the jobs, and operating procedures are unique and innovative: production teams of hourly employees function without supervision, select their own leaders, select, train, and evaluate new team members, and manage their own budgets, quality control, and personnel. The performance in these plants, when compared with that of similar plants operating on traditional patterns, demonstrates what innovative efforts can achieve.

☐ An established plant has abandoned the traditional organizational structure in favor of a business-team structure. The plant is organized into six business teams, each consisting of the necessary production and support activities. Support activities such as engineering, accounting, scheduling, quality control, and maintenance now function more effectively as a team with manufacturing people.

☐ An entire division of the corporation retains the traditional organizational structure but has formed an independent business-team structure for each of its eleven product lines. The teams are composed of both management and nonmanagement people from various segments of the organization. They operate as small, independent companies, may borrow and loan money from other teams, must pay a dividend, and report regularly on performance to divisional top management acting as the board of directors.

☐ In many parts of the corporation, clerical and professional people have personalized work schedules such as flex time.

In 1976 an employee survey was introduced as a measure of several areas of work life, including the physical work environment, economic well-being, the development and utilization of employees' skills and abilities, employee involvement and influence, and supervisory and work-group relations. During each of the past two years, nearly all salaried employees of General Motors were surveyed, and increasingly, hourly employees are being encouraged to participate in the survey. The survey is helpful in evaluating both progress in improving the quality of work life and the effectiveness of specific projects. In addition, many operating units use the information from the survey as a springboard for employee feedback and the initiation of involvement activities.

In 1978 a comparable measurement device was made available to General Motors' franchised dealer organizations to help them to evaluate the health of their organizations and devise more effective management and organizational systems to meet the changing needs, values, and expectations of their work forces. At present, several hundred North American dealerships are participating.

The particulars of Quality of Work Life, however, are less important than the learning that has occurred. The close relation between an organization's performance and its members' feelings about the organization, the work climate, the quality of management, and employee-management interaction was clearly identified. The project demonstrates that both performance and human satisfaction can be improved by creating conditions in which people can become more involved, work together, and experience personal growth and development.

To summarize in the words of the speech cited earlier:

> We think we're on the right track and making progress. We also know we don't have all of the answers. But, today in General Motors, perhaps more than ever before,

> *there is a greater appreciation of organizations as entities*
> *and greater appreciation for the need to respond creatively*
> *to a changing work force and changing business envi-*
> *ronment. In the broadest sense, this is what "Quality of*
> *Work Life" is all about, and this is what good management*
> *is all about.*

A Summary and a Challenge for Academic Continuing Education

Many academic continuing education functions appear to have grown like Topsy and present a bewildering array of programs with no apparent planning or philosophical base. One can only conclude that in many cases, they have grown in response to particular external stimuli or the economic needs of the institution. The volume of activity and the legitimacy accorded it by the faculty and administration appear to ebb and flow with the volume of available eighteen-year-olds or funds from various sources. This is very understandable and practical, but hardly a solid base on which to build a viable, long-term function for meeting the educational needs of society.

The phrase, "Physician heal thyself," may be most descriptive of the situation facing many academic sources of continuing education. Opportunities abound, but many institutions are ill equipped to respond to them because their own house appears to be fragmented and confused.

Those campus institutions that are vital and responsive to the environment—and there are many—must clearly have taken the time to articulate the philosophy behind their continuing education function and to develop the policies that will guide it over the long term. They will also have established both short- and long-term objectives on all facets of their business, the business of the total academic institution.

This philosophy, these policies, these objectives, cannot be departmental; the total institution must be prepared, or educated, to recognize and support continuing education as an integral and important function of the university or college. The reward systems for administrators and faculty must be structured to facilitate this process.

When continuing educators and their organizations have identified what business they are going to be in, how they are going to run it, where they are headed, and how they will know when they get there, the answers to many other questions become routine. What needs will we respond to? What are our economic requirements and how will we meet them? What research is required? What should the programs be? Who will develop them? Who will teach them? How will we ensure that the instruction is appropriate? All such questions require work, but they are relatively easy to resolve once an organization knows where it is going and is committed to getting there.

In industry, there is virtually no topic or teaching methodology in the technical and professional programs conducted by internal sources—save certain unique and customized instruction—that could not be handled as well or better by academic sources. The competency and capacity for aggressively servicing the business market, and many other segments of society, exists on our campuses. When academic institutions truly decide to enter the market in a substantive way, when competition drives up the quality of programs, and when institutions learn to cooperate with business in calculating and meeting its national and, indeed, world needs, their markets will be unlimited.

DISCUSSION

Bob Kost summarizes the challenge: "Major industries maintain very large staffs of their own to meet their continuing education needs, but they do so principally because they can't find viable providers through academic sources. We simply would not hire people and maintain them on the payroll if there were an alternative, but so far we haven't seen an alternative. The point is simply this: There are very few unique things internal to a company of a continuing education nature; these things could be done as effectively —or more effectively—if the academic community would take the initiative to go after that kind of business. But we don't see that happen, even though we'd rather buy than make."

"And yet you say providers must adapt to the needs of industry," *Mort Gordon* points out. "What do you mean, adapt?"

Bob replies, "It does little good for industry to spend its money with academic sources if the outcomes don't provide an advance for the business."

"And some of us are uneasy about what that means philosophically," *Mort* says, "and maybe we're not poor enough to go that far."

"I'm not suggesting that industry should impose its philosophy on academic institutions," *Bob Kost* says, "but I am suggesting that when academic institutions serve industry—or any other segment of society—they should be helpful. And I wonder why the leadership of the academic world can't come to a point where they can establish a philosophic base for their continuing education processes. When it comes to research, for example, academic institutions don't seem to have any philosophic problems. We recently paid a professor from a prestigious eastern university—the one you identified a little while ago as a johnny-come-lately in continuing education—$300,000 to do some research on the service end of our business to find out what we can do to help improve service to customers at the dealer level. We found it very helpful, meaningful research. I also mentioned the contributions of the Institute for Social Research to General Motors'

Quality Work Life project. To be sure, the services came from individuals and not the institutions per se, but neither Harvard nor the University of Michigan had to revise its institutional philosophy for them to do it!"

Not all academic institutions will be able to compete . . .

"That's all well and good," *George Robertson* says, "and I think many colleges and universities will move into your market because of declines in demand for their traditional products. But the fact is that in practice not all academic institutions will be able to compete; many lack the competencies, and probably even more lack the will to provide for industry's needs, simply because their traditional self-concept doesn't include such services.

"We are, in fact, likely to see a good deal of market displacement and realignment among providers of adult education. Some colleges will compete more aggressively in traditional kinds of continuing education. The resulting pressure in that segment of the market may drive other colleges, especially the community colleges and technical institutes, to provide more services directly to business and industry. And of course, we should remember that those who are already 'inside' industry have been quite effective in competing with outsiders. We can be certain that they will adjust the decision point for the make-or-buy decision in order to guarantee their own survival."

"And it's not an either-or situation," *John Ervin* points out. "Persons in the work force constitute a significant majority of the participants in higher continuing education. They turn to continuing education providers for satisfaction of a variety of needs and purposes. Industrial and other work settings can focus on abilities and skills basic to functioning on the job, while educational institutions can focus on knowledge and concepts which broaden the view of persons toward themselves and the world of work. It can be beneficial to the worker if corporate entities and educational institutions work seriously at developing areas of collaboration which make maximum use of the strengths of both."

How long is a degree any good anymore?

"What I'd like to do," *Phil Frandson* suggests, "is look critically at academia in the context of what it traditionally says it has to offer: knowledge and concepts all wrapped up in that piece of paper called a 'degree.' There's not much dispute that the degree has an indispensable place in the mechanism of economic life, but the question is just how long is a degree any good anymore in connection with work? The rate of career change in this country is about every five to eight years, and when the forty-year-old person who's fed up with work comes to the campus for help, the university sits there and says, 'OK, become a freshman again!' An institution that is geared only to saying, 'You've got to go back to *go!*' doesn't seem to me to be adjusting itself very well to reality."

"Yes, but before we go too far on that line," *Milt Stern* says, "it seems to me that you have to accept the position that what people glibly call career change is really nothing more than getting another job."

People somehow muddle along . . .

"I'd like to underline Milt's point about the overrating of the change of career, the career crisis," *George Robertson* adds. "The great majority of people somehow or other muddle along, and adjust and adapt, and take a course here or get a new job, and you get a learning period on a new job—they don't fire you right away if you can't do it! The catastrophic enforced career-change is not so common. The idea that people have forgotten everything every five or six years and have to go back and become freshmen, I don't think is one that really arises all that often."

"But it does come up," *Milt Stern* says, "and when it does it's very visible in the university, as when a student returns, not having finished a degree or having changed fields slightly and discovers that the university regulations are really kind of crippling and stupid! Viewed cosmically, it's a small matter, but it's an example of what can be analyzed into a very big thing."

Bill Griffith shakes his head. "I'm not going to make an apology for the fact that universities are not terribly creative about accepting people of mature years," he says, "but I do think there's something fundamental about our understanding of education that had better be clarified.

"If you're coming to the whole process of learning with a model of 'no transfer of learning'—and there are many people who take that position—then it's quite clear that the training in which you teach people specifically what you want them to do, in which order, puts the university in the position of being a trade school, and that will require a hell of a lot of retraining, because it assumes little or no transfer of learning, and what it's teaching is specific skills.

"But if your philosophy—if your understanding of learning —includes some belief that transfer of learning does occur, then there must be some justification for teaching more than just what a person is going to be able to do tomorrow in the world of work.

"What should concern us is how much we have distorted—as a society—the meaning of a college education. Perhaps the best thing that could happen would be to have so many people with degrees that the economic value of the degree would drop so that it would no longer serve as the major incentive for people to pursue learning. And I think maybe that's happening.

"But my point is, to the extent that the university wants to be a trade school you've got a constant problem of reschooling. But to the extent that your perception of the university is that its major responsibility is to teach the generalizable, and it is the responsibility of the subsequent employers to teach the specifics, then you worry about different things."

"I wonder, though," *Phil Frandson* says, "how adequate is the generalized university education that people get? It seems to me that what really happens every five to eight years is that the typical adult is confronting a reoccurring assessment of values in a rapid and accelerated way, and it has nothing to do with the job. The job may have relevance—and so may a lot of other events in family life and society—but what happens is that the person says, 'I'm ready to go back and study philosophy again, or history, or literature, or whatever,' and the university doesn't provide it except out in the margin, and you pay for it, and it doesn't add up to anything.

"The generalizable basic education I got from the age of eighteen to twenty-five I don't think is anywhere near adequate! It doesn't serve me at the age of forty when I find the whole society value-system in flux. I want to reevaluate, and I want to do it in the heart of the university. I don't care to do it out there in what the university says is a very marginal activity. And I want to be recognized as a mature, experienced person, not as a freshman again."

"That's a different point, though," *Milt Stern* says, "a parallel point."

"OK," *Phil* agrees, "but what I'm saying is that not just career change but also reassessment of values is accelerating in the same sense, and I guess I think neither academia or industry—whatever the philosophy of learning—is dealing with the problems appropriately."

What about paid educational leave?

"Well, then," *Bill Griffith* returns, "what about paid educational leave? I've heard nothing mentioned so far in our conversations about that possibility. I wonder why it is that both in Europe and now apparently in the United States, educational institutions are going to be the last group to discover that such a thing exists and is growing. I don't understand why if money is the important thing, or merchandising and marketing is the big thing—why paid educational leave has not come up as a topic for consideration by this group. What is the stand of NUEA on paid educational leave? I'm struck by its absence from our deliberations."

"There are some reasons," *Roz Loring* says, "why people have at least delayed their wholehearted investment in paid educational leaves. The largest single pool of untapped money that most of us know about is the labor unions's kitty for their workers. Yet the use of that is somewhat less than 3 percent, and one reason—from the workers' viewpoint—is that management is not doing anything to facilitate taking advantage of it. Management is setting up various kinds of prerequisites—for example, that it must be directly related to the job they're currently doing, which will not help them to advance or progress; a worker can't study liberal arts or the fine arts or subjects for personal development unless they're directly work-related."

"Don't you have to say that *some* companies are that way?" *Bob Kost* asks.

"Obviously no statement covers everybody," *Roz* replies, "but there are enough beginning studies available to say that workers don't know how to use the pool of money that's waiting for them. Of course, they may, themselves, not be interested in using it; their values may not lead them in that direction. But for whatever reason, so far people are not using what's already there."

Here *Bill Griffith* interrupts. "But you could understand philosophically that you can regard this as a transaction, and if the buyer is not buying, it could say something about the product."

"Right," *Mort Gordon* agrees. "And it goes back to institutional rigidity. Correct my numbers, Bob, but in the UAW contract there was $900 per worker per year! And in the Detroit area, I was told, one tenth of 1 percent—not 3 percent—of that money ever gets spent! And the main reason, I think, is institutional rigidity."

"But there is the Wayne State project," *Roz Loring* suggests, "which is for workers, and which gives them a degree, and has all kinds of flexibility. I just read a proposal from the National Endowment for the Humanities to extend that to thirty institutions around the country. There are a growing number of institutions that have indicated they're quite willing to accept nontraditional formats."

"Yes," *Bob Kost* says, "there are certain institutions aggressively trying to tap the potential market. Wayne State is one, and so is Oakland University, in the Detroit area. But in general I still find there's a lack of aggressiveness coming from the academic side."

Industry has not held education high in its value system . . .

"I'll accept part of what you say," *Phil Frandson* tells him. "There's a lack of aggressiveness in our institutions, that's true, but that's not the only burden. Another burden is that it should be understood that our American institution called industry has not traditionally held education very high in its value system.

"Our country is loaded with industries that really hold education out only as a kind of status quo carrot, and they don't relate learning to its use and meaning in work life. Education isn't really related to incentive plans and continuation within the system. If it were, you'd be pushing it more, and we'd be out cultivating it more, because it would be useful to our students, and there would be a symbiotic relationship."

"It seems to me one of the things that's overlooked," *John Ervin* says, "is that you can't escape the impact of previous educational experience. If public education has been such a total disaster area for a lot of people—and it has been—it's unreasonable to assume that all those people will willingly plug into a system which is pretty much the same. We've got plenty of research on the relationship of life-style to learning activity that says, 'Those who have most want more, and those who have least couldn't care less.' And it's still true! So part of what we have to do is to go back and do something about the other part of the educational system!"

"What we're talking about, really, is the whole value which education has in the eyes of the American public," *George Robertson* says. "We question it all the time! And if a young person questions the value of going to college, I would think that someone who's making a good salary and has a pair of children to support might well not be much interested either."

We've entered the field ourselves . . .

And yet, *Bob Kost* says, "I still believe that the academic community could do the job if it would go after it, but we just don't see that happening on any significant scale. We've engaged in quite a few studies of other companies, as well as our own, and the market is just so vast that we've entered the field ourselves, in a very quiet way. We're beginning to provide certain services of a continuing education nature to banks, to hospitals, to savings and loan institutions, to wherever we sense a market—and that is going to add a complexity to the whole issue of competition among providers. What I'm saying is that the market is so sizable, and the traditional sources are in such disarray, that those of use who operate within a profit-oriented company see opportunities there."

"That says something about our genius in program planning, doesn't it?" *Bill Griffith* asks. "Here's this big pot of money growing; we have the support of labor and management; the money is there, scarcely being tapped; we are blithely ignoring it. Is it because we really don't like to serve that segment of the public?"

"What I think it says," *John Ervin* puts in, "is something which comes naturally to General Motors, and that is segmenting the market so that as you begin to develop products, you look at that segment of the market which will make this a profitable entry, and so you disregard all the other kinds of populations. Now, I hear over and over again that $30 billion bandied around as a kind of absolute which suggests a kind of uniformity within that series of populations. But it's not so. And if we paid more attention to a careful segmenting of the market, that, in fact, would become the basis for developing some cooperative relationships or complementary relationships that all of us as providers ought to be looking at."

There are opportunities for collaboration . . .

"As I keep saying," *Bob Kost* returns, "there are many opportunities for collaborative efforts among academic institutions that would better serve us than our constant building of internal resources, but let me give you a very recent example from the state of Michigan. We have, as many companies have, a concept of career planning for our employees' career development program. We asked a college consortium of several Michigan institutions if they would address that issue and provide for our employees, on a tuition basis from us, training that would help those employees develop their objectives and interests in terms of career opportunities that are available within the company. Those institutions met with us and discussed how they might wire this together, and so forth and so on. But the project fell apart because some of the institutions felt they could get a larger market share on their own, some felt the need for an advance commitment on student enrollment, and others were just not particularly interested. I don't know all the reasons—it just fell apart because the institutions couldn't come together."

"And yet," *Grover Andrews* points out, "there is one state that has been successfully trying to get collaboration and coordination for continuing education by both public and private institutions, and that's the state of Virginia. They did it by legislation based on the recommendations of a planning committee. They divided the state into six continuing education regions and, by law, mandated that all public institutions work together within each of these six regions with a continuing education board. Any private institution could cooperate as an equal member, and it is working reasonably well. However, I agree that the most difficult part is getting the institutions to agree to cooperate in program planning and development, in new program areas, in developing new outreach programs to serve the citizens of the particular geographic region."

"Whatever the reasons," *Bob Kost* says, "it is very difficult to get institutions to work together. And more than that, I have to keep chiding the continuing education units within academic institutions, because invariably the way they become involved in working with industry—if at all—is through *our* initiation and only rarely through *their* initiation!"

We send our people out . . .

Roz Loring counters: "Maybe I'm speaking from a minority viewpoint—the private university—but we send our people out; we don't wait for you to come knocking on our door! And I meet faculty members from the School of Business in the same offices! We're there to see what the training needs are of people in particular firms and corporations, industries or whatever they are. Private universities have always been concerned!"

"It's not just private institutions," *Mort Gordon* says. "Milt Stern works at a public institution and he's interested in industry for many reasons. And one of them is that his people are supposed to develop courses for subjects and populations that can't pay all the costs; so he's supposed to figure out how they're going to be paid for. The only way he can do this is to make a lot of money on business-oriented programs that he can squeeze the corporations for. And institutions, including my own, make a lot of money in continuing education this way. So if Milt makes money from General Motors, he can then take the money and use it for broadening access on a low-fee basis—or no fee basis at all! But if individual members of the faculty at the University of California or Michigan, or wherever, are permitted to go directly to General Motors—as Bob says they do—where the hell are we or Milt going to get the money to broaden access?"

"If you're talking about financial benefits," *Bob Kost* adds, "let me give you just another small example of where institutions are having financial difficulties in attracting students and they have fixed facilities as we have that need to be maintained. Annually—and this is just a single company example—we're spending on the order of $300,000 on just the rental of university facilities around the country for training programs of various kinds. It's just another example of industry's supporting academic institutions through lean times, and I guess I'd rather pay to support an educational institution than to support a hotel or motel.

"But in all of this talk about money, one of the things it seems to me academic institutions lose sight of—in terms of the strength that they have—is that the other providers, such as myself, want more than anything else to have academic legitimacy for the things they do. There's this whole new move through the American Council on Education and a variety of sources to get credit equivalents. So, in the discussion, one point would be that continuing education programs on the campuses should never lose their linkage to the mother institution. That's part of their power, and I think, from my point of view, that this urge for our sources to have the same legitimacy as your sources is a very powerful thing!"

What is good for General Motors . . .

"That brings me to what I've said before and want to say again," *Bill Griffith* says. "Universities have historically appeared to outsiders as inefficient, confused organizations. Because of the autonomy of professors, it is not as easy to identify purposes and structures or to apply management-by-objectives, as it would be in a business or industrial organization. To advocate that universities become more like business organizations in philosophy and operation would reduce their capacity to serve society. Universities must voluntarily refrain from doing those things which other institutions do equally well or better. Society and industry will best be served by universities which do not accept a behaviorist model as the true approach to education, but instead live with ambiguity as they deal with philosophical issues. What is good for General Motors in terms of management, structure, and philosophy is almost by definition antithetical to the notion of a university. Each contributes, but to do so each must each maintain its uniqueness."

Mort Gordon nods. "Everything you say is true," he says. "Everything we *all say* is true. And yet even if all those things taken together are true, the educational institutions still haven't done enough; they still haven't, even at Wayne State, where they're getting sniped at by the rest of the faculty for doing what they're doing.

"It seems to me we haven't done enough; we're not flexible enough; we're not hungry enough; we're not eager enough; we're not smart enough. We should be reaching more people more ways more effectively. And an awful lot of those people—one way or other—are all gathered together out there in something called business and industry, waiting for us!"

FINAL COMMENTARY

The world of work demands continuing education. Vocational advancement, and training for career change, are clearly prime motivators of individual participation; increased quality and productivity are corporate needs. But despite huge sums of money available for individual tuition assistance or contract courses, industry feels that too few universities are aggressively seeking to identify and meet those needs and too few of the programs offered are adequate in content and instructional design. Therefore industry continues to do much of its own training and increasingly is receiving academic accreditation for that training.

It may well be that many colleges and universities will persist in feeling that adjusting their programs to fit business and industry requirements is inappropriate to their philosophy, in feeling that they can best serve society as unique institutions dedicated to seeking and teaching the generalizable while other institutions deal with the specific and applied. Nonetheless, at a time when the value of education itself is being questioned, there is strong pressure on higher education to regain public support—and in the process gain much needed immediate fiscal support—by providing continuing education specially designed for adults engaged in the world of work. There is also pressure on industry to place education higher in its value system, not just training to increase job skills or courses leading to college degrees, but also education to improve the quality of life both on and off the job.

Certainly the diverse learning needs of employed persons and the ready financial resources to defray the cost of meeting those needs offer vast opportunities to all continuing education providers to serve appropriate segments of the industrial market.

3 THE COMMUNITY COLLEGES

Paper by George H. Robertson

BIOGRAPHY

GEORGE H. ROBERTSON is president of Mohawk Valley Community College in Utica, New York, a position he has held since 1974. A native of Scotland, he emigrated in 1952 to Canada, where he worked as a technician and engineer while earning his B.S. and M.S. degrees in mechanical engineering from the University of Toronto. In 1961 a part-time teaching position developed into a full-time teaching career at Ryerson Polytechnical Institute, and he served as chairman of the Departments of Mechanical and Civil Technology from 1964 to 1967. As chairman he had responsibility for evening extension programs in the Technology Division. These spurred his interest in adult education, and by part-time study he earned an M.A. in adult education from the Ontario Institute for Studies in Education. When the Ontario System of Community Colleges was established, he served as dean of faculty at Sir Sandford Fleming College in Peterborough, Ontario, a school with a strong record of providing adult education in sparsely populated areas. In 1975, while serving as President of Mohawk College, he completed a Ph.D. in higher education from Florida State University.

Robertson's special interest in linkages between the college, the community, and the workplace has led him to participate in community activities and in professional assignments in such groups as the Board of Directors of the Utica Chamber of Commerce, the Industry/Labor/Education Council of Mohawk Valley, the New York Regents Advisory Sub-committee on Vocational Education, and the SUNY Chancellor's Advisory Council of Presidents for Public Service.

INITIAL COMMENTARY

Most community colleges had a modest beginning. Starting as "junior colleges," and in many cases as the two-year appendage to the local high school, they were frequently housed on an upper floor of the high school building and staffed by high school teachers. In recent years the community college has emerged as a rich and powerful institution, epitomized by the huge multi-campus operations such as Miami-Dade Community College in Florida, the Dallas County Community Colleges in Texas, and the Orange County Community Colleges in southern California. But there is still great variety in community colleges. Some have displayed flamboyant instructional innovation, while others have been content to be "cut-rate, small-scale variations of the first two years of a liberal arts college," and still others have become college-level versions of the technical high school.

It is in the area of continuing education that the community college is most renowned and controversial. Competing, usually successfully, with high school adult programs, with four-year college and university extension divisions, and with professional schools and associations, community colleges have moved confidently into the continuing education business. Heavily subsidized in most cases by local taxes, community colleges rode the crest of the support-to-education wave of the 1950s, coasted virtually unscathed through the student unrest of the 1960s, and, until the Proposition 13 philosophy permeated the country, seemed destined to sail serenely on their course. As George Robertson points out, their resilience should not be underestimated; they are prepared to remain in the thick of the power conflict in continuing education. Indeed, in view of their history of innovation, their sense of mission, and their record of achievement, the community colleges will assuredly prosper, although they may have to temper their desire to be all things to all people.

George H. Robertson

The Community College in Continuing Education

Continuing education has always been competitive. Profession-als in the field tend to be entrepreneurs. They have had to learn how the forces of supply and demand regulate their program. They have had to learn the meaning of enlightened self-interest, to make their programs self-sufficient while fulfilling society's needs. And they have generally been self-sufficient operators on the fringe of their home institutions, especially in money matters.

Today, competition results from new opportunities for service, from an increasing demand for continuing education, and from the challenges posed by declining enrollment in traditional college pro-grams. While a good number of colleges and universities have always given special attention to continuing education, the new demand has only recently pushed others into the field, often with the sole pur-pose of generating additional income. Few colleges and universities have been untouched by the decline in the traditional college age-group. Most institutions are taking steps to ensure their survival; many are shifting their programs to attract a larger share of the traditional age-group, and still others are adjusting their traditional goals to suit "new clienteles."

Considering how closely the public interest is associated with education, this competitiveness should be tempered by some reason-ably clear ideas of institutional mission, just as competition in the economic marketplace, for example, is limited by commonsense re-straint and by laws that protect the public interest. But resolution of the current challenges to continuing education will not be easy. In many areas, competition has already led to conflict. Institutional survival is often at stake: we can expect the competition to get worse before it gets better.

In this competitive environment, there is both bad news and good news for community college programs. The community colleges are probably the least powerful of all educational institutions in academic prestige. We can expect to hear all the old arguments of senior institutions, especially that community college instruction is not "col-lege quality." Transfer credits may once again become the major issue they were in the 1950s and early 1960s. As financial resources dimin-ish, we can expect heavier lobbying from senior public institutions and private institutions for greater public support. In particular, they will argue that community colleges were created to meet the demands of an extraordinary surge in the birthrate, and thus they should be the first to be dismantled as the birthrate has declined. The community colleges will find themselves pressed toward the bottom of the academic totem pole.

Yet in spite of their historical disadvantages, and notwithstanding the status of traditional academic institutions, community colleges appear to have many advantages that enhance their ability to survive. They have a local base of support, as well as a commitment to universal access, a concept with great appeal in this country. In inflationary times the community colleges are the only educational option for many citizens. In many program areas, the community colleges virtually control the market—for example, in two-year technical and vocational programs. Most significantly, community colleges are a well-defined movement, thoroughly committed to the ideals of lifelong learning, adult education, and community service. And they have effective lobbyists to help achieve these goals.

Community colleges were conceived as a balance against the university's commitment to elitism and intellectual rigor. The prime mission of the great universities was the preparation of an elite in government and the professions, and the extension of knowledge through research. Access, remedial instruction, and vocational specialties below the baccalaureate level, are of little concern. By contrast, the community colleges have a local base in almost every community, a commitment to access for all who present themselves, the concentration of occupational skills at a level below the baccalaureate, and the commitment to public service at a very practical local level.

The greatest challenge to the community colleges come from that great middle range of American colleges and universities, those with a mission that extends over a broad range. The middle group are in competition with the great universities and with the community colleges. These institutions are highly adaptable, and can change their mission to face opportunities or problems, like the onset of declining enrollment. Many have embraced open door admission, vocational programs, and an upgrading of their admissions advertising. They have also moved into nontraditional areas, community service and continuing education.

The blurring of distinctions between these institutions has been encouraged by rapidly rising college costs. Students of sound academic competence but moderate means follow the two-plus-two pattern of college attendance, starting at the community college, then transferring to another college. Competition from four-year schools, over programs as well as geographic territories, has put heavy pressure on community colleges.

This pressure is likely to force the community colleges into providing even more effective services to its traditional daytime clienteles. It will encourage improved service to previously neglected groups, especially those in business and industry. This is a positive development, as is the increase in rigor and quality of transfer programs. There should also be a payoff in upgraded services for the part-time continuing education student. The local community college will become more important as commuting costs increase, as discretionary income decreases because of inflation, and as community colleges win greater acceptance academically as a result of the two-plus-two pattern.

The ability of the middle-group institutions to compete in occupational programs is limited by their lack of personnel and equipment. The curriculum device of injecting a few courses in business or applied science works tolerably well in daytime course programming, for students who can be drawn into a modified liberal arts program. For the adult, part-time continuing education student, however, occupational courses are the prime necessity, and not supplemental. Community colleges should have a similar advantage in meeting the specialized needs of business and industry, with contract or in-plant courses. The liberal arts colleges generally lack the specialties needed in business and industry, as well as the experienced faculty.

Some academic institutions can define their market by specializations; community colleges are not free to specialize. They cannot be all things to all people, but the truth is that they intend to be many things to many people.

In planning for survival, most institutions inevitably concentrate on tactics and neglect strategy. They focus on aggressive salesmanship and pay little attention to their mission and its flexibility. But continuing educators face changes on a scale that requires them to clarify their mission for the future. For community colleges, the prime mission is to provide access to higher education. They accomplish this with the open-door concept and occupational programs for families that have no tradition of college-going. Their local base makes access easy and affordable. And because the "open door" was opened too late for many citizens, the community colleges also have remedial adult education as an integral part of their mission.

The community college is by no means the only institution to serve the public purpose of universal access, but it does have a clear-cut and uncomplicated commitment to that mission. The mission for access naturally applies. More importantly, it extends into areas of service that involve new students in full-time programs. In addition to services to traditional adult college students, the community colleges have an obligation to provide an "open door" to new adult students, that is, those who have not completed high school.

This is an important and distinctive assignment for adult educators in community colleges. The times seem to be moving in directions that are encouraging to community colleges, especially in continuing education.

The prospects for continued relevance of the community college mission can be found in emerging new clienteles and growth areas, as well as in some traditional ones:

☐ *College graduates* are increasingly participating in adult education programs, either voluntarily to enhance their job skills, or under the pressure of licensure requirements. This prosperous and sophisticated group also sees educational activities as an important part of its discretionary use of money and leisure time.

☐ *Industrial and business corporations* are demanding specially tailored programs for their employees, some with specific job application, and others for general enrichment.

☐ *Government agencies* at every level are increasingly interested in training programs for civil service employees. Government is becoming aware of the need for educational components in community development and information programs.

☐ *Americans who have not completed high school* comprise a large part of our population and are in need of basic education. In many cases they need instruction that will make them "college material."

☐ *National programs to relieve unemployment and assist those on welfare* will continue to require assistance in their educational components.

☐ *Women* looking for job-related educational opportunities will need to be aware of the new kinds of careers available to them, and this trend should place more women in technical and management education programs.

☐ *Elderly citizens* will require programs enabling them to lead a quality life in retirement.

☐ *Young people from families who have not traditionally valued education* will place increasing demands on education. This group will increase the need for developmental education.

These opportunities are likely to catch the imagination of continuing educators, especially those in community colleges. Most of these clienteles will require access to education on a *local basis*, within a few miles of their home or work, and on a *part-time basis*. Presently, there are not great numbers of adults seeking full-time education for career change or a major reorientation to work or life. Work-study, career education, and cooperative programs are developments that point away from a significant demand for full-time study. The pattern seems to be for the integration of career and education, for the young as well as the old.

Effective service to these clienteles will also require special attention to the administrative and technological aspects of education:

☐ *Financial assistance* needs of part-time students are as important as those of full-time students. The logic of subsidizing the working student, the bureaucratization of financial aid programs, and repayment concepts need to be seriously considered before we commit ourselves to financial aid for this expanding group.

☐ *Counseling* requirements of part-time students include assistance with study skills and program planning, but may require additional career counseling and aptitude testing. Minority and disadvantaged groups, women, and the elderly may each require special attention. But we should beware of imposing unnecessary counseling as a matter of routine.

☐ *Educational technology* (radio, television, computer instruction, audiovisual systems) has not had its desired impact on formal full-time instruction, but may be helpful to part-time students. It may broaden access to education for some, but may never replace the need for social and intellectual contact in the classroom.

☐ *Textbooks* have made instructional advances, with integrated study outlines and teaching manuals, which may be more effective and useful than educational media such as television. Educational technology in this form can help deliver effective adult education services, and insure that a greater number of people have access to college opportunities.

Perhaps it is inevitable that a community college specialist takes the point of view that the community college can provide almost everything for everyone. Whatever our reservations, it is difficult to dismiss the view of the community college as a kind of ubiquitous, universal provider of continuing education, within its academic and geographic range. One explanation for this is that the community college lacks the sense of autonomous self-interest that is found in the great universities and middle-range schools. The community college is a purely responsive institution, responding to the needs of the community, students, and the traditional academic institutions. Many other institutions share this sense of service; however, with them, it exists in tension with the idea that the university has its own autonomous purposes that do not necessarily jibe with universal access and community service. The community college has no such dilemma; it simply accepts traditional college objectives as additional demands, to be added to all the other demands from clienteles and the community. In this manner, the ideal community college is a pure adult education service, in which the distinction between full-time instruction and continuing education has for all practical purposes been eliminated.

Community colleges can coexist with other academic institutions. It is probably impossible to avoid resentment from the front-line competitors, to say nothing of the public secondary schools that fear displacement from their traditional roles in continuing education. Most continuing education providers will survive, but not simply by exploiting continuing education. The problems resulting from short-falls in full-time enrollment cannot be solved by simply embracing continuing education. In the end, shortfalls in full-time enrollment will require adjustments in daytime programs.

The community colleges are not without problems in the delivery of continuing education programs. Many faculty and administrators are academically conservative, as indeed they are in other institutions. Staff development and even retraining is needed here. Part-time faculty need to be selected and treated with care because of their importance to the continuing education program. Finally, community colleges are just as likely as any other institution to go their own way, and often need to be dragged into cooperative activities with other institutions. Like other institutions, they should focus on what they are qualified to do.

The community colleges can be a convenient center for cosponsored offerings by other institutions and providers. This arrangement would permit other institutions to make use of the community colleges' numerous convenient locations, thus improving access and availability for many specialized or high-level programs. It goes without saying that some universities and colleges will provide a similar range of services for their local constituencies, or specialized constituencies; but these will tend to be special cases.

For the future, I quote the recommendations directed to community colleges by the 1979 Assembly on Lifelong Learning, sponsored by the American Association of Community and Junior Colleges:

1. That community colleges make an institution-wide commitment to lifelong education. Institutional policies should reflect this institutional commitment. Policies and practices that are barriers to lifelong education should be revised.

2. That community colleges join with other community organizations to sponsor local assessments and other activities that will result in a current picture of unmet lifelong educational needs. Implicit in this recommendation is the belief that community colleges can work with other organizations to solve social problems. Moreover, community colleges should develop programs which respond to the identified needs of specific segments of the population, such as the economically and educationally disadvantaged, minorities, women, older persons, and physically handicapped.

3. That such assessments of needs then be translated into statements of priorities that can be used by policy makers. The statements of needs and priorities should be developed in cooperation with interested community organizations. The interested organizations should unite in presenting their statements of needs and priorities to local, state, and federal funding sources, as well as to business, unions, foundations, and other private agencies that can provide support.

4. That community colleges cooperate with other community agencies to conduct hearings on lifelong education and how to best meet identified needs. Recommendations should be made known to the appropriate community and political leaders.

5. That community colleges collaborate with other community agencies to define the clientele to be served through lifelong education, to shape educational programs to meet consumer needs, and to provide access for all clientele into appropriate programs.

6. That community colleges seek private and public funding to enhance the professional development of counselors, faculty members, and administrators so all staff may better meet the needs of the adult learner.

7. That faculty members be aware of the roles they play in regard to lifelong education and receive special training in working with adult learners.

8. That college presidents take the initiative in bringing together community representatives from all organizations and institutions which provide lifelong education experiences and that the various groups join together to sponsor a community educational information center. The information center would offer educational brokering services, information on various resources, as well as counseling and referral services. Local, state, and federal support should be sought for the information centers.

9. That community college trustees familiarize themselves with local needs for lifelong education and provide local leadership in the development of policies to facilitate lifelong learning services. Trustees should also help interpret the services to the community to help build support for them.[1]

The intent of the community college movement is clear enough: community colleges should be committed to lifelong education, and the term *lifelong education* is used to encompass most of what has variously been described as continuing education, adult education, university extension, and so on, as well as traditional "two-year" career and transfer programs.

It is unlikely that the community colleges, in spite of their commitment and sense of mission, will be successful in everything that

[1]From *Policies for Lifelong Education* by James Gilder, editor. Report of the 1979 Assembly. American Association of Community and Junior Colleges, 1979. Used with permission.

they attempt. They, like other "providers," can expect heavy weather in the next few years. But we can expect that the public purpose of near-universal access to all kinds of higher education will be extended to most Americans throughout their lives. Apart from some fine-print guarantees for the preservation of traditional academic quality, most American colleges and universities surely support that objective.

DISCUSSION

"The score is not in," *Bill Griffith* remarks, "as to whether the community college is truly a missionary or a compassionate prostitute. It could be either."

"Missionaries," *Mort Gordon* points out, "usually get eaten by crocodiles!"

George Robertson smiles. "What I want to say is that the two-year colleges are perhaps the major provider of adult education to the large mass of citizenry and therefore they ought to be viewed very critically in any discussion of adult education. I think that as we look forward to the adjustments of the years that are coming, the community colleges have good enough reasons to believe that they will survive, doing at least as much as at present; and other institutions are going to be under similar pressures. I don't see a cataclysmic future. I think we can see things proceeding much the way they are, with slightly different arrangements."

Mort Gordon shakes his head. "Public support, meaning 'financial support,' for the community college can hardly continue the way it has been much longer. I think that you're all going to be in one hell of a lot of financial trouble and very soon. I think this will come about, and a major change in your philosophical position will follow. You'll change your philosophy when you find out you haven't got money. Philosophy is in part a function of budget. But, anyway, if you look at what has been happening to Americans' expenditure patterns in the last five years, you'll see that this whole country is going into debt at a faster rate than ever before in history. And if you add to that the whopping increase in the cost of gasoline and not much increase in the standard of "living"; you're going to have to start spending less money on some things so we can keep our automobiles, which we have to do. There's no choice in our society. Other societies have choices, we don't. What are they going to save money on?"

"They're going to save it on education," *George* agrees, "but the community colleges are still going to provide the service to the limit of our ability. We'll do that by all sorts of means that are very nicely fitted into an adult education philosophy—the involvement of volunteer instructors, specialists from the community, who are willing to give their time. I know that happens, because we have run courses with volunteers in the past. I've had courses run through the Workers Education Association in Canada. And here in the United States, we've had some experience with lawyers and medics who come in as a routine matter, doing instruction at our very low rates of adjunct pay. They come in regularly as adjunct faculty members. We don't begin to approach the cost of their services. All of these things will happen. That's the religious side of the community college: if it needs to be done, we'll do it."

It costs money to build a church . . .

"But it still costs money to build a church," *Bob Kost* points out.

And *Mort Gordon* says: "I want to make sure I understand you. Do you say that even if money is *seriously* curtailed—then what? You're still going to do pretty much what you're doing?"

"We're going to do as much as we can," *George* says.

"You're going to do as much as you're doing?" *Mort* retorts. "I think you're going to do a third as much as you're doing, a quarter —that's what I think."

George shakes his head. "The funding patterns are shifting. We will be able to derive funds in ways that will allow us to spend money differently, for things we had not been previously funded for. I don't know that you're right in thinking that the community college's share of the pot is going to drop off that much. We're not living in a fool's paradise in New York. Maybe we're doing some other kinds of foolish things, but the financing pattern for our particular college has been desperate for some time. When Proposition 13 came out in California, our county executive brought in his new budget and said, 'We've had Proposition 13 in our county for the last seven years.' We've had these reactions to excessive taxation already. We've got them, but we know how to live with them."

"You mentioned," *Phil Frandson* says, "that if funding should go down further, volunteers will be one alternative. Would you go in a direction of pricing, marketing, self-support?"

"We charge what is necessary to support the course in many cases," *George* responds.

"I know *we* do," *Phil* agrees, "but I just wondered whether you perceive, as an alternative, a fully cost-burdened program in the community college. I think the community colleges I watch are facing that alternative. Most of the gigantic programs in the areas outside the traditional undergraduate curriculums are subsidized heavily. And they're going to have to go. Their leadership is going, too—staffs are being laid off. Now they're going to really have to get into the business-oriented side of being a provider if they're going to do anything."

"Sure," *George Robertson* says. "That's what I mean. We'll try by any means possible. I do believe that the community colleges have got a much more clearly understood mission of service than most other educational institutions, and I think they'll try to do what they're designed to do, no matter what."

"That's a nifty thing to say," *Roz Loring* says, "but in the Los Angeles Community College District, which is a large one—fourteen of them—the first thing that went with Proposition 13 was community service."

"But they'll get back into it!" *George* insists.

"It will be different, though," *Phil Frandson* points out. "It will have to be volunteer work or charging. What else is there? Prayer? George has spoken with a kind of religious fervor. He's spoken of 'the movement.' And you're right—that is different. I don't find that my faculty colleagues are imbued with the spirit of the things that we teach in the graduate program—I don't hear that much. You do. It's coming through to me that you've got a spirit!"

The community colleges are where it is these days.

"I mean it," *George Robertson* says. "When I use the word *missionary*, of course, I do it with a certain amount of irony. But I do think that when we look where the money is, where the activities are—it seems to me the community colleges are where it is these days."

Bob Kost adds: "I assure you that the community colleges will continue to enjoy considerable revenues from the business and industries they're associated with, but when economic times dip and funds become short, it certainly will slow the growth of activities and services that are provided. We face the issue of discretionary spending, and I'm not sure we will spend it on community colleges the way we have in the past."

"Another thing I think we have not brought up," *Bill Griffith* suggests, "is that the publicly subsidized community college has had great difficulty, in more than one location, in trying to give away programs that the customers buy through private trade and technical schools. This is something that we need to think about. Why is it that in the most underprivileged areas the credibility of the private trade and technical school is higher than the credibility of a nice middle- or lower-middle-class-oriented community college?"

Everything to everybody . . .

"A point I'd like to hear some discussion on," *Phil Frandson* says, "is a point I think George made several times, the idea that community colleges should provide almost everything to everybody."

"I'm intrigued by a dozen different things," *Bob Kost* says. "I'm very perturbed by the idea of anyone's being everything to everybody, because I understand how one moves into a void in the marketplace when there is no other option; and perhaps, in fact, the reason the community colleges are so effective in the marketplace is that major institutions, for whatever reason, haven't seen the need or developed the desire to compete in those markets. But I'd be very apprehensive of the ultimate result in quality if community colleges try to be everything for everybody."

"I don't think we're willing or able to do that," *George* says. "When I say—and I do say it—that we should provide almost everything to everyone, I mean we should provide everything within our kind of funding limitations and within our mission of instruction. If we offer instruction—and we do in the technical programs—practically equivalent to that of the junior and senior years of some university programs, then to everybody who needs or wants them we *should* offer those programs and that instruction. I believe, whatever instruction is available in the institution should be made available to as many people as we can get through the door and who want to buy it. We should not, however—and the main reason is that we can't—get into the business of providing for the professional associations' needs, and we can't get into the business of regularly providing junior and senior and graduate instruction."

"That's not the way it's been operating in California prior to Proposition 13," *Phil Frandson* says. "Community colleges define their community, which ranges from adults with little or no schooling to doctors. With respect to doctors, some community colleges have been offering continuing education programs for physicians, programs which have benefited from state support. Because of state underwriting, a fifty-dollar one-week short course on the latest research in cancer can be offered with instruction provided from public and private research universities as well as from practicing physicians."

"I agree that I find that a little inappropriate," *George Robertson* responds. "I have a rather orderly engineer's mind which that kind of thing offends but which does help in thinking about things. I've been sitting here trying to draw a kind of time continuum related to the structural things I described. I see the first stage as being what might be called postsecondary and precollegiate, and I think that in that area the universities do not compete directly with the community college. There's a whole range of content there that no one else gets into, and I think we could agree that that's a job the community college can do a little better in and do a little more of, even though the universities are by and large better funded in a developmental program than community colleges.

"The second stage is during the first two years of college work, and at that point there's competition between community colleges, four-year colleges, and universities. Of course, there are different kinds of universities—some of them are service stations, and some of them aren't and aren't going to be, and they won't compete.

"Within the third and fourth year, however, the competition starts to diminish a little. The community colleges are essentially out of the act, but the four-year institutions and the universities are still trying to work out some modus operandi.

"After the undergraduate years, with the entrance to graduate school, it's clear—and this is a tremendous preoccupation with people here—the competition with the nontraditional providers is what's the big issue.

"And I think there are four areas in this continuum, and the solutions in each area are not the same, and the competition is not the same.

"The continuing education of professionals can take place only within the university or with somebody who's got similar levels of competence. You can't—or shouldn't—do that at a community college. (I guess they've been doing it in California—I believe you. But I would prefer not to see it.) I think the professional associations in engineering, medicine, law, and whatever groups identify themselves through forming into associations—especially the ones related to the license to practice—certainly have a role.

"And then there are scholarly things, in the sense of traditional university interests in humanities, fine arts, and the sciences. I can see these areas of competition in the postgraduate professional continuing education field, and most of the time the discussion seems to keep coming back to that question: What happens after the individual gets a B.A. and gets out to practice a profession somewhere?

"It would be helpful to me if we talked about some of those other three blocks: preadmission, prior to the normal levels of competence for university admission; the two years in which the community colleges and other two-year institutions have an operating license and their resources are pretty effective; and then the third and fourth year, where the competition is mostly among the universities and colleges. Is it not right that these areas might be a useful framework for a discussion of continuing education, as distinct from continuing education for a profession?"

Whose mission are we really talking about?

"It's a very interesting time line," *Roz Loring* agrees. "What you get is a sense of movement, and then you're either on another plateau or there's kind of an overlap that takes place. It's at these moments of overlap that the sense of competition is felt most keenly. There's a sense of, Whose mission are we really talking about?

One of the things that has occurred to me as I have been listening to this so far is that you've brought out most clearly your own sense of mission—more clearly than some of the rest of us. And what's disturbing perhaps, in the notion of competition, is not to be able to get a sense of mission from those others who are outside educational institutions. Or else it looks to us as though their sense of mission is to make money; and that somehow disturbs our sensitivities and our value systems."

"The competition of the people who are simply in the business to make money," *George Robertson* says, "is not something we can do much about, can we? They'll take students away from us quite cheerfully and do it very effectively for a variety of reasons, not necessarily related to quality, but rather to people's perception of what they're buying. However, the moneymaking issue I'm not too sure is a big issue. I think it may be a red herring. If people want to engage in an instructional enterprise in order to make money, that can happen. And it doesn't necessarily mean it's a bad thing."

"I didn't mean that," *Roz Loring* says. "I just meant that it seems as if you've got a single string in your bow, and somehow I like to think of complexity. I'm moving to an awareness that for each of us there are some deeper meanings we haven't touched on to do the kind of work which you find challenging and absorbing. And hopefully you can rationalize it by making it sound useful as well.

"In other words, if we change the mission statement to some degree, these moments of overlap that you were defining would perhaps be something you could deal with more rationally and move on to worrying less about the competition and more about the best way of providing educational opportunities for the students."

Conflict and competition are obvious . . .

"Just an observation," *Grover Andrews* says: "Conflict and competition are obvious around the table between the providers represented—or not represented—here. And one thing I kept hearing—I can say this now because I've been outside institutions for eleven years, not working directly with an institution—I've heard each of you from your own perspective throw out the word or phrase *service*, *public service*, and so on; but I think one thing I did not hear or read in the papers was, What do you mean by *service*? I think the role definition for *service* would be significantly different for a prestigious, rather large, private institution and for a legislatively designed comprehensive community college system. But there must be some common strains and some definition of this if order is to come out of chaos. 'In public service' in some people's definition includes continuing education; in others' it excludes it. In the commercial world it may not include education at all; the borrowing, with or without your knowledge, of some of your key individuals with expertise to apply to a very practical problem has nothing to do with the educational function or mission of an institution at all.

"To go back just briefly to the Carnegie studies of the 1970s and the little book that Perkins wrote on the university's organization. He addressed a very good chapter to the concept of service, and outlined the various conflicting positions that are inherent in this unless it is made operational within the institution, made part of its mission and purpose."

"I have concerns, too, about 'public service,' " *John Ervin* says, "and I'll probably come back to that. But right now I'd like to speak to another point. It seems to me that one of the things I didn't hear about providers is recognition of the fact that they're all trying to do the same thing. And I don't mean just the content competition George outlined. Part of the problem is that all of you seem to be targeting on the same population, and the great unwashed and unserved still don't get served, even in the community colleges. One of my own concerns with that movement is that I've seen community colleges in which all the minorities are in nontransfer programs, just piling up, piling up! And here these middle-class, affluent kids in the technical and transfer programs are right beside them and they go out into industry or on to college, and the minorities just pile up! And yet community colleges keep making these big claims about serving! Hell, they ain't serving! They're catering to essentially the same kinds of populations that the other higher education institutions have been serving all the time. One of the questions we need to address is, How do we really open up access so that we make the nonproductive more productive as we develop our society? How do you do that and still have a place for everybody else to make the buck they have to?"

"I guess I can't deal with that because it is a tough one, and I don't know anybody who has the answers," *George Robertson* says. "But at the beginning level, Ontario illustrates an especially good approach to adult retraining and dealing with basic literacy. And South Carolina is pretty hot stuff in getting community colleges to provide for illiterates. Open colleges are showing up all over the country and getting state support—funding from the state and from the local community. Besides which we're being pretty thorough and ingenious in arranging for credit, and therefore funding, to be available for all sorts of things. There's flexibility of funding, even within the existing patterns, and local support is forthcoming when you show the ability of doing the job that the local people want to have done."

You hear a lot about technology . . .

"Along the line of things you hear a lot about," *Phil Frandson* says, "is the implication of technology for the provider—the electronic world."

"Walk around any university and open closet doors," *Mort Gordon* says. "Thousands of dollars' worth of equipment sitting there."

"That may be true for universities," *George Robertson* says, "but not for community colleges. The mistake that the universities and others made was to assume that educational technology was going to be the whole world. We had television courses for credit; we had newspaper courses for credit; we had videotaped lectures, and audio-cassette lectures; and all of that hardware and technology is just one side of it. I think perhaps the more serious impact will result from the technology of instructional concepts—the whole notion of instructional objectives, outcome measures, and so on. That hasn't taken over completely either, and, thank goodness, it won't. But it has an impact on everybody who is the least bit interested in how to teach a little better. I think these great waves of excitement come and go and leave a little residue and add to the completeness of systems. My own feeling is that future technologies may come and we may spend a bundle on them again. But it probably won't have any greater impact than present technology."

"The way you said that," *Mort Gordon* says, "a figure comes to mind. You know, we have the technologic age, like the Mesozoic age. They go up to the beach and a residue is left, and then the waves retreat, and then a million years from now there will be this layer with all kinds of semiconductors!"

"We are still learning about learning," *John Ervin* says. "Some time ago I sat in on a national meeting in Arizona and we had great excitement about international faces and voices from London, Michigan, and California, and all those remote places, through the wonders of electronics and satellites. And what did they do? They lectured! The lecture method is the least effective method we have. And what you do is render it even less effective by putting it on a television screen and having it talk at you. And I think that's what much of the technology has done: it makes it even more apparent that we haven't learned enough about learning!"

"I agree with that," *Milt Stern* says, "but what has happened is that in the last twenty-five years a whole load of seductive ideas has come down the pike related to education: hardware ideas, teaching machines; let's have this, let's have that! And colleges, in particular, have invested in them and lost their shirts. I'm struck with the fact that community colleges don't accept the notion of reality. They just don't accept it. It will be forced on them, and it may be forced on them much sooner than you think."

The community college will survive . . .

George Robertson smiles. "There are plenty of grim realities in upstate New York," he says, "and I face them every day. But I think the community colleges are going to survive and prosper, because in the community colleges it seems to be quite likely that the continuing education specialists are going to be in charge. The missionaries are in a good position to take over because of the decline in the available population of young people, and it becomes clear that not only survival but mission are all quite compatible, and that funding runs along with both, quite conveniently.

"I think we may well see a number of the two-year institutions, other than the specialized technical institutions, become essentially a matrix of adult education services, with the traditional departments as inclusions in that matrix rather than the other way around, which is the way it is in most of them at the present time.

"We are likely to be in a position to want a very special kind of adult education assistance from the adult educators. We need to retrain our faculty and administrators. We will be a large market ourselves for the services of the adult education departments at most universities.

"I don't know whether community colleges, in general, or in all states, or in all communities, are going to be able to make the transition. For some of them the transition may be just too difficult. The times may never be right. Some of the colleges are probably going to go down the tube because they simply cannot conceive of themselves as anything but a kind of cut-price lower order of the senior institutions. Some of the more recently established community colleges in the East—even colleges established in the last five to ten years—still set out to become small-scale variations of a liberal arts college. Those places, I suspect, will probably die before they can make the adaptation, or else they'll use up so many presidents and deans that nobody will go to work for them.

"I think the emergence of the kind of organization pattern I see as beneficial for most community colleges is not going to happen in all places. But in those places where it does happen, the adult educators will end up being in charge and their problem will be to retrain or repersuade the mass of faculty and administrators; and that shouldn't be so hard, because most of them have the good sense to see that continued employment depends on continuing education."

FINAL COMMENTARY

Supported by local taxes and accessible to a broad local constituency, both geographically and through their "open door" admissions policy, community colleges historically have been able
to provide their services at a lower cost than have other academic
institutions. However, taxpayer revolts cut community college
financial support at the same time competition for students of all
ages increased.

Despite the challenge by other institutions, community colleges
may still emerge as a dominant force in continuing education because
both faculty and administration of community colleges are generally
committed to the mission of providing almost everything for everybody. They believe they are more likely than their peers in other
institutions to aggressively seek to understand the principles of adult
learning, to design appropriate curriculums for new clienteles, to
utilize new technologies in instruction, and to develop local networks
of cooperating agencies to maintain and increase their share of the
continuing education market.

Not all community colleges will be able to adjust to the new realities of finance and competition; some will revert to being junior colleges; some will cease to exist. But those who seize the initiative in
local leadership, in joining with other agencies in cooperative ventures in continuing education, and in providing special services
needed by part-time career-oriented mature students, may achieve
the goal envisioned by pioneers in the community college movement: they may become a pure adult education service in which the
distinction between full-time instruction and continuing education
has been eliminated.

4 THE PROFESSIONAL ASSOCIATIONS

Paper by Lillian Hohmann

BIOGRAPHY

LILLIAN D. HOHMANN is an associate of Blessing/White, Inc., Chicago, a consulting firm offering employee development programs to industry. She graduated from Pennsylvania State University and has an M.A. in adult education from the University of Chicago. She has had wide experiences as an educator and researcher for business and professional organizations.

She has been a member of the faculty of the Cooperative Extension Service of Rutgers and the Evening Division of Northwestern University, where she offered courses in "Preparing Women for Management" and "Managing the Training Function." She has also been a staff member of the Center for Continuing Education at the University of Chicago, developing short educational programs in various fields. As administrative director of the Education Foundation of the National Association of Bank Women, Hohmann had responsibility for a nationwide nondegree management program serving commercial banks. As a research associate for the American Hospital Association's Hospitalwide Education and Training Project, she was involved in national research on centralized training.

In addition to her teaching, research, and administrative duties, Hohmann has served as a consultant to a variety of professional associations, including the Medical Library Association, the Society of Heart Associations Professional Staff, the American Society of Association Executives, as well as to the U.S. Department of Commerce, the Kenwood Truck Company, Chubb Insurance Group, and National Broadcasting Company affiliate stations in Cleveland, Chicago, and Washington, D.C.

INITIAL COMMENTARY

There is widespread agreement that professionals must keep up-to-date in their fields to ensure ever-improving professional competence in service to their clients. Agreement on how to accomplish this is far from unanimous, but continuing education is at least one element of almost every suggested solution. Professional continuing education has become one of the most hotly contested fields of action in education. Professional schools, university and community college extension units, and professional associations vie with each other, and with individual entrepreneurs, for the professional continuing education dollar.

According to Lillian Hohmann, four issues are paramount: Does continuing education actually improve practice? Can an effective model for designing and delivering professional continuing education be developed? Should professional continuing education be voluntary or mandated? Is cooperation between providers possible or desirable? Competition in the marketplace is matched by controversy in legislatures, within licensing and accrediting boards, within institutions of higher education, and among professionals and their associations. Recently, with the rise of consumerism, even the voice of the general public, ultimate beneficiary or victim of the level of professional competence, is being heard.

Lillian Hohmann

Professional Continuing Education

How Can the Professional Associations and Other Providers Best Interact?

Several years ago, a poignant but gently humorous cartoon in *The New Yorker* showed one lemming commenting to another as they and a few thousand other lemmings approached a perilous cliff, "Don't you think we could have gone to the mountains this year?" Like lemmings, continuing educators appear to be rushing off en masse to produce more and more programs. Glossy flyers from academic institutions, professional associations, and aggressive new proprietary groups daily cross the desks of professionals, announcing important and timely programs taught by important and timely instructors. To reach the professional, there is a new breed of continuing educator—the marketer—and the professional is no longer just another participant, but *the market*.

This intense interest in the professional has many explanations, among them the fact that educational institutions and professional associations have been seriously shaken in the past decade by social, political, and economic changes affecting their clientele and membership, their programs, and their finances. With deep concern many have engaged in thorough self-examination, in order not only to survive, but to set new service priorities to foster excellence in professional performance. Others have precipitously taken off to the sea for the veritable golden treasure of the professional continuing education market.

The situation is compounded by increasing numbers of occupational groups who are calling themselves professional associations and are at various stages of "professionalizing." Major issues such as licensure and preservice education, resolved by some groups years ago, are still in the future for others; and there is practically no communication about continuing education across professional lines. Thus continuing education for the professions means continuing education profession-by-profession. Each profession goes it alone, struggling to define such central issues as professional performance standards, appropriate educational programs and techniques, member/learner motivation, and effectiveness in job performance of continuing education. Cyril Houle noted many years ago the advantages of a comparative study of professional continuing education; he hoped for the development of taxonomies of methods, evaluation of methods in different settings, and development of patterns of program delivery.[1] Yet today the impressive work done by some professional groups is hardly known outside their own industries and schools.

Against this background, it is clear why a discussion of professional associations and their access to continuing education is pivotal to a discussion of power and conflict, and competition and cooperation, in continuing education. Professional associations are both the providers and the buyers of educational services; their members are academic continuing education's largest market and also its greatest competitor. Academic institutions are encouraged to initiate broader programs of continuing education, yet the professional association insists that it identify the continuing education needs of its members. Despite the dilemmas, and the lack of cooperation in most programs today, the professional association and the academic institution each has a legitimate role in developing professional continuing education programs; each has special strengths that can be enhanced and certain limitations that can be minimized if each plans carefully its relations with the other. The initiative for cooperation must come from academic institutions; continuing educators should begin to examine professions more carefully, with less predictable prejudice and immediate criticism of their educational programs, and with a fuller understanding of the complexity of professional politics and decision making.

The Professional Association as Continuing Educator

De Tocqueville was one of the first to comment extensively on the American propensity to organize; however, even he would find mind-boggling the complexity of organizations today. There are associations, associations of associations, associations that manage other associations, councils, forums, and round tables. Each claims a special category of professional territory and works diligently to protect its hegemony.

The educational role of professional associations is taken for granted; most members attend meetings to learn "new ideas" by "sharing" information with other members. The associations become battlegrounds, however, when steps are taken to formalize the education function into programs that have regulatory overtones. The debate over this role of the association focuses on such questions as: If influence over members' professional behavior is a legitimate function of the association, by what mechanism should it operate? How

[1]Cyril O. Houle, "The Comparative Study of Continuing Professional Education," *Convergence* 3, no. 4 (1970): 3–11.

can the effectiveness of that mechanism be regularly and reliably evaluated? What role should continuing education play in regulating member behavior? If professional associations do not regulate behavior or provide continuing education, who will? and If government decides to regulate behavior and academic institutions provide continuing education, what does an association have to offer its members? These questions are important and timely in view of the widespread concern over the quality of professional performance, and the increasing tendency of government to regulate professional behavior with continuing education requirements. Partial answers can be found by looking briefly at some of the mechanisms used to influence professional behavior.

1. *Licensing* is a government regulatory power intended to protect citizens. In varying degrees from state to state, workers from hairdressers to real estate brokers to horseshoers are subject to licensure. Licensure exists in areas where unqualified practice poses a potential risk to the consumer's life, health, safety, or economic well-being, and where the public cannot accurately judge a practitioner's qualifications. Licensure is usually not the result of consumer demand, but the response of government to petition by professional groups hoping to protect their own interests. It has generally been accepted as useful and important in protecting consumers despite the close ties between professional associations and their licensing boards. The future of licensure is uncertain; many states are following Colorado's lead in passing "sunset" laws that terminate all regulatory boards every six years and reinstate them only after public review of the continued need for their existence.

2. *Peer review* receives mixed evaluations for its effectiveness in influencing the behavior of members of a professional association. Many feel that by its very existence the organization serves as a constant reminder to members to monitor their professional activity themselves, and that the strong desire to do a good job and be respected by peers is sufficient control. Others suggest that associations like unions cannot effectively influence their members because they are so busy defending professional behavior. Most associations have ethics committees, but they are seldom used unless members have been involved in significant public misbehavior.

3. *Certification* programs have probably been an important device in encouraging professional competence. Most associations have continuing education programs and examinations by which they award their members a certificate, and they encourage consumers to use certified practitioners as a means of improving the profession's image and consolidating the membership. However, as a control mechanism of performance, their effectiveness is questionable. More than one half of the state medical and dental associations require

some form of continuing education as a condition of membership, but a member is rarely dismissed for nonparticipation. In addition, the programs usually consist of traditional lecture courses with examinations that are often outdated.

4. *Mandatory continuing education* results when state governments, usually under pressure from consumer groups, become convinced that professional associations are unable or unwilling to police their members. As a control mechanism of professional performance, mandatory programs may at first appear to be sound: exposure to continuing education should result in better performance. Yet there is little evidence that exposure to education (mandatory or otherwise) results in improved performance. This question is hotly debated, and the discussion suggests that numerous additional factors—such as personal values and attitudes, readiness to learn, personal and social environment, performance feedback, and organizational support of new ideas—mediate the learning experience. In addition, mandatory programs are plagued with logistical problems—record keeping, the time and place of courses, minimum enrollments, and so forth—that minimize their effectiveness. But, the most serious problem facing mandatory programs is programmatic and the questions are basic: How will educational needs be determined? Who are the providers? How will the providers and participants be financed and regulated? How will a marketplace with numerous providers be coordinated to ensure consistent quality? These problems are difficult to resolve because mandatory requirements have attracted marginally qualified providers and hastily planned programs into a greatly expanded marketplace.

If none of these mechanisms provide an adequate answer for the professions or consumers, what can be done? The solution proposed here has two parts; the second will be addressed in closing. First, the responsibility of the association to establish performance standards and to monitor the behavior of its members in return for societal privileges must be reaffirmed. A profession is partially defined by a body of knowledge and a code of ethics; its members voluntarily adopt certain values and norms of the profession. If continued competence is not among those values, the profession gradually weakens, its domain diminishes, and it is replaced by stronger professions. The professional association, then, must voluntarily and aggressively pursue continuing education as an organizational priority.

Organizing for Continuing Education

Despite words to the contrary, associations as organizations often fail to support their own ideals. Edgar Schein states the problem clearly:

The initial purpose of a professional association is usually to protect and enhance the profession through 1) defining its boundaries and setting entrance criteria, 2) lobbying with local government for varying degrees of autonomy or self-government by setting up and legalizing licensing procedures, and 3) conducting essentially public relations activities on behalf of the profession. However, as these associations mature, they often prescribe norms which are presumed to be good for the professional and client alike yet which may be in the interests of neither.[2]

Interviews with the training directors of associations confirm that the politics and public relations of associations frequently distort the real needs of members and alter the direction of good planning. Associations, like other groups, have problems in defining goals, conducting long-range planning, coordinating internal relations, and providing educational programs that address important issues in the field.

Thus a major problem in professional continuing education is organizational. Fortunately, rarely does an association have problems in all areas at the same time. But because associations are voluntary and their members geographically dispersed, communication and unity of purpose are difficult to maintain. Innovation of any kind is risky when members lack the perspective of past and future in the profession, rarely know more than a few members of the association, do not know the association's staff and officers, and have memberships in other organizations, often specialty ones. The apparent power, wealth, and singleness of purpose of an association may be as much image as reality.

A recent survey by the American Society of Association Executives contains data that suggest the associations' difficulties in providing quality continuing education. In 1977 the new education section of ASAE undertook a profile study of member groups, representing a range of trade and professional associations. The seventy-five respondents were predominantly professional associations (the American Medical Association, American Hospital Association, the American Society of Landscape Architects) representing both traditional and emerging professions. The data include important information in several areas:

1. *Program objectives and planning:* In the ASAE study, only slightly over one half of the associations had written objectives for the continuing education function. Without objectives, the barriers to long-range planning are significant. An important correlation was

[2]Edgar H. Schein and Dianne W. Kommers, *Professional Education* (New York: McGraw-Hill, 1972).

shown between the age of the education function and the age of the association. Although the average age of the associations was fifty years, one half of the associations formalized their continuing education programs in the past decade. The continuing education function is immature.

2. *Internal competition:* The continuing education programs compete with other association programs, especially those with public relations value, such as conventions, publications, and lobbying.

3. *Staff:* In an association the staff of the continuing education program have little autonomy and are subordinate to volunteer committees of association members. The staff are expected to be team members, and only occasionally leaders. Although salaries are good, the lack of recognition can cause morale problems. Internal mobility is limited, and professional educators in association work frequently move from association to association.

4. *Directors' education and experience:* For most directors of the education program, association work was a new career. While the majority had education experience, few had been in professional continuing education for more than five years. Seventy-five percent had graduate degrees and 20 percent had a professional degree or doctorate.

5. *Staff size:* The typical continuing education staff is small. The study showed a range of one to thirty full-time staff members, but the average size was six. The problem of small staffs was compounded by the fact that the directors carried other major association responsibilities. Only 21 percent of the respondents in the study spent full time on continuing education.

6. *Role perception of the directors:* More than one half of the directors saw themselves as little more than seminar schedulers, although the majority would have preferred a role as education specialist, consultant, or change agent.

7. *Advisory boards:* Boards are usually composed of members of the association who have very little knowledge of the entire field. Members are typically selected as part of the slate of the president-elect. The boards rarely meet more than two or three times a year. In some associations, little is expected of the education advisory board due to the lack of preparation of new members or the lack of policy and procedure. In other associations, the work load of the education advisory board is overwhelming. In some associations, it is staff strategy to control the information flow to committee members in order to prevent their interfering in long-range activities; in others, staff are the pawns of certain committee members ambitious for higher status in the association.

8. *Program:* Nearly all the associations in the study provided short-term learning experiences for their members, but only one third sponsored certificate, licensure, or degree programs. Program priorities are determined largely by staff observation, but also by

regular surveys and committee input. Program development was predominantly the work of staff and advisory boards. Programs are taught predominantly by volunteers and paid presenters, but some associations employ staff instructors or secure instructors through academic institutions.

From these data it is clear that professional continuing education is traditional and voluntary both in its planning and in its delivery. It is likely to be a new function for the association and its purpose is not clearly defined in terms of the association's overall goals. The staff has heavy administrative duties that compete for time it should devote to program development. Academically and professionally prepared, the staff is nevertheless new to continuing education. Collaboration between associations, academic institutions, and other agencies would be an obvious remedy—if only to the extent of pooling resources and improving the quality of offerings. But although most organizations talk of the need to cooperate, few take steps toward real cooperative ventures.

Cooperative Relations

We know very little about cooperative relationships in continuing education. However, a study of nearly 1,000 National University Extension Association and ASAE members now in progress by the University of Chicago has produced some preliminary data. The study is investigating relations between university extension programs and professional associations with respect to joint sponsorship of nondegree continuing education. The study focuses on *process*—who did what and how—rather than on *program*, which will be dealt with in subsequent studies.

Only 53 percent of the professional associations had participated in a cooperative relationship compared with 85 percent of the university extension programs. Predictably, lack of staff and time and minor disagreements over procedural issues prevented many relationships from getting off the ground. Whatever the reason that many other professional associations did not establish contact with university extension programs, it was not because they received continuing education programs from the professional schools of the university!

The study explores how the relationship between the two groups began, how the needs were assessed, how objectives, curricula, and instructional methods were developed, how faculty were selected, and how the joint effort was administered and marketed. Each party to a reported cooperative venture perceived itself to have taken the major responsibility on each of the issues, with "joint effort" second. Both groups agreed that "public or member demand for new (or traditional) programs" and "industry/professional problems or crises" were the main reasons for the focus of the program. (Governmental regulation was not a significant factor in influencing the contact between the programs, or in shaping curricula.) The programs were offered in a variety of forms, from single-day workshops to full-term courses, the traditional full-term format predominating.

While universities were satisfied with the outcome of the relationship, professional associations were less satisfied. The toughest problem in the relationship for both groups lay in "defining the 'turf' of each organization." Universities also ranked high: "university housing inappropriate for professional adults," and "our overhead investment much larger than expected." Association concerns were "other organization's planning group too large," and "inadequate business procedures at the other organization." The major benefit of the cooperative relationship was "new rewarding professional friendships."

The data suggest that the critical problem in continuing education is not program development; good program development is not dependent on the nature of the provider. The critical problem is *delivering* quality programs to learners; the answer might be in cooperation among providers—if providers knew how to cooperate. To ensure that they learn to do so, we need to develop organizational models of cooperation between different providers. These models should establish the range of the issues to be resolved in funding, staffing, administration, timetables, marketing, evaluation, ownership, and so forth. Some important clues to these models are unfortunately locked away in the files of organizations that have developed original and successful continuing education programs using the resources of both universities and associations.

In the absence of a true model based on adequate data, three models of current practice can only be sketched now, but can be elaborated upon as experience broadens.

☐ The *service model* is the classic operational form. The continuing education function is viewed as a modern-day missionary to knowledge-hungry practitioners. A program is respectable just because it exists, and although excellence is desirable (and often achieved), an organization is successful just for being. Programs are created haphazardly because the organization is *reactive*.

☐ The *marketing model* is an operational type rapidly gaining ground over the service model. Its sophisticated techniques of product marketing enable the continuing education program to be *proactive*. Learners are referred to as "market segments" and programs are "packaged" for eye appeal as much as academic appeal.

In both models quality is determined by what works in the marketplace, and improvements in content are determined by experience or third-party interference. Program evaluation is limited to assessing the satisfaction of participants and counting their numbers; improvements in the effectiveness of learning are left mainly to guesswork and speculation. Both university extension and professional association programs are likely to adopt these orientations; for some institutions it is the only realistic posture in a hostile and highly competitive marketplace.

□ The *performance model* is an emerging orientation whose proponents are concerned with learner performance. For example, concerned with the quality of professional service, some professional groups have exhaustively studied their members' practices and used the results to develop continuing education programs that stimulate self-learning.

A major difference in this third model is its assumption about the relationship between learner and institution. With primary emphasis on learner outcome, participants adopt the role of self-learner and institutions assume a supporting role.

The service model should foster complementary relationships between university and association programs, insofar as one group views another's alternative offerings as evidence of need and not of competition. In some ways this is a version of the classic marketing maxim according to which one business does better *because* there are competitors. The flaw in the service model is that the program developer becomes the ultimate determinant of need, curriculum, and instructional method. Proper credentials, and sometimes just salesmanship by the potential program developer, are all that is required. For some programs curriculum is determined by who is available and willing to teach at a given time.

The marketing model should foster competition. The program director must be continually aware of who is doing what for whom so as to ensure a share of the market. Quality is an important consideration in programs, but staff time is largely devoted to the "bottom line"; the ultimate measure of success is the solvency of the operation and the number of participants.

The performance model would appear to be the most rewarding, the most logical choice for continuing education providers; and, for professional associations, absolutely essential to survival. But it isn't the first choice for the majority because of the required investment of money, time, and staff.

Such then are some advantages and disadvantages of the three most widely practiced models of program delivery. Another question is: What are the advantages of cooperation? Some answers are suggested here in outline form.

Advantages of cooperation for the field of continuing education

☐ greater knowledge of the field of continuing education among professional groups

☐ broader and more appropriate use of adult education technology and methods

☐ professional growth of adult educators

☐ hastening of the emergence of comparative continuing professional education for researchers and practitioners

Advantages of cooperation for association/profession

☐ assurance of a market for programs each association is best suited to provide

☐ better coordination of offerings; omissions and duplication avoided

☐ closer link between preservice and continuing education

☐ better definition of competence in a given field

☐ enhancement of profession in society

☐ more reliable consumer guidelines

☐ acceleration of professionalizing process for emerging professions

☐ strengthening of affiliate groups; attraction of new members

Organizational advantages of cooperation

☐ better institutional performance; greater contact between the professional world, academic institutions, and professional schools

☐ better understanding of institutions; exposure of outdated values

☐ sharing of resources (personnel, space, finances) producing higher-quality programs

☐ employer and employee would share responsibility for continued professional competence

Disadvantages of cooperation for field of continuing education

☐ a coherent program of national scope may limit cooperating providers to the largest and best financed

☐ program planning and implementation may take so long that programs are outdated

☐ curriculum could become complex system of assessments, study modules, and courses; motivated self-learner loses interest

Disadvantages of cooperation for association/profession

☐ a program that is too broad and universal could fail to satisy licensing boards or to prepare professionals for examinations

☐ resources of professional school could be spread too thin in an effort to provide continuing education

☐ graduates of high-quality programs may have placement problems

☐ association membership could diminish if continuing education becomes widely available

Organizational disadvantages of cooperation

☐ planning/implementation process too complex for anticipated outcome; parties become discouraged

☐ evaluation inadequate or unacceptable to one party

☐ financial resources insufficient to accomplish goals; parties in the joint activity unsophisticated in financial planning, grantsmanship

☐ programs too ambitious for long-term administration and record keeping

☐ dominance by the programs of leading institutions; smaller and newer programs discredited without serious examination

☐ career mobility of program developers creates reliance on second generation without training, experience

Consumer Education as an Alternative

If cooperative institutional efforts fail and the future of professional continuing education is dominated by self-interest and intense competition, the only realistic alternative becomes the *continuing education of the consumer*. Consumers are the ultimate judges of the quality of work offered by a professional, either directly as recipients of services, or indirectly as citizens and voters on public policy. Consumers ultimately decide whether a bridge, a building, a medical remedy, a sermon, or a legal opinion is satisfactory. There are encouraging cases of sophisticated consumers' having altered professional practice and continuing education.

Some traditional hospitals have come perilously close to losing their maternity wards because of empty beds; the business has moved to hospitals where psychoprophylactic obstetrics was practiced. Obstetricians have been forced to reshape their skills by educated patients who know the pros and cons of various childbirth procedures. This sophistication among consumers of medical services has irreversibly changed the clinical techniques of obstetrics and the patient-obstetrician relationship. Teaching consumers how to judge the performance of professionals is not a new idea. For many years professionals have printed information booklets on the qualifications of professionals and have encouraged consumers to ask questions. They have helped consumers identify good services and good products.

A failure of continuing professional education is its failure to promote self-learning at the early stages of professional training. Rather than persist in the endless quests to define professional learning needs—quests that look suspiciously like market research—let us collaborate in reaching consumers. How different a world it will be in continuing education if professionals are forced back to the books to answer questions they haven't encountered since graduate school. *Then* continuing education can speak to learning needs and be assured of learner motivation, professional standards, and performance.

The 1980s will demand more of professionals than public relations and promises to remain competent. The tremendous growth in the numbers of professionals, and FTC investigations into the largest professional associations, will force practitioners into greater competition for survival. If professionals have anything to learn from retailing, it is that consumers are fickle. They are no longer rooted in small communities with a handful of familiar professional faces to choose from, but are urban and urbane.

Of course, the proposal to abandon professional continuing education and focus on consumers would have few takers. Associations would not be able to participate, for political reasons, and any other groups tackling the area would find the problems monumental. Nevertheless, accountability must be addressed soon. The failure to promote self-learning is a serious reproach to the educational community and the professions. Cooperation, rather than competition, could overcome the vulnerability of each, and create a climate for creativity and excellence.

DISCUSSION

Phil Frandson opens the discussion: "Cy Houle reminds us that the performance of one half the members of a profession is below average. So, he asks, what's the best model for diffusing new knowledge?"

"I'd like to respond to that," *Lillian Hohmann* says. "I think there are differences in how that might be handled, depending upon the profession. For example, the dentist who operates essentially in isolation might be reached in quite a different way from a social worker with a large government bureau; and I don't think we know very much about a method or any number of methods that work best for different kinds of professional settings—for highly technical professions, say, as compared to highly social, human-resources professions.

"As a result, across the board continuing education in the professions is in very bad shape. It's not well developed, not at all developed, even though some of the major professional associations have launched significant programs. And now legislators have moved in and said, 'You professionals aren't doing very well and we're going to send you back to school. We're going to mandate your continuing education in the face of your incompetence!' I don't think that's the answer, and I'm not the only one who feels that it's an impossible burden on professional associations, the licensing boards, and the schools to provide the right mix in the right places for the right kinds of people.

"That suggests to me that the opportunity is ripe for excellence in cooperative relationships between professional groups and university extension divisions to provide continuing professional education. But because we don't know very much about it, I think the political problems of cooperation have far overshadowed the potential. You get in each other's way in terms of providing continuing education, and then competition takes over because of the breakdown in what should be a cooperative relationship.

"Instead of professional associations' providing programs in cooperation with either professional schools or educational extension divisions, what happens is that brochures are being printed by any number of providers with no quality control whatsoever. It's an open market. I think the professions are suffering, and the universities are suffering."

Diffuse new knowledge to the top 5 percent . . .

"But no matter who provides continuing education, or how well or how badly it's done," *Phil Frandson says,* "one argument is that you're never going to diffuse the newest of knowledge to the bottom 50 percent. Yet the mandatory continuing education laws are directed at that segment. On the other hand, the best way, some arguments go, is to diffuse new knowledge to a very rarefied few—the highest-quality, the really stellar people in every profession! Once you get that very small 5 percent of the bell curve, you are then making the greatest investment, and you can call it cost-effective. It may be argued on that basis that those 5 percent are the ones who will really influence change and ultimately affect the bottom half. That's contrary to most models which most of us in continuing education think about. I'm just wondering if that isn't an extraordinary and very powerful thing that all of us in education should deal with—I'm wondering, What is the right group to reach?

"And a seat-of-the-pants reaction to my own question is that most professionals follow the leader—not the professors, not the university, not our continuing education program, but the best among us. And even though the best are variously defined, they are those people who are at the top of the list. I would suspect that it is those types in the professions who are most open for continuing education, not the people who are at the lowest levels of practice—those whom the legislators and consumers are out after. Those are actually the least likely to come into the continuing education program."

"I think it's true," *Mort Gordon* says, "that research does indicate that the bottom 30 percent or 40 percent don't go anywhere, and don't know from nothing—but the fact is, that's the best argument for compulsory professional continuing education I've heard yet. You're never going to have a chance to teach the lower half anything (never mind for them that we're not talking about *new* knowledge—we'd be happy if they learned the *old* knowledge!) but if you send soldiers after them and bring them in, then at least you've got a chance that they might learn something! You're talking me into compulsory professional education for the sake of the 30 percent or 40 percent on the bottom who never attend any of these things and won't unless you make them!"

There's the impact of the reward system . . .

"A very important point in this whole thing for many of the practitioners," *John Ervin* points out, "is the impact of the reward system, because modification of the reward system does an awful lot about the willingness to become involved with new knowledge. Part of the reason librarians, public school teachers, and others don't participate except under pressure is the reward system. You're on a salary schedule. You can beat your brains out, and nothing happens. You do nothing, and the salary schedule rewards you."

"That's another of our failures," *Lillian* says. "Learning should be its own reward. It's fun to learn; it's fun to think . . ."

"That's just one of the things we say," *John Ervin* interposes.

"I know," *Lillian* agrees. "But can we move it ten degrees nearer to the center?"

Roz Loring has been waiting for a chance to break in. "I've been thinking of another aspect of the difference between the top and the bottom in the professions," she says. "It's intriguing to note that the *most* prestigious of the professions—which I guess we could agree upon if we had to—as well as the *least* prestigious of the professions have many members who join organizations. Some of the *most* prestigious professions seem to have required licensing, and some of the *least* prestigious professions or occupations seem also to have required licensing. The rest of us in the middle—we're kind of sliding through, not important enough for anybody to worry about."

"That touches on the thing that disturbs me most," *George Robertson* says. "It's a problem that almost leads you to despair. I'm thinking of the engineers and others who operate in fields that do not require professional licensure—like the aerospace industry. There's no state requirement that says you have to be a registered professional engineer if you are developing solid-state circuits. And yet these people are right on the cutting edge. They're teaching themselves and learning all the time, and working closely with universities in their science departments. It strikes me that we use licensure as a good excuse for encouraging a few and driving others out of particular professions. The ones that really bother me are the wealthy professions—medicine, dentistry, and law—where it's quite clear that the massive public interest is in having them competent! We should hope that the licensure examination begins to mean something and that we'll put some of these birds out of business if they don't measure up. They have a license not only to practice medicine but also to make a bundle of money at it."

Start with 'in the public interest' . . .

"I start," *John Ervin* says, "with the issue I think you're raising, and it's contained in the expression 'in the public interest.' That has been the rationale of much that has been developed for distribution to a variety of publics. But what's actually going on is that people who function within a field of work which involves special skills, techniques, and so forth, find their positions enhanced by the designation 'profession.' Licensing regulations and procedures become useful for selective addition and selective elimination. It grows out of their need to protect their own status. Associations which emerge as vehicles for assisting in the definition of what those regulating procedures will be are simply another way the profession maintains itself by helping to determine what those regulating procedures will be and do.

"The collective self-interest becomes increasingly important, and the public interest is more narrowly defined. Cooperation with other associations is less important than improving conditions of the membership. Competition is avoided only when it seems counterproductive to the aspirations of the membership. (That's kind of a double negative.) What I mean is that when we talk about cooperation and competition, those are not as important in the professions as is the matter of their own self-interest. Education and programming then become more a matter of satisfying maintenance requirements than continued professional growth and development. 'In the public interest,' in that sense, narrowly defines their real interest, but the overt rationale remains 'the public interest,' although what they're really talking about is 'what's good for us'! It seems to me that's the context within which we look at cooperation and competition between the professional associations and all the other public providers."

What about the locus of power?

"That really speaks to a point I think we need to deal with," *Milt Stern* agrees. "I wonder, What do you think about the issue of the locus of power? The locus of power might be in continuing professional education and is related to the issue of relicensure and the composition of state boards of relicensure. I don't suggest that we would exclude professionals from these boards. As a matter of fact, I think there's nothing so easy to co-opt as a public member of a professional board if he doesn't know anything. But if you were able to put something like continuing educators of quality on such boards, or if specialized members of the lay public for a given profession were represented—is this a possible answer?"

"I would think so," *Lillian* says. "In many professions there is a continuing problem with licensing boards—they don't have enough competent people on them."

"We have had public members on our boards in California for some time," *Phil Frandson* points out, "and I don't know how others feel but I have seen no evidence that the public-member role has increased the disciplinary role.

"And now we're in another phase in some states—unless regulatory boards can justify their worth, they will go out of existence. Can regulatory boards establish their worth by making an impact on the issue of quality, on discipline, on levels of practice?"

"I think one of the big problems in professions is there just isn't yet an answer to professional behavior," *Lillian Hohmann* says.

"It's the old question," *Phil Frandson* says: "Who should control quality? You say it's the practitioners?"

"Yes and no," *Lillian* says. "The problem is that it's the professional school that is regulating or defining what a competent professional is *at entry level. But that's where it ends.* The professional school takes no more responsibility for its members."

The best bet for improvement is 'performance standards' . . .

"And that brings us directly to one of the most interesting things I found in your paper: performance standards," *Grover Andrews* says. "Apart from the power and the politics that we were just talking about, I really believe that you've got the heart of what might be the best bet for improvement of the profession and the role for continuing education if you mean by *performance standards: where* standards are set, based on performance criteria; *how* they can be developed as a basis for education; and then *how* the results can be validated."

"Unfortunately," *Lillian* says, "when I've talked to different professional associations about this, they start off by talking really impressively about performance standards, and then . . ."

"You've got a dilemma," *Grover* agrees. "The dilemma is that most of the educational institutions in this country do not structure education in terms of performance criteria. They look at input, not outcome. They assume that if you go down the tube a certain way, you're going to come out able to do this or that or whatever. A lot of people speak the rhetoric, but they do not have the performance criteria established, and more than that, they do not have the evaluative system to verify performance. In other words, the dilemma you're in is that if you emphasize performance, where are you going to get the training? Most of the institutions are not really equipped. But I do know of one dental school—Kentucky—that changed its whole curriculum and its whole mode of operation to performance. Their faculty spent a large number of years in developing their whole program into performance criteria. The entry point and exit point are no longer fixed in time. They're totally based on when a person can demonstrate competence in dental work of all types. And there is a great deal of interest in this. And that's good!"

Continuing education is oriented to what individuals say they want . . .

"As preprofessional training," *George Robertson* agrees, "but it's truer to say continuing education in the institutions is oriented to what individuals or individual groups say they want than that the institution has initiated some type of performance-oriented program. You come to me and say, 'I've got a group and we need a place to meet and we may need a teacher,' etcetera. OK. You say you know exactly what the performance is that you're trying to achieve and you want us to sit down with you and try to help structure a program, drawing on the expertise and resources the university has, and if we agree, you will enter into a working relationship in which we'll be trying to help you achieve your performance standards, figuring out the best way to do that and how to measure it. But the problem in the past has been that we're not equipped to do that. Probably not even Kentucky! The association has a different set of goals from ours—operationally, functionally, substantively."

Mort Gordon says: "Professionals, present company included, become who they are as a consequence of getting socialized in the profession. When you go into a continuing professional education program, if your professional education wasn't done right in the first place, you've become socialized in the wrong way, and it confirms the socialization. For example, in those associations that do their own continuing education because they don't think the universities can do it, or they don't want so many people having a voice, or whatever . . . who does the planning and teaching? Where do they find the people to do this?"

"Definitely volunteers," *Lillian* says. "Members of the association from practice. From the field."

"These are all natural-born teachers eight feet tall?" *Mort* asks.

"That's right," nods *Lillian*. "That's exactly what the problem is!"

Professional education is too important to be left to the professions . . .

"And I guess that's why I think continuing professional education is too important to be left to the professions," *Mort Gordon* concludes. "It can't be, because if there is anything wrong, they did it in the first place."

"And in that connection," *Milt Stern* says, "I thought that Lillian had a very interesting point to make—that business of consumer education. You're suggesting that the professionals themselves, and the associations themselves, educate the consumer. That's kind of rubbing their noses in it. I just wonder what ideas you might have about how you might bring to professional associations that wonderful and delightful idea of educating consumers."

"My thought there," *Lillian* says, "is that we seem to be getting greater and greater and larger and larger cycles of continuing professional education, yet we've still got problems with doctors who don't practice good medicine and dentists who don't practice good dentistry, teachers who don't teach well, and so forth; and so maybe what we ought to do is forget about trying to reach all those people and about dragging them back into school, and try to remember that we were supposed to have inculcated lifelong learning at the university and forgot to do that, or at least didn't do that. So if they're out there, practicing bad dentistry, forget about trying to reach them—get the customers lined up, teach them what a poor job of dentistry is like, if you can, and let the practitioner beware. How do you do that? In neural surgery I suppose that would be very difficult. But in dentistry or medical technology or engineering, it might be possible to teach what a good bridge is."

"There is a growing need for programs on how to choose and evaluate your doctor," *Phil Frandson* points out, "but schools of medicine and the profession are reluctant to support such programs."

"Of course," *Mort Gordon* says. "At least, in anything like the short run neither the associations nor the medical schools are going to participate in a program that educates the consumer unless they're forced to. I'm sure that's a kind of altruism I wouldn't, myself, be sure I wanted to affect what I do for a living. As we've said before, professional associations are dominated by the professionals. It can't be otherwise. Who else is going to dominate them? Professionals are looking out for the profession as defined by the leading professionals. I'd like to educate consumers, but I can't imagine the professions' wanting to do that—unless they were under the whip!"

Continuing professional education is not a failure . . .

"And in that connection, I'd like to comment on something else that both the paper and our discussion seem to be suggesting, and that is that continuing professional education is a failure," *Bill Griffith* says. "I happen to think that there are a number of fairly serious professional organizations involved in effective continuing education. For example, the Veterinary Medicine Association has spent a lot of time and money, and has used consultants wisely, to put together self-administered diagnostic tests so that individual members are able to assess what they don't know they don't know. I'm not repeating myself—that's intentional—because one of the hardest jobs we have in continuing professional education is that people don't know what they don't know and therefore they are not motivated to try to learn anything. So the fact is that we do have professional associations behaving, I think, rather ethically. The anesthetists, I believe, have very similar kinds of programs, and a number of the journals have self-administered tests with answers and guides to where you can find the information that will help you to arrive at the same or some other conclusions. I'm just disturbed a bit that we m come out of this meeting with the blanket statement that continuing professional education is a failure. Is that what you mean?"

"Of course I didn't mean that all continuing professional education is a failure," *Lillian Hohmann* says. "But I continue to be disturbed that only a few of the associations are doing the kind of thing you point out that the veterinarians are doing. Most are still at the happiness-index level. They have that one single evaluation question, 'Do I keep you happy?' And I think that's the predominant tool in continuing education also. 'Would you come back?' 'Would you recommend it to others?' It's almost the notion 'Have I entertained you?' Not 'Will you use some of this information in practice?' but rather a perception that you were, by and large, pleased by the event and that, after all, that's why you came to Hawaii to the annual convention. I think that's unfortunate.

"And I see what I think is an equally unfortunate trend—professional associations' now getting into large-scale continuing education as a money-maker. It's the same kind of phenomenon that's corollary to the university. After all, the professional association can only charge so much for membership; there's only so much the members are willing to fork over every year. So how do associations make money? They diversify. They offer more products—and the more products you offer, the better. One of the big money-makers the professional associations, especially the new ones, have just discovered is continuing education, because this can be mainlined into the office budget if just anybody will stand up there and keep the audience really happy for the afternoon."

Roz Loring says: "Although we may not yet have been able to find the best way to validate the value of continuing education, I have to agree with Bill Griffith that we miss seeing what has been an enormous growth in the capabilities of the health professions, specifically, the impressive technical advances which have taken place. They could as well be laid to continuing professional education as to anything else, since most of those advances came about because practitioners as well as professors have learned better how to bypass hearts or whatever. It seems to me that we have some fine empirical knowledge that a good deal of benefit has been derived from continuing professional education. Whether the practitioners would all pass tests or not, I'm not sure. But on the other hand, if we use certain kinds of criteria, we could say that continuing education for managers in business administration must have been some kind of success because of the growing numbers of people who are taking part. They must think somebody got something out of it."

What's a good program anyway?

"With so much stuff going on," *Mort Gordon* says, "I'm willing to believe that there are some very good continuing professional education programs run by whomever, some mediocre ones, some awful ones. But to deal with Roz's first point, what's a good program anyway? And what's the difference between a good one and a rotten one? And who knows what the crucial elements are: money and/or leadership and/or the particular profession? Is it easier in veterinary medicine to put together a good program than it is in social work? Do we know that even?"

"I think this is what continuing education as a field may need to define," *Lillian* says. "How do we come up with what is a model program or any number of model programs? Common elements that are ways to evaluate outcomes? In medicine, for example, if 50 percent of the time you get well spontaneously—so that all the continuing education in the world may or may not affect whether a patient gets well—then maybe it doesn't make any difference how or if we offer a model for continuing education in medicine.

"I guess I believe, though, that it probably *does* make a difference, and that we ought to be about the business of joining professional associations, and that educators should make it their business to try to figure out how to do the job better. There are too many physicians who do not go back for continuing education, too many veterinarians who are not going to take the self-assessment test. The top 5 percent—the leaders—will, I think, do that. The next group may stumble on something in the journal and do something. But it's the group that isn't learning that really endangers the professionals and the profession itself, as well as their own practice. That's the group we're talking about here. That's where it is."

FINAL COMMENTARY

The frustration of continuing educators seeking to contribute to improved practice in the professions is exemplified by the dramatic difference between four suggested strategies to achieve that end: (1) concentrate on the top 5 percent of the professionals in the belief that the field will follow the leaders and that when performance at the top improves it will also improve at the middle and bottom; (2) mandate and enforce continuing education and periodic relicensure for all professionals; (3) declare a moratorium on professional continuing education and concentrate on consumer education; (4) rely on the personal integrity of each professional by providing self-learning packages, which include self-scoring tests, and hope for the best. The central problems are that while professional schools generally define and apply standards for entry into a profession, the professional associations, which take over from that point on, are usually more protective of the professions than regulatory. Available continuing education programs, whether sponsored by professional associations, academic institutions, or entrepreneurial organizations, are frequently designed to raise money rather than standards. Despite the difficulties, so many vital interests are involved that the future appears to demand increased cooperation between all providers of professional continuing education in order to encourage universal participation by professionals in programs that demonstrably improve performance.

TWO

Continuing Education Organization and Operation

How Should Continuing Education Be Evaluated, Financed, Organized, and Staffed?

5 ACCREDITATION

Paper by Grover J. Andrews

BIOGRAPHY

GROVER J. ANDREWS recently rejoined North Carolina State University as assistant vice-chancellor for extension and public service and professor of adult education. He received his Ph.D. from the same school in 1972 with a dissertation on "Public Service in Higher Education: A Status Study of Accreditation in Adult and Continuing Education Programs." He was also assistant to the administrative dean for university extension at North Carolina State from 1967 to 1968.

Over the last seven years, Andrews served as associate executive secretary of the Commission on Colleges, Southern Association of Colleges and Schools. He directed the research that led to the adoption of a new standard for accreditation in adult and continuing education in the Southern Association. He directed the research that led to the guidelines for putting into effect the Continuing Education Unit (CEU). He also developed a series of accreditation seminars held in each of the Southern Association's eleven states.

Recently Andrews was selected by the Council on Postsecondary Accreditation (COPA) to direct a national project (funded by the W. K. Kellogg Foundation) to develop evaluative criteria for the accreditation of nontraditional education. Following the recent publication of the study's final four-volume report, he was again selected by COPA to direct a national project, now underway, to investigate education provided to military bases by postsecondary institutions.

Andrews has held administrative positions at Baylor University, George Peabody College (from which he received two degrees), the University of Arkansas at Little Rock (where he was also assistant professor of English), and Meredith College, Raleigh, North

Carolina. He has published extensively on accreditation and the CEU and is a frequent speaker to such groups as the Regional Accrediting Associations, the American Council on Education, the National University Extension Association, the National Association of Land Grant Colleges and Universities, the National Association of Summer Sessions, and the American Association for Higher Education.

INITIAL COMMENTARY

Accreditation, in the past, was essentially ignored by those in adult and extension education. When "adult education" had to do primarily with literacy and citizenship education for immigrants, competency—not credit—was the goal. When "adult education" became a movement in the 1920s, enlightenment and enrichment were its goals, and credit was a non sequitur. "Extension education" went in two directions, both directed to a rural, agrarian constituency: one led to the improvement of agricultural practice; the other provided for the delivery of the content of non-agricultural campus courses—but did not lead to the awarding of degrees—to individuals some distance from the campus.

With increasing industrialization and urbanization, "evening colleges," extending and replicating the "day school," began to emerge. Increasing demands for credentialing by agencies outside the educational enterprise led to the awarding, first, of "credit" to the part-time student and, ultimately, of the "degree" to those who completed the curriculum. (Typically, a "two-year" or "four-year" degree took eight to fifteen years to complete!) During the last two decades a new movement, the "nontraditional," has emerged, and credit and degrees are being offered for "life experience," "contract projects," and "learning activities" that would have seemed academically questionable to even the most revolutionary and radical extension educator fifty years ago. Add to these the variety of programs in "continuing education," and the result is increased pressure for "accreditation." Indeed, the pressure for accreditation has been exacerbated by the creation of a host of accrediting bodies: voluntary regional associations that accredit institutions; specialized professional associations that accredit specific programs; and associations of proprietary schools that accredit noncollegiate organizations formerly ineligible for accreditation. And the involvement of state and federal regulatory agencies in accreditation adds still further pressure.

Despite these developments, continuing educators have universally resisted getting into the accrediting business themselves, relying on the institutional accreditation of regional associations and maintaining that content, not credit, is their product. But in the competition for survival within institutions, specialized accrediting associations have demanded control over continuing education by deans of separate schools and colleges, and not by the centralized continuing education unit. As a result, many continuing educators see outside accreditation as a major threat to their capability to deliver programs. Continuing educators are now discussing special accreditation. As Grover Andrews shows, the accreditation issue brings power and conflict in continuing education into sharp focus: continuing educators are concerned not only about competing groups within their own institutions, but about the intrusion onto their "turf" of other academic institutions' programs, and of programs developed by "outsiders," whether by nonacademic organizations sponsored by accredited institutions in name only, or by entrepreneurs not associated in any way with academic, or accredited institutions.

Grover J. Andrews

Continuing Education Accreditation

Who Should Be Responsible, and What Standards and Ethics
Should Be Developed?

Though continuing education has been defined in many ways by many different individuals and organizations over the years, the National Center for Higher Education Management Systems issued in 1979 a new compendium of definitions that identifies *continuing education* as "the philosophy and the process under which an institution, organization, agency, or individual provides organized learning activities for the professional or personal development of adults whose primary role is something other than that of a student." The compendium extends the definition to include *continuing professional education* as "instructional programs, courses, and seminars contributing toward certification, credit, degree, licensure, or the improvement of the competencies of participants in the professions."

Other definitions of terms that are related to continuing education and that are relevant to this paper are as follows:

Adult Education: "Instruction designed to meet the unique needs of persons—beyond the age of compulsory school attendance—who have either completed or interrupted their formal education and whose primary occupation is other than full-time students."

Extension Education: "Education offered outside the normal physical confines or formal framework of an educational institution. It may include such activities as short courses, conferences, institutes, independent study, and credit or noncredit courses offered in off-campus settings and/or via television or other media and correspondence."

Lifelong Learning: "The process by which a person acquires knowledge and skills throughout his/her lifetime, in order to maintain or improve occupational, academic, or personal development."

Recurrent Education: "The distribution of education over a person's life span, which makes it possible to alternate between work, leisure, and education in a nonsequential manner."

Accreditation: "The process whereby a recognized state, regional, or national agency or association grants public recognition to a unit of an educational organization indicating that it meets established standards of quality, as determined through initial and periodic self-study and evaluation by peers. The essential purpose of the accreditation process is to provide a professional judgment as to the quality of the educational institution or program(s) offered, and to encourage continued improvement thereof."

Scope of the Field

The range and scope of the field of continuing education is unlimited and currently has had few restraints placed on it and few boundaries established. Herein lies one of its greatest strengths and also one of its most serious weaknesses. The strength obviously is in the diversity of the field—a strength to respond to any educational need of any adult no longer involved as a full-time student—and in the ability of the continuing education administrator or educator to respond to an educational need quickly and imaginatively.

The potential weaknesses of such an uncontrolled and open approach are many, however; the most significant ones appear to relate to an unevenness in the quality of programs offered and a duplication of effort by the multitude of providers. Until the past decade or so, few efforts were made in any of the arenas of "continuing education" pertaining to setting standards or establishing criteria for program development and evaluation, or concerning ethical practices among the providers. Most of the recent efforts in these directions have been made by the voluntary accrediting agencies for postsecondary education and by the various professional organizations and agencies. A recent development has been the move by a number of professional organizations to secure legislation by state assemblies interlocking licensing or certification with continuing education and, in some cases, specifying (directly or indirectly) a particular provider.

In 1974 the first national accrediting agency for continuing education was established, the Continuing Education Council, now called the Council for Noncollegiate Continuing Education (CNCE), to provide accreditation to the variety of noncollegiate organizations, agencies, associations, and businesses that offer continuing education for their employees and constituents. The CNCE was officially recognized by the U.S. Office of Education in 1978. It has not yet been recognized by the Council on Postsecondary Accreditation (COPA), the official body for voluntary nongovernmental accrediting agencies.

Another national development in continuing education that may affect quality and ethical practice in the field was the creation of the Continuing Education Unit (CEU) by a National University Extension Association (NUEA) affiliated National Task Force in 1968. While the CEU is a quantitative unit of measure for participation in continuing education programs, the criteria for use of the CEU when properly applied provides the framework for qualitative improvement in continuing education programming. The National Task Force for the CEU was reconstituted in 1978 as the Council on the Continuing Education Unit as "a nonprofit federation of education and training organizations and individuals devoted to the constructive and consistent use of the CEU and to improvement of the quality and effectiveness of continuing education training and development."

While each of these accrediting bodies and organizations is dealing with the qualitative issues in continuing education within the context and scope of its current operations, none to date has a system capable of addressing the depth and breadth of the complex, multidimensional field of continuing education. Of the six regional accrediting associations, only three have developed formal procedures and criteria for review and evaluation of continuing education in their accreditation processes. A significant number of the fifty-five specialized professional accrediting agencies recognized by COPA has included continuing education in its accreditation procedures. Both the regional associations and the specialized agencies, however, deal only with established postsecondary institutions. And while both the CNCE and the Council on the Continuing Education Unit are organized to work with the nonpostsecondary providers of continuing education, such as business and industry, professional organizations, government agencies, and community and other social organizations, the scope and range of their work to date is rather limited when measured against the total field of formal sources of learning for adults in the United States.

The Johnstone Study of the early 1960s indicated that some 25 million American adults were involved in some form of learning activity. Samuel Gould, in his final report issued in 1972 for the Commission on Nontraditional Study, indicated that 80 million American adults were in need of further education at the postsecondary level. More recently the Future Directions for a Learning Society Project of the College Board issued a report in 1978 that distinguishes 58.4 million adults who are engaged in formal learning, of whom 12.4 million are in schools and institutions and 46 million are in nonschool organizations (see Table 1).

What Should Be Done? And Who Should be Responsible?

The real questions to be addressed are: What should be done to promote quality in continuing education programming? How can this be done in such a large, complex, and diverse field? and Who should be responsible for the assessment and evaluation of continuing education programs to ensure quality and integrity regardless of the provider?

TABLE 1: FORMAL SOURCES OF ADULT EDUCATION AND LEARNING (1978)

SOURCES	SCHOOL/ NONSCHOOL	NUMBER OF LEARNERS (IN MILLIONS)
Agriculture extension	NS	12.0
Community organization	NS	7.4
Private industry	NS	5.8
Professional associations	NS	5.5
College and university part-time	S	5.3
City recreation	NS	5.0
Churches and synagogues	NS	3.3
College and university extension and community education	S	3.3
Government services	NS	3.0
Public school adult education	S	1.8
Federal manpower program	NS	1.7
Military services	NS	1.5
Graduate and professional education	S	1.5
Trade unions	NS	0.6
Community education	S	0.5
Free universities	NS	0.2
Total school		12.4
Total nonschool		46.0
Grand total		58.4

Sources: Lifelong Learning Report (1978), Richard Peterson et al. (1978), and *Chronicle H. E. (1978)*

While there is a need for a more complete and uniform review of continuing education activities by all the regional and specialized accrediting agencies, this would still only address the work in this field by the established postsecondary institutions. Though there is much room for expansion and improvement by these agencies to provide for a consistent evaluation of continuing education through the existing accreditation system, there is not the level of concern over the work of the established postsecondary institutions that exists concerning the other types of providers. The Council on the Continuing Education Unit is limited in its scope of operation in that it works only with those institutions, agencies, and organizations that are using the CEU, and its functions are primarily certification, information, and research. The Council for Noncollegiate Continuing Education also has a limited scope of operation and has not yet gained the legitimacy and acceptance necessary for national significance. The National University Extension Association has been exploring the feasibility of developing an "accreditation" function, but no decision has been reached, and even if such a function should be developed, its scope of influence would be minimal because of the association's limited membership; in fact, it would for the most part be a duplication of efforts by the regional and specialized accrediting agencies.

A more comprehensive project currently being developed is the proposed "National Project to Assess the Quality Assurance Factors in Continuing Education: Accreditation of Continuing Education" by the Council on Postsecondary Accreditation. The COPA study is to be cosponsored by the American Council on Education and the National University Extension Association. The project is being designed to be sufficiently comprehensive in nature to include all types of providers of continuing education and to study and assist in improving their practice relating to the three basic functions of continuing education programming. These functions are—

1. cultural enrichment and personal development
2. licensing and certification
3. conferral of degrees and other formal credentials

The purposes of the COPA study are as follows:

1. to survey the process of continuing education and the relation of that process to the educational objectives of the learners

2. to identify the criteria and standards necessary for conducting and for improving the quality of continuing education programs

3. to determine appropriate methods for the assessment and evaluation of continuing education, presently and in the future

4. to develop policy for the evaluation and accreditation of continuing education, for use by institutions of postsecondary education, the Council on Postsecondary Accreditation, other approval and certifying agencies, other educational agencies and organizations such as the American Council on Education and the National University Extension Association, and other providers of continuing education

5. to determine the type of productive relationships (and ethical practices) that should exist among the various groups, agencies, and providers

6. to compile contemporary national research data, thereby identifying trends and issues in a rapidly moving field

To achieve these goals, the COPA study is being planned in five phases:

Phase I: a preliminary survey of the literature and state of the art

Phase II: research of specific functions by task forces

Phase III: the determination of the criteria and methods for evaluation

Phase IV: the development of a policy for the accrediting and evaluating continuing education

Phase V: the determination and proposal of follow-up activities for implementing the findings

Admittedly ambitious in its primary goal—to make a comprehensive study of all of continuing education nationally—the COPA project has the structure to bring representatives of all major providers (and their constituents) of postsecondary continuing education into a working relationship to determine issues of quality and evaluation.

Regardless of *who* should be responsible for standards of quality, evaluation, and ethical practices among the providers, consensus can probably be reached among the providers and constituent groups, except for the charlatan-type of entrepreneur, that such should be done. The motivating principle that can stimulate consensus is the "assurance of quality in continuing education programs for the consumer." Standards and criteria for continuing education should be such to provide a reasonable assurance to the constituent concerning the purpose and quality of the programs and of fair and equitable practice by the providers.

In considering appropriate standards and criteria for the evaluation and accreditation of continuing education, at least the following concepts should be studied in detail:

1. *the purpose, goals and objectives, and commitment* of the institution, agency, or organization, as well as those of each program

2. *organizational structure,* including management, faculty, and personnel, as well as matters of governance and controls and of policy

3. *financial matters,* including operational resources, charges, policies, and accountability

4. *program development and planning,* in such areas as curricula, instruction, learning resources, crediting, recruitment policies and practices, needs analysis and planning, and external relationships

5. *credentialing,* including credentials to be awarded, certification and licensing relationships

6. *evaluation,* internal and external, encompassing the achievements of both the institution, organization, or agency and the students

7. *relations with other providers,* in such areas as ethical practices and including relations within the profession

Such considerations are essential in developing standards and criteria for the evaluation and accreditation of continuing education, and others may emerge as research progresses. Any system for accreditation should also include procedures for review and evaluation as well as the development of standards and criteria.

Alternatives

A number of alternatives appear to be available for the development of a system of review and evaluation and possible accreditation for continuing education regardless of the nature and character of the provider. The following alternatives are presented for discussion. Experience, reflection, and research will suggest others.

Alternative 1

Redesign the present voluntary nongovernmental accrediting system (regional, institutional, and specialized) to extend eligibility and incorporate any provider of postsecondary continuing education into the system. While this may appear to be inconceivable, some recent developments in the established agencies indicate an outside possibility. Currently the Western Association has accredited the graduate institute of the Rand Corporation, the New England Association has accredited the educational institute of the Arthur D. Little Corporation, and the North Central Association has accredited the General Motors Institute. All of the regional and institutional associations and most of the specialized associations have revised their criteria for membership to include proprietary institutions.

Alternative 2

Encourage and support the Council for Noncollegiate Continuing Education in strengthening its accreditation program so that its range and scope of operation shall expand to encompass (a) all noncollegiate providers or (b) all providers, including collegiate and postsecondary institutions. A basic problem exists with the acceptance of this organization because of its conditions surrounding its origins, the legitimacy of the operations, acceptance by the collegiate community, and the duplication of efforts with the regional, institutional, and specialized agencies.

Alternative 3

Encourage and support the Council on the Continuing Education Unit in expanding its operations to include all providers of continuing education to: (a) establish standards and criteria for evaluation of continuing education programs regardless of their use of the CEU and (b) develop a program of recognition and certification or accreditation. The Council was established to work exclusively with institutions, agencies, and organizations that have adopted the CEU. This would mean a major role change for the organization, which may not be appropriate. But it should also be noted that the CEU was originally intended to be used by all providers of continuing education programs—educational institutions, business and industry, organizations and agencies, and professional societies.

Alternative 4

Propose the establishment of a federation or consortia of existing organizations and agencies (regional, institutional, specialized, NCE, CCEU, NUEA, and so on) for the development of a policy and procedures for coordinating standards, criteria, and evaluation of continuing education programs. The task may be impossible because of the organizational and philosophical differences of the groups concerned. A major difficulty would be in securing their agreement on a common objective.

Alternative 5

Propose the establishment of a new national organization to institute standards and criteria and an evaluation process for the recognition, certification, and/or accreditation of all continuing education providers. The normal resistance to the establishment of a new accrediting body may be insurmountable. The obvious problems of gaining support for the concept, of financing it, of developing an appropriate organizational structure and process, and of securing recognition and legitimacy would be major hurdles. These problems would be somewhat lessened if the new organization were developed as a part of an established agency such as the NUEA.

Alternative 6

Propose that the U.S. Office of Education establish a recognition and certifying component for all continuing education providers. Historically the accreditation function for education has been and currently is independent of the federal government. The education community's resistance to the proposed change would be justifiable and insurmountable.

Alternative 7

Encourage, support, and work with the Council on Postsecondary Accreditation in the implementation of the proposed National Project to Assess the Quality Assurance Factors in Continuing Education: Accreditation of Continuing Education. This is probably the most viable of the alternatives. If implemented, this study would be comprehensive enough to include all of the major providers of continuing education and should produce the data base essential for evaluating the alternatives available. It should also be remembered that COPA was designed to address the accreditation of "postsecondary education."

Ethical Practice

Regardless of which alternative might emerge as an acceptable approach for the establishment of standards or criteria and an evaluation process for the certification or accreditation of continuing education programs, it is essential that the standards and criteria give the provider clear guidelines for developing acceptable programs and that the evaluation process give the consumer reliable assurance of the integrity of the enterprise and the quality of the programs offered. Standards of ethical practice in continuing education should be a part of the certification or accreditation process and should concern at least the following:

1. the professional responsibilities and integrity of the personnel, staff, and faculty

2. integrity in admissions and recruitment, record keeping, student relations, personnel relations, publications, financial matters, and organizational practices in general

3. fair practices in relations with other institutions, agencies, or organizations

4. acceptable practice in program development and implementation procedures, including completion requirements and outcome utilization

5. full disclosure of accurate and pertinent information concerning the policies and procedures of the institution, organization, or agency and concerning its status or recognition in the education community

Continuing Education as Business

Standards and criteria for evaluating program quality and institutional, organizational, or agency ethics will become increasingly important as continuing education becomes more of a "business enterprise" for all providers. Competition among the providers will intensify as the lifelong education movement becomes more firmly established. Traditional colleges and universities will probably move more rapidly into continuing education programming to maintain a stable operation as the pool of eighteen- to twenty-two-year-old students decreases in the 1980s.

The potential economics of the continuing education market is overwhelming. The figures of 58.4 million adult learners given by the Future Directions for a Learning Society of the College Board (1978) is a good indication of the potential dollar market as well as of the potential student market. If each of the 58.4 million adults spent an average of $100 per year on continuing education, the dollars available to providers of continuing education would be 5.8 billion. The $100 figure is probably low, so that the total would in fact be far greater than 5.8 billion.

The continuing education student deserves a reasonable assurance that the money and time invested in further education will be well spent, that the programs are of high quality, and that the providers are dealing with them fairly and with integrity. There may be other alternatives available to the field of continuing education to bring about these assurances. For the moment, however, it appears that the development of a uniform system of standards, criteria, and evaluation to ensure quality in programming and ethics in practice among all the providers of continuing education for the adult student is the most promising option. Such a system could take the form of accreditation or certification.

References

Accreditation and Institutional Eligibility Unit, Office of Education. *Nationally Recognized Accrediting Agencies and Associations: Criteria and Procedures for Listing by the U.S. Commissioner of Education and Current List*. Washington, D.C.: U.S. Department of Health, Education, and Welfare, 1970.

Accrediting Commission for Senior Colleges and Universities. *Handbook of Accreditation*. Oakland, Calif.: Western Association of Schools and Colleges, 1975.

———. *Non-credit Programs of Continuing and Extended Education*. Oakland, Calif.: Western Association of Schools and Colleges, 1978.

———. *Policy Statements*. Oakland, Calif.: Western Association of Schools and Colleges, 1976.

Andrews, Grover J. *A Study of Accreditation in Adult and Continuing Education Programs*. Atlanta: Southern Association of Colleges and Schools, 1973.

Commission on Colleges. *Accreditation Handbook*. Seattle: Northwest Association of Schools and Colleges, 1977.

———. *Manual for the Institutional Self-Study Program of the Commission on Colleges*. Atlanta: Southern Association of Colleges and Schools, 1977.

———. *Standards of the College Delegate Assembly*. Atlanta: Southern Association of Colleges and Schools, 1977.

Commission on Higher Education. *Characteristics of Excellence in Higher Education and Standards for Middle States Accreditation*. Philadelphia: Middle States Association of Colleges and Schools, 1978.

———. *Handbook for Institutional Self-Study*. Philadelphia: Middle States Association of Colleges and Schools, 1977.

————. *Manual for Chairing a Middle States Evaluation Team*. Philadelphia: Middle States Association of Colleges and Schools, 1978.

Commission on Institutions of Higher Education. *Guidelines for Institutions Offering Advanced Degree Programs*. Chicago: North Central Association of Schools and Colleges, n.d.

Commission on Nontraditional Study. *Diversity by Design*. San Francisco: Jossey-Bass, 1973.

Council on the Continuing Education Unit, *Continuing Education Unit, Criteria and Guideline*, Silver Springs, Md., April 1979.

Council for Noncollegiate Continuing Education. *The Growing Edge*, 2, no. 3 (Winter 1979): 1–4.

Council on Postsecondary Accreditation. *COPA: The Balance Wheel for Accreditation*. Washington, D.C., 1978.

————. *National Project to Assess the Quality Assurance Factors in Continuing Education: Accreditation of Continuing Education*. Draft proposal. Washington, D.C., 1979.

Education Division, *Lifelong Learning and Public Policy*. Washington, D.C.: U.S. Department of Health, Education, and Welfare, 1978.

Houle, Cyril O. *The Design of Education*. San Francisco: Jossey-Bass, 1972.

National Center for Higher Education Management Systems. *Adult Learning Activities: A Handbook of Terminology for Classifying and Describing the Learning Activities of Adults*. State Education Records and Report Series, handbook 9, draft 6. Washington, D.C.: National Center for Education Statistics, 1978.

Peterson, Richard, et al. "Toward Lifelong Learning in America: A Sourcebook for Planners." Report prepared by the Educational Testing Service, Berkeley, Calif., 1978.

Ray, Robert F. *Adult Part-time Students and the C.I.C. Universities: A Study of Credit and Degree Earning Opportunities for Adults at Eleven Midwestern Universities*. Iowa City: Division of Continuing Education, University of Iowa, 1977.

Selden, William K., and Porter, Harry V. *Accreditation: Its Purposes and Uses*. Washington, D.C.: Council on Postsecondary Accreditation, 1977.

Yearbook of Adult and Continuing Education, 1978–79. 4th ed. Chicago: Marquis Academic Media, 1978.

DISCUSSION

"Accreditation is normally a very controversial area," *Grover Andrews* begins. "People either believe in it and like it; or they don't believe in it and don't like it; or they believe in it and want to change it or they don't believe in it and don't want to change it, because they just don't want to have anything to do with it.

"I came into accreditation eleven years ago after thirteen years' experience in five different types of institutions, including three private institutions; and after having been in it eleven years, even with its faults—and they are many—I have seen the very positive things that accreditation can do. I've had a personal interest in trying to use the accreditation vehicle to work within continuing education to bring about improvement, particularly with the development of standards in Region III of NUEA; and now, with the procedures we have for continuing education within the colleges and universities in the southern region, I guess they're our strongest advocates."

"You're prescribing a cure, but I don't know yet what the disease is," *Mort Gordon* says. "More important than that, to me anyway, is the fact that if elementary and secondary education are accredited and credentialed and certified—and they are, and it's a big mess—why should we assume that instead of improving, we're not going to get things homogenized *down* rather than *raised*?"

"I understand what you're saying," *Grover* says, "but I still think that accreditation or certification (I'm not making a case for either —one over the other) can bring a great deal of order to the field. That's a very simple statement about a very complex problem. Let me go back just one minute. Originally, when accreditation started in this country, it was started by the postsecondary institutions, the universities. New England was the first region, then North Central and Southern came along, and then Middle States within about two years. We've almost come full circle. The prep schools, the academies, at that time were turning out such poorly prepared students that the universities organized to set standards for those schools or academies so that if they met those standards, their students could have access to those universities. And it worked. Now what has happened since that time, since the late 1890s, is that the standards have evolved for colleges in various regions, and even though there are differences in operation there are some common elements."

"We've changed things that are historically based when they are no longer needed," *Roz Loring* points out. "There are social inventions that are made because the situation requires it. I understand what you're saying about the 1890s. We even had a period, as I remember, when we didn't allow alcoholic beverages to be sold in this country. But we changed that. So even though something once was precious and needed and good and valuable, it may not be appropriate today; and to proliferate something which seems not to be necessary, with few exceptions, seems to me to be creating a monster."

More than just colleges and universities . . .

"I'd like to bring another aspect into this," *Bill Griffith* says, "because we have perhaps narrowed our consideration excessively. When we're talking about accreditation, we need to think about more than just colleges and universities. If we're talking about adult education, I've been party to the development of a set of standards for the accreditation of separately administered high schools for the North Central Association.

"I believe that in many of the high school systems the adult programs were really inexcusable and that it was, in fact, quite worthwhile to set standards to be above most practice in terms of the hours of accessibility to teachers, in terms of courses, in terms of qualifications of faculty. Those were approved then by the North Central Association of Colleges and Secondary Schools. And as a result of it, I think that there is some more responsible programming taking place for adults in the North Central Region than there was before.

"I would mention also that there is an organization with which I expect you're familiar, the National Association of Trade and Technical Schools. Well, I have served on accreditation or visitation teams for NATTS. I think, frankly, they have done quite a bit to raise the standards of educational programming for adults. They have done a tremendous amount to get rid of misleading advertising. They have done a tremendous lot to provide additional counseling for students. They've done an awful lot to make sure that what the school says it is doing, it is actually carrying out. Here again there may be more efficient ways and there may be other groups who could accomplish the same thing, but it was not apparent to me who they were or, if they were at work in the field, that what they were doing was effective. And so I was willing to give some of my time to that effort."

"Let me go along with what Bill is saying," *Grover Andrews* says. "Those were efforts to get at the institutional base. You go outside of that for all the other kinds of providers, and according to the latest college board information, of the 58 million or so adult learners (postsecondary) only 12.4 percent are served by higher education institutions or schools. That means that 46 million of them are getting their continuing education from someone other than the educational institutions that we've been talking about, those that have accrediting bodies of some kind; but probably no more than half of those have specific standards to deal with continuing education.

"Part of the problem that we have had in trying to get full acceptance of a very simple standard for continuing education has been trying to convince the individuals in the field that what we were talking about was good from the point of view of basic processes which would facilitate improvement of product and not be inhibiting to innovation. The whole purpose of continuing education is to be able to turn around very quickly, to respond to needs in delivering programs—and many providers tend to think that if you standardize, it automatically rigidifies something and would inhibit if not kill innovation. That's not true. Noncredit continuing education students deserve at least a reasonable assurance that what they are getting will have quality, will have utility, and will be useful to them in whatever productive manner they wish. Without some system to at least facilitate giving that reasonable assurance, it's questionable in many cases. I think the bottom line is that the individual—regardless of whether it's an adult or whoever—deserves some assurance of quality."

Money is the reason for competition. . . .

"I approve of accreditation," *Milt Stern* says. "That's the first thing I should say. I think it is an absolutely necessary function and probably one of the major defenses of institutions today, and of the whole field of continuing education. But the issue of quality control, I'm sorry to say, is a hypocritical front for the money interest of several kinds of institutions, both educational institutions and others. Money is the reason for competition. That's the only reason. And the sooner that is recognized and washed out in terms of discussion of accreditation, the sooner we'll be able to talk without hypocrisy about the issue of quality. To establish each institution's rights to survive as an institution, we now raise the flag of quality as a cover for fiscal or financial interests. Once you get that out of the way, I think you will have a much clearer perception of the real quality of these institutions. Some of them won't be too good; some of them will be good. But you will be able then to talk about them much more clearly."

"I'm not going to argue that money isn't a large part of it," *Grover Andrews* says. "For example, I know a man and his wife who have *one* contract and last year they made $225,000 in providing continuing education to 700 individuals! That's the profit they make! And that's just one example."

"I guess I'm sitting here very tender about all of this," *John Ervin* says, "looking at some of the fallout and the impact of the actions of accreditation which is designed to deal with standards, quality, money, whatever. I'm looking at an institution which had done programming both within a school of business and within a continuing education unit: because of the impact of special-interest accrediting standards, the continuing education unit was forced out, and a very interesting thing happened. As the continuing education organization was denied the possibility of granting degrees to part-time business programs, the faculty—adjunct and regular—went across the street to a small women's college which didn't have a single business person on the faculty! And they started to grant degrees, both B.A.'s and M.B.A.'s! A very interesting kind of fallout from an attempt to spread salvation, goodness, and light! What you get is programming which then continues to operate outside the purview of a school that is accredited by the regional association, as a result of a specialized accrediting association's purported attempt to get quality! That, it seems to me, is a part of this whole discussion of power and conflict! It really is clearly a matter of power and has little to do with quality."

Accreditation reports are political documents . . .

"To illustrate this last point," *Phil Frandson* says, "in many accreditation reports there are things that would certainly convince anyone not to send their best friend, child, mother, anybody, to the school in question. They're dreadful evaluations of what are—indeed what other evaluation agencies have declared—very fine schools! What is going on here? The professional association sends a team of practitioners and professors, and they hear, 'We don't have a decent budget around here; we don't have appropriate teacher-student ratios. Do you know how much money is in our budget for new books?' They hear absolutely everything possible that is awful about the place. You can be sure that it is all going to be written down. And who is going to read that report? Those who can, if pushed, provide more resources. In sum, accreditation reports are political documents that give the professional schools some leverage."

Regional accrediting associations are the best hope . . .

"I guess I have to go along with all the negative things that have been said," *George Robertson* comments, "and yet I come back to Middle States and the other regional associations. I have a feeling there is not much the continuing education people can do to get their institution to wipe out Middle States. I suspect their colleges and schools have voluntarily gotten together and formed a marriage which no man or woman is going to put asunder. I don't judge that we're likely to back away from the voluntary accreditation by the regional agencies.

"And having said that, I see the specialized accrediting agencies as a real problem because they're trying to impose standards of the professional groups upon institutions. Because of the specialized agencies, we can't afford to build any medical schools anymore. They tell you the kind of building you can build. Even in America you can't afford it. The things which they impose upon the institutions tend to be unrealistic wish lists that probably are not absolutely essential to the preservation of minimum reasonable standards as compared to what the regional accrediting groups do, and they frequently give contradictory instructions in relation to other specialized groups.

"The other problem is the threat by the state to say that voluntary accreditation is not adequate for their purposes. That's what happened in several states. The higher education boards have said, 'The regional association guidelines just are not tough enough anymore! We've got to have some real teeth in our accreditation!'

"I think that I would see the voluntary regional accrediting associations as perhaps the best hope we have of a reasonable, moderate, and accurate system of accreditation over which we have a degree of control as professionals. Otherwise, it will be that professional engineers and M.D.'s and other specialists are imposing the standards on the educational institutions. The other side of the coin is that the state will impose more severe and more unmanageable controls. I think voluntary accreditation groups are perhaps the best we can hope for.

"My problem is, What is the process by which the efforts of the regional associations can be extended to cover continuing and adult education in good, healthy ways? Of course, we have some indications of that. Some associations seem to have fallen on this little phrase, 'the one-college concept,' which I'm afraid has been an attempt to impose daytime standards and practices on adult education programs. If you follow the one-college concept, the intent of that and the effect would be to refute or damage the opportunities available in continuing education. The other route that seems to be followed now is inclusion of continuing education specialists in accrediting teams. I think that would be a healthy move.

"But with regard to the expansion of the voluntary accrediting system to provide some kind of umbrella to the groups that never ever volunteer—I don't know about that. I have some trouble wondering whether it would be worth it. I see the problem as to hang in as well as we can with the regional groups as a means of beating off excessive and severe government intervention, and also as a means of moderating the intervention of professional associations and of extending the gentle coverage of voluntary groups to continuing education. As to the expansion to other kinds of institutions, other kinds of instruction—I don't know."

The others are going to undercut you every day! . . .

"But don't you see," *Grover Andrews* points out, "in this whole business of power and conflict and competition—if the regionals are saying one thing to the universities, and no one is saying anything to the others, then the others are going to undercut you every day! Even the community colleges will be undercut, as well as the universities!"

"One example I can cite," *Phil Frandson* says, "is the time that a

regional association accrediting team went to a university, and applied its criteria, and a million-dollar continuing education business—brokered throughout the country—was virtually shut down
immediately on the grounds that it did not meet the regional accrediting association standards. There was absolutely no internal academic control. The curriculum and instruction were determined by
coordinators in the states where the programs were offered. In
short, the program had little or no academic relationship to the parent
institution."

"That's a good example," *Grover* agrees. "I assume there are
others. And there are two ways to look at this. Some say, 'Let the
university clean up its act and don't worry about it!' We come back to
our topic, power and conflict, and talk about the role of the universities and colleges in resolving it. But I happen to be greatly disturbed
that much of the postsecondary education in this country is out of the
hands of the educators, the professional educators in our institutions. That disturbs me. I think, in order to get our hands back on this
changes are going to have to be made."

A lot of people drown each year. . . .

"But you're making an assumption I don't get," *Mort Gordon*
objects, "which is that the stuff which is not in the hands of the
educators is not as good as theirs—or is seriously enough less good to
warrant setting up a special structure. This assumption has to be
based on one hell of a lot of examples. A lot of people drown each
year. That doesn't mean that we set up cops to keep people from
going swimming. Maybe that's a lousy analogy. But even so, I see
more papers flying around, more accreditation teams going to
Hawaii and exotic places while I go to Cleveland. I know a guy who
went to Cleveland twice!"

"One philosophy goes," Phil Frandson says, " 'OK, you have
peer review and peer accreditation. It ought to be based fundamentally on a set of standards agreed to by everybody in the field—
everybody gets credit against that particular standard.' Then we've
got another system that they try to juxtapose on the first which says
that what each of us ought to be doing is to develop a separate plan
for our institution or unit or maybe the whole university: we're to say,
'We think this is what our mission is—these are our goals and this is a
plan of getting there.' The accrediting groups will come in as a group
of peers who will look at our plan, which says what we want to do in
our institution, and then will evaluate how well we are achieving our
plan. That's quite a different thing from the first one—philosophic,
practical, everything. Which way is this thing going?"

"Either way, one thing needs to be added," *Grover Andrews* says:
"Is the purpose worthy for postsecondary or higher education, what-

ever kind of education is represented? Regional associations for years have said they would evaluate institutions on the basis of their statement of purpose and goals. They never said, 'Is that statement of purpose worthy?' As one writer has commented, what if a group of individuals who are thieves goes out and forms a college—a college of thievery? Their purpose is to teach people to steal and steal without getting caught. Now, if their graduates do steal and they don't get caught, they are achieving their purpose and they would be accredited!"

Accreditation is a gimmick . . .

"I'd like to get us off this lovely intellectual level," *Roz Loring* suggests, "and speak against the whole proposition. I think we have become such a credentialing society that where there is no one giving credentials, we insist there be one. I think we have become so committed to the notion of being validated that we'd like to be validated in as many ways as anyone can conceive of. I simply regard this as a gimmick. You may want to cure a few ills, but the cost of curing those ills may be more than the cure is worth. I believe, for example, that we are really speaking about licensing here, that in fact accreditation amounts to licensing, and that we have not yet faced the reality of what a licensing situation means when we have so little evidence that all earlier forms of licensing have worked. Let's take the Carnegie unit, for example—one hour of credit for one hour of class per week per term—which was used throughout this country as though it were uniform. Everyone of us knows that some institutions will not accept Carnegie units from other institutions who are accredited and that it is very possible within the same institution to have the same course with the same course number taught differently by two different faculty members.

"We have tried over the years to invent methodologies for ensuring quality and equality, and it seems to me, to the best of our ability we have yet to find one that is foolproof or manipulation-proof, however you want to describe the behavior of people. I think we can tell, when pressed, which we believe are the most qualityful institutions or programs or whatever; and our judgment, if we could get consensus, would probably be right. But to license people on the basis of that, it seems to me, is very scary. If I were going to ask anyone to license me, I would go to the government and not to any institution outside the government, because if the government wants to know who it gives money to, then let the government decide who's worthy of receiving its money. And let them not use us to validate what is basically their problem. If what we're talking about is protecting people from fraud, there are legislations and rules and regulations; and people can file suit, and have collected and can collect

money, for having been led down the primrose path and paid their
good money in the process. Who needs it? is my question."

I'm more frightened by private power than I am by government. . . .

"I have to agree," *Mort Gordon* says. "I'm more frightened by
private power than I am by government. I don't like this whole thing.
I don't want the government, least of all the federal government,
telling me what to do—they're doing so much good for us already, I
can't stand it!—but at least it is possible to get them to stop. They
have, over the years, made some changes, because in a slow, difficult, cumbersome, expensive way, citizens have had access to the
government. But you get a private power out there, and suppose that
after it gets started and all set, we decided we don't like it. What are
we going to do about it?"

"With regard to federal intervention," *Milt Stern* puts in, "there is
a notion of an automatic basilisk-approach to federal intervention.
You can't look at the idea of the federal government without looking
at it in a mirror as if it were a Medusa and you'd turn to stone if you
really looked at it. I think, though, it would be well to look at it,
because from our point of view I think it's possible, at least, that we
would be served well by a closer relationship with the Division of
Eligibility of Agency Evaluation (DEAE). I do not think that professional schools would be served that way. I do not think that industry
would be served by such involvement on our part. I do not think that
a whole range of competitors would be served. But I think *we* would
be served."

"This point has come up I don't know how many times," *Mort
Gordon* agrees, "and we're not through with it yet—about the role of
the federal government and so on. To make an obvious point that
everyone, present company included, often overlooks: You get into a
situation and pretty soon somebody says, 'Yeah, if we do so and so,
they will come in, and then you'll have control and bureaucracy and
whatever goes on in that monkey house in Washington,' and then
we're off and running.

"For many Americans—or most Americans or all Americans
—the federal government is the enemy, and that's crazy, because
then we get the government we deserve; if we treat the government like the enemy, they are the enemy! But that's not my point.
My point is, there is a tendency to treat the issue as being the
following: You have freedom, ecstasy, love, and if you don't watch it
they will come in and *they* will control you. You have a perfect situation now—everything is fine; instead of that you're going to give
up all these great and wonderful things that we have and let the
federal bureaucracy come in and screw it all up. And we do it all the

time! The issue is *not* between *federal* control and *no* control, *federal* control and *light* control, but *control* by the feds versus *control* by the large corporations, *control* by the large universities, *control* by the large private institutions, *control* by God knows what! It's one kind of control versus another, not one kind of control versus freedom and ecstasy! No way!"

Why is it such a hot issue?

"Why is this such a hot issue?" *Phil Frandson* says. "There is a division of opinion among continuing education leaders in higher education regarding the need for continuing education to accredit its members. Some feel this function should be the sole responsibility of regional accrediting associations, together with the special-interest accreditation by professional associations. Others feel that existing accreditations are inadequate because they are too broad and thus do not articulate the special quality-needs of continuing education."

"I can say," *Milt Stern* adds, "that there is a decisive change of attitude on the board of NUEA, and I think that there is much more interest in the idea of being accredited, for the simple reason that there is an assumption—and I suppose it is partially true—that a continuing education accrediting body would have much more strength and more clout than a representative on either the regional bodies or other professional specialized accrediting bodies."

"What I have to say," *Grover Andrews* concludes, "is that in the Southern Association we conducted some very extensive research just a couple of years ago in which we asked all of our members to evaluate the accrediting process, including the cost; we asked whether it was worth the cost, and whether they wanted the process to continue or did they want to replace it with something else. Ninety-five percent of our 700 institutions that participated responded, and 98 percent said they wanted to keep the process! If you ask me what I think we ought to do, I cannot honestly give you a plan and say here's the *one*! My point of view is, nonetheless, that we do need to develop, somehow, a single national system of either certification or accreditation or something like that for continuing education."

FINAL COMMENTARY

Accreditation of continuing education has become an important topic for two reasons: the protection of "turf" and the protection of the student. The protection of "turf" is both internal and external to the institution. Internally, the continuing education programs' autonomy is threatened by specialized accrediting agencies (associations of business schools, colleges of education, colleges of engineering, and so forth) which require that those particular schools or colleges —not a centralized unit—control continuing education curricula that concern the agencies if they wish to gain accreditation. Externally, both territoriality and credit- and degree-granting authority is threatened by proprietary schools and other entrepreneurs engaging in national (even international) marketing of programs. And now these programs and agencies are being accredited by both traditional accrediting associations and newly created ones. The protection of "turf" and the protection of the student by some form of quality assurance in continuing education are not mutually exclusive concerns, although the protection of "turf" stems primarily from *fiscal* concerns, while the protection of the student is an *ethical* issue.

It is likely that the national accreditation of continuing education programs—if accreditation occurs—will result from the action of one of four existing agencies, or from some combined effort by them: (1) regional accrediting associations, (2) the National University Extension Association, (3) the Council of Postsecondary Accreditation, and (4) the federal government. Each group is studying the issues; each is capable of moving into a position of leadership; and each has proponents and opponents. Continuing educators still have time to influence the activities of accrediting agencies and the establishing of standards; but that time is probably growing short.

6 FINANCE

Paper by Rosalind K. Loring

BIOGRAPHY

ROSALIND K. LORING, dean of the College of Continuing Education at the University of Southern California since 1976, has been identified in a national poll of leaders in the field of continuing education, conducted by Morehead State University, as one of the top adult educators in the United States. Before coming to USC, Loring was with University Extension, University of California, Los Angeles, for twenty years, serving in a variety of capacities, including coordinator of special programs, Department of Liberal Arts; director, Department of Daytime Programs and Special Projects, and associate dean.

In 1976–1977, Loring was president of the Adult Education Association of the USA, and had previously served on its executive board for three years, chaired its national conference in Los Angeles in 1971, founded its section on continuing education for women, and participated on a number of its commissions and committees for more than ten years. She has also been active in the National University Extension Association, as founder of its section for continuing education programs for women; as chair of the "View of the Future of Continuing Education" committee (1974–1976); as a principal speaker at the NUEA annual conference (1975) in San Juan, Puerto Rico, on "Charting the Future in Programming"; and in planning the Division of Special Needs session in 1974 on "Identifying the Challenges of Non-traditional Clientele."

As author or editor, Loring has produced more than two dozen books and articles on continuing education. She has also provided professional consultation services to a number of organizations, including the U.S. Information Agency, the National Endowment for the Humanities, the National Vocational Guidance Association, the

130

American Council on Higher Education, and UNESCO. She was a faculty member and chair of the Continuing Education Section of the Salzburg Seminar in American Studies in Austria in 1978 and faculty member of the Harvard University Management of Lifelong Education Program in 1979. Loring was appointed by President Gerald R. Ford to the National Advisory Council on Extension and Continuing Education, where she has served since 1976.

INITIAL COMMENTARY

No topic is more universal in education today than finance. Finance has always been of concern, but in the halcyon days of the 1940s and 1950s—the days of the GI Bill, of increasing college enrollments, of expanding curriculum—getting funds for education was an exhilarating adventure, not a desperate struggle. In those days only continuing education was a poverty partner, scrounging in the marketplace for single dollars while the rest of the institution dealt in the hundreds of thousands. Now, conventional wisdom has it, the roles are reversed. There's billions in continuing education; deficits everywhere else.

Rosalind Loring suggests that it "ain't necessarily so." Yet there's no doubt that continuing education has a fine financial future:

☐ *if* present population trends continue.

☐ *if* present technological change and occupational obsolescence continue.

☐ *if* adults, who in the past have rejected further schooling, embrace the idea of lifelong learning in large numbers.

☐ *if* legislative bodies, who in the past have rejected subsidizing adult schooling, appropriate large sums in support of continuing education.

☐ *if* business and industry, which in the past have limited tuition assistance and their own internal programs to narrowly defined job-related courses, recognize continuing education as a corporate "good."

☐ *if* educational institutions, which in the past have focused on youth education, adopt continuing education as a central mission, support it rather than expect to be supported by it, and recognize participation in it prominently in their reward systems for faculty.

☐ *if* continuing educators, who in the past have either dissipated their energies bewailing their second-class status or alienated academia with huckstering, grasp the significance of their new opportunities and respond with quality adult programs.

Rosalind K. Loring

Dollars and Decisions

The Realities of Financing Continuing Education

The sources of money for continuing education describe, define, and delimit all of the processes, the programs, and the operating philosophy of any unit of continuing education. Such major issues as autonomy versus dependency, cooperation versus separatism, and relationships within or outside the institution or the unit itself are all made clearer when one knows the source of its funding. In addition, such operational issues as personnel selection, administrative structure, and, indeed, the best way to search for students to match goals, are also set within the source, or sources, of funding. Our objective here is not to remove the mystique altogether, since, of course, there are individual differences. There is always that extra spurt of overcoming and transcending one's basic given, but the *zeitgeist* of any continuing education program is made known through the decisions that must follow dollars.

Although lifelong learning has been acknowledged through national legislation, there has been a significant lack of investment compared with that in youth education. The results have been inequalities in access to education because of inequitable nationwide funding philosophy, policies, and practices. Historically, continuing education has never been a high funding priority within any institution, within state or federal government appropriations, or in private organizations' grants or gifts. Now, in an era of inflation and rising operating costs, resolution of the complex issues of continuing education finance is more crucial than ever. Within the context of competing institutional and societal demands for the available dollars, continuing education rarely comes in second or third, but, instead, way down the line on budget.

The issues of providing financial support for continuing education are institutional and individual. The institutions are numerous: the traditional postsecondary institutions—universities, colleges, and community colleges—and other providers—business and industry, labor, professional associations, and community organizations. There are, of course, some crucial differences. For example, all except educational institutions make the decision to provide their services without outside interference. They have the pleasure of determining the quality, content, duration, and inclusion or exclusion of adult learners, because the source of funding is their own organization. We also see community organizations and professional associations competing with academically-based continuing education for federal and state support, corporation grants, and individual gifts. For these groups, however, continuing education is not the primary mission, but a discretionary service. On the other hand, the central mission of continuing education in postsecondary institutions is the development and implementation of learning opportunities for adults.

Because of the growing interest of many institutions in providing continuing education, there has been a surge in numbers and diversity of programs, with great variation in quality and areas of concentration. What has made this enormous flowering so diverse has been the patterns of provider and user. For example, business may provide its own training for its employees, or, alternatively, it may send its employees to an educational institution for a specific course, certain credentials or degrees, or highly specialized information. Voluntary associations and universities or colleges have jointly planned and presented community development activities. The collaborations of professional associations with educational institutions have contributed to an increase in technical expertise, which communities need. Nevertheless, at least half of all continuing higher education (education beyond high school for adults) is carried on by postsecondary educational institutions. Therefore, the realities of financing continuing education within postsecondary institutions and the responsibility of continuing educators to constantly generate income are central themes.

In academic institutions, with a few encouraging exceptions, continuing education programs have been forced to be self-supporting operations with all of the attendant frustrations and constraints and opportunities. Still, the number of students has grown enormously over the last two decades, perhaps because

> more than any other form of education, continuing education is market-sensitive. It is conducted on business principles related to supply and demand, income and expenses, product and advertising, with slim margin for error and tight management of personnel and facilities.[1]

Financial Values

Some institutions deal fiscally with credit programs quite differently than they do with noncredit; indeed, major sources of federal funding insist upon a separation. Other institutions, because of

---

[1]Rosalind K. Loring, "The Continuing Education Universe—USA: A Multi-Faceted Picture." Paper presented at the Salzburg Seminar in American Studies, Salzburg, Austria, August 1978, p. 33.

philosophy and sources of funding, do not make distinctions. Private postsecondary institutions, for example, frequently treat credit and noncredit alike, since the entire institution is self-supporting. Scrambling for the same pools of money, therefore, is speeded by the differences of emphasis, but the values of the institution force a focus, issue by issue. This is the case because all institutions have a set of values through which the everyday world is filtered, categorized, and made operational. This values perspective guides policy development, decision making, and the conduct of activities. Two values in postsecondary education that interrelate, but frequently conflict, are the continuing educator's belief in universal education in all areas, and the institution's wish to be selective with regard to students and curriculum. Traditional institutional elements usually focus on serving the full-time, eighteen- to twenty-four-year-old student who is degree oriented. On the other hand, the continuing educator typically views education of the adult as a lifelong process in a democratic and rapidly changing society that more and more requires ongoing learning.

Now, however, the learning populations are blending together. Adults are increasingly participating in degree, for-credit, and certificate programs. Traditional students are becoming more part time and more diversified in their interests. As traditional curricula have changed in response to the interests and demands of traditional students, so the adult students returning for a formal education have impacted academic institutions. The basic question of whether or not the university or college should play a role in providing for various disadvantaged populations (the unemployed, mid-life career changers, women, senior citizens) is now asked in different terms. New questions have arisen: Are part-time learners jeopardizing or contributing to the financial survival of the institutions? Will there be an institution as we have known it? Are continuing education activities seen as solutions for the university facing changing demographics and not for the benefit of the learner?

Community colleges, which were established to meet the early postsecondary needs of their communities, have demonstrated that education is increasingly important to groups formerly outside the mainstream of society. The economy has accelerated concern with ways to meet threatened economic disaster, and, true to character, Americans are turning to education for solutions. So the doors of higher education are opening for those who have never crossed these thresholds before, thresholds built of funding policies and aggravated by the cost of preparing to serve adults. Most adults seeking education are confronted with almost insurmountable barriers, beginning with a general belief on the part of lawmakers and educational administrators that adults are more capable of educational self-support than younger students, and exacerbated by the concept that adults should, in addition, contribute to the financial well-being of the institution. A number of policies mitigate against adult participation in learning in regular institutions of higher education:

1. higher charges for a single course per unit than for full-semester registration

2. charge for student services, although they are not often utilized

3. lack of needed services, such as study skills development, career-change counseling, child care, parking, convenient faculty office hours

These conditions are intensified by forces outside the university or college, as evidenced in the patterns of federal, state, and local student assistance programs that have primarily benefited the eighteen- to twenty-four-year-old student. Most institutions have learned to survive within the current funding patterns and the more or less reliable sources of money traditional students have provided. In doing so, they have been forced to compromise access to education for the adult learner. To change these funding patterns in order to benefit neglected populations is perceived as risky, for it means a shift from a reliable source of income to one far less reliable and certainly less familiar. The institutions' management teams of faculty and administrators and the various agencies providing student support still are not convinced that part-time or nondegree students are serious and competent learners.

On the other hand, continuing educators are better able now to convince their institutions that providing opportunities for the education of adults is less risky than they thought. The changes in ability of students, the growing confluence of the needs and interests of all students, and the fact that many adults, either themselves or through their employers, are able to pay all or part of their costs have made continuing education units more viable fiscally on many campuses. Unfortunately, much of this activity is in the context of career or employment opportunities. Interest in the "traditional" programs of nontraditional education (liberal arts, public policy, community development, and the like) has diminished greatly over the last decade. When speaking of financial viability today, one must specify content fields.

The Current Financial Scene

Despite the statistical aging of the population and the fact that adults are the new majority in postsecondary institutions, data regarding adult learners are difficult to secure and confusing when obtained. For example, Edward Durnall, in 1978, reports that there is a decline nationally in the enrollment of part-time students in credit courses at colleges and universities, and he recommends that institutions look both to the national economic pattern, where the shrinking discretionary incomes of adults may account for their discontinuing education, and to the fact that postsecondary institutions are not producing what adult learners want and are willing to pay for.[2]

However, a more recent report[3] analyzed enrollment trends at 1,663 colleges and universities. Garland Parker defined the part-time learners as degree-earning undergraduate or graduate students pursuing anything less than 75 percent of a full-time academic load. He found that enrollment of the part-time students increased by 1 percent in the fall of 1978 over enrollments in 1977, while the number of full-time students declined by 0.9 percent.

This report is certainly more consistent with the experiences of many who have witnessed, within the last five years, increasing numbers of adults returning to colleges and universities for credentialing through either certificates or degrees. The disagreements about the number of part-time learners are largely a function of definition. Whether one considers the part-time learner as a student taking less than 50 percent or less than 75 percent of a full academic load makes a significant difference.

Specific trends are, however, clear. For example, 9.8 percent of all those who receive Basic Educational Opportunity Grants are adults who perforce meet one or many of the criteria earlier established as a definition of the continuing education student.[4] Graduation exercises across the nation are being photographed less by loving parents and more by admiring children. Everywhere we see evidence that adults—searching for social mobility, greater economic stability, and even confirmation of ability—are finding satisfaction and success on college campuses as students.

Another indicator of this trend is that the average age of undergraduate students has moved from eighteen to twenty-four to, depending on the institution, twenty-seven to thirty-two. Surely the returning veterans of Vietnam, with their vouchers from the Veterans' Administration, have augmented the enrollment lists of community colleges as well as four-year institutions. What remains for us to decipher for the future is where the next groups will come from,

[2]Edward J. Durnall, "Noncredit Continuing Education Guidelines for the Future," *Lifelong Learning: The Adult Years*, February 1978, pp. 18–21 and 26–27.

[3]Garland G. Parker, *Collegiate Enrollments in the U.S., 1977–78; Statistics, Interpretations, and Trends in 4-Year and Related Institutions*, Iowa City, Iowa: American College Testing Publications, 1978.

[4]Alan P. Wagner, "Financing Postsecondary Learning Opportunities Through Existing Federal Student Aid Programs," *School Review*, May 1978, pp. 410–35.

when the next surge of students will arrive, and what will be the sources of their financial support.

With respect to the support of the part-time, *noncredit* adult learner, the picture is less favorable. The needs of this population have historically been met through a separate unit of continuing education. In public universities and colleges the decision to fund various components of continuing education is made at the state level, and in community colleges at the local level. As a consequence, less federal support has been appropriated for noncredit than for credit activities. The extent of support for noncredit programs within private universities and colleges is impossible to estimate because of widely varying policies.

It is in the noncredit area, however, that some of the most extraordinary and creative ways of resolving the cost of financing have occurred. Programs designed for a specifically targeted clientele have brought students by the thousands to classes, conference centers, lecture series, television viewing, and independent study.

The financial support that some institutions provide is extensive and varied. Some universities and colleges pay the salaries of administrative staff, while requiring that the program staff, and the credit, certificate, and noncredit courses for which they are responsible, be self-supporting. Ways of covering operating costs vary, as do ways of providing services such as counseling and registration. On the other hand, some postsecondary institutions provide classroom space and public relations support for many programs. Frequently, two key elements of the institutional infrastructure—fund raising and the management of government and foundation contracts and grants —are also provided. Again, as in identification of federal support, data are needed, but all evidence points to far less support for noncredit than for credit.

Funding Sources

An overview of continuing education finance, as summarized from the National Center for Education Statistics data, shows that 56.7 percent of continuing education participants pay for their career and personal improvement education, employers finance 27 percent, and public funds support 16.7 percent. Other sources, including private organizations such as churches, foundations, and the like, although they are involved in funding to some degree, were not statistically sufficient to be individually included in the final report.[5]

[5]Mary A. Golladay and Jay Noell, *The Condition of Education, 1978: A Statistical Report*, National Center for Educational Statistics, U.S. Department of Health, Education and Welfare (Washington, D.C.: U.S. Government Printing Office, 1978), p. 11.

The categories of funding sources for adult learners include both public and private as well as intrainstitutional support described earlier. It is in the government and private sources that the greatest growth is possible, especially for low- and middle-income persons, and for ground-breaking experiments in teaching and learning. The government picture alone is extraordinarily complicated, and, of necessity, the description of each alternative will be brief.

Public Support

An examination of public support of continuing education, whether at the federal, state, or local level, shows no single guiding policy or organizational structure, but rather reveals a decentralized, fragmented, uncoordinated, and sporadic effort developed over a long period of time as a result of accepted political lobbying-based processes. Policy—in this case, nonpolicy—is replete with political machinations and maneuvers. Aaron Wildavsky, in discussing the federal efforts, pointed out:

> Because most of the budget is a product of previous decisions, the largest determining factor of the size and content of this year's budget is last year's budget. The budget is like an iceberg; by far the largest part of it is below the surface, outside the control of anyone.[6]

In spite of the zero-based budgeting discussions, the budgetary process is incremental, and program funds are neither reduced nor increased drastically, unless, of course, they are discontinued. Each program has its advocates, each represents a special population, and all present their best case for continued and increased funding to the Office of Management and Budget and the appropriate government agency, as well as to members of Congress, the state legislature, or the local college district. Political pressures and competition are great. Such a process, with all its flaws, does work and thus is not likely to significantly change in the near future even if continuing educators become more involved in the process. This is not to say that fragmentation cannot be reduced by such measures as the new federal cabinet-level Department of Education, which could make it easier to coordinate educational activities with other government providers such as the Department of Labor.

The Federal Effort's Premises

Federal influence and involvement in education is through enforcement of judicial decisions related to equal treatment and

[6]Aaron Wildavsky, *The Politics of the Budgeting Process* (Boston: Little, Brown, 1974), p. 216.

through financial provisions for (1) direct institutional support based on program-specific grants, (2) individual student subsidization usually based on need, and (3) loan funds,[7] as well as through tax incentive programs and other proposals yet to be passed and appropriated.

This patchwork of federal policies has had uneven effects in states and institutions. Federal definitions concerning the education of adults tend to be restrictive, with the result that many organizations are excluded from the policy framework. A number of continuing education providers are ineligible for federal funds, and participants attending such institutions cannot be awarded federal financial aid. For example, the federal definition of postsecondary education includes only formal education at an accredited institution. With the intent being to protect the public, other forms of deliberate learning do not qualify for federal support. This issue raises questions by both policy makers and consumers. How can federal policies best advance the national interest? Should funds be allocated through state agencies or be granted directly to institutions or to individuals? How should state and local needs be reconciled in national planning?

Pamela Christoffel presented a broad picture of recent federal support of lifelong learning by analyzing the *Catalog of Federal Domestic Assistance*.[8] She concluded that in 1976 the federal government expended over $14 billion in support of college-age youth and adults engaged in training or education, representing a substantial increase in funding over the previous four years. The image that emerged from her investigation shows no single agency or department charged with responsibility for oversight and coordination of more than 270 federal programs dispersed throughout twenty-nine cabinet-level departments and agencies. Her work complements the recent work of the National Advisory Council on Extension and Continuing Education, which compiled a list of all federally supported programs for education of adults. Primarily noncredit, these included programs in aging, business, community development, drug abuse, education, environment, health, arts and humanities, law enforcement, manpower, social welfare, and miscellaneous programs, which include civil defense, civil rights, and rehabilitation.

In Christoffel's report, when financial aid for veterans and BEOG/SEOG are removed, only a fraction of program money remains to provide learning opportunities for adults over the traditional college age. Educational programs that focus specifically on adults and their

[7]Douglas M. Windham, "On Theory and Policy in Financing Lifelong Learning," *School Review*, May 1978, pp. 535–43.

[8]Pamela H. Christoffel, "Current Federal Programs for Lifelong Learning: A $14 Billion Effort," *School Review*, May 1978, pp. 348–59.

needs account for only $545 million, or 4 percent of the total $14 billion. Seventy percent of this $545 million goes to three activities: cooperative extension programs of land-grant universities; adult components of vocational education grants to the state; and adult education grants awarded through state agencies, that is, Title IA, HEA.[9] Four learner groups have been given priority in these programs: workers, urban youth, women, and older adults.

Significantly, three out of four of these programs have fallen outside the jurisdiction of the assistant secretary for education and the U.S. commissioner of education (the chief educational officer responsible for educational policy development and implementation). The majority of these educational activities are designed to help the various federal agencies achieve essentially noneducational objectives in such areas as health care, conservation, and the like. Not designed with continuing education institutions or students in mind, such programs aim at alleviating pressing social problems.

The primary method for the distribution of federal program funds is through competitive grants and projects that require annual application. When postsecondary institutions receive this type of sporadic support, financial security necessary for long-range planning and development is drastically reduced. Of course, others argue that these monies are to be viewed only as seed money, and that the government expects publicly funded programs to be eventually integrated within institutions and supported by participants' fees. This expectation that continuing education for adults will be self-supporting is expressed again and again in federal practice, but its validity has yet to be established. Again, since the primary goal of the program is not education, there is little or no concern for the maintenance of institutional excellence or capability.

Federal Student Assistance Programs—Entitlements

Some of the major student assistance programs mentioned earlier that benefit primarily the eighteen- to twenty-four-year-old postsecondary student also have potential benefits for lifelong learners. They include the Basic Educational Opportunity Grant (BEOG), the Supplemental Educational Opportunity Grant (SEOG), College Work Study (CWS), National Direct Student Loans (NDSL), and Guaranteed Student Loans (GSL). Barriers to greater participation in these programs for the adult learner are as numerous as are the proposals for their reduction. An examination of the BEOG program by Alan Wagner estimates that lessening three specific restrictions on qualifications would benefit approximately 860,000 to 949,000 adult

---

[9]Penelope L. Richardson, *Lifelong Learning and Public Policy* (Washington, D.C.: U.S. Government Printing Office, 1978), p. 6.

learners at a cost of approximately $250 to $280 million. First, the BEOG "eligible program" requirements are:

1. Students must be enrolled in programs leading to a degree or certificate.

2. The program must be of at least six-months duration.

3. The program admits as regular students only those persons having the equivalent of a high school diploma.

Accompanying these requirements for an eligible program are certain provisions that limit severely the participation of adult post-secondary learners. The most important of these provisions are:

1. The eligible program must provide degree- or certificate-creditable courses.

2. The eligible students must be enrolled on at least a half-time basis (more liberally interpreted this year).

3. The adult students are expected to make contributions toward educational expenses in relatively greater amounts than traditional students.

4. At full funding the minimum grant cannot be less than $200.[10]

It is the last three requirements that Wagner uses as the basis for estimating that we could provide for almost one million new adult learners at a cost of less than $300 million. Each of these provisions, of course, reflects specific views of appropriate ways to enact legislation intended to benefit students completing degrees, especially those from low-income, disadvantaged families. With the growing recognition that each of the provisions mitigates against people who fit just outside these provisions in some way or other, numerous proposals have arisen. The first, to eliminate credit or certificate programs as a prerequisite, seems to be potentially the most expensive and the most in conflict with the original intention of the legislation. Wagner suggests rather that the last three be removed in order to accommodate adult and part-time students.

The second eligibility restriction of the BEOG is that a student must be enrolled at least half time. Assuming that half time constitutes eight units, this represents a substantial burden for most adults who are working full time and possibly supporting a family. While some adults can manage this burden, many cannot. Of those adults who do enroll less than half time, many face financial barriers that can be overcome by the elimination of this half-time enrollment restric-

[10]Wagner, "Financing Postsecondary Learning Opportunities," p. 415.

tion. Wagner estimates that its removal could result in 100,000 additional adult learners at the postsecondary level.

The third restriction of the BEOG is that adult students are expected to contribute much more toward their educational expenses than the eighteen- to twenty-four-year-old traditional student. At the same time, the expense allowances are clearly more consistent with those of the traditional student than those of the adult student. For example, it was said that single, self-supporting students generally incurred expenses from $450 to $600 greater than BEOG cost-of-attendance allowances. While inflation has driven costs higher and higher, the BEOG nontuition cost (housing, meals, books, and so on) allowance remains at a $1,500 ceiling. Wagner estimates that elimination of this barrier would result in larger awards to cover real costs.

The last barrier requires that, at full funding, the minimum grant cannot be less than $200. But since the full award for the BEOG is first calculated as if a student were attending full time and then adjusted according to the actual number of units taken, this eliminates as many as one quarter of the eligible part-time adult students because their pro-rated awards are frequently less than $200. Elimination of this barrier would benefit approximately 80,000 adult postsecondary learners.

Each of these items, of course, has its difficulties. For example, the cost to any institution to process and administer paperwork alone is so great that there is a lessening of enthusiasm with a lessening of the amount accruing to the institution. Half the cost of a community college course is very small indeed, perhaps smaller than the sum necessary to process the person and the procedure.

It is also true that the major requests seem to come from the noncredit side of the ledger. As indicated earlier, the course costs here are so prohibitive as to be beyond the scale currently envisioned by anyone familiar with government spending.

Similar provisions apply to SEOG, CWS, NDSL, and GSL. These programs, in concert with the Veterans' Special Benefits (the GI Bill), have formed the basis of the federal effort based on the concept of providing greater equity to certain segments of the population. Currently the middle class, who are being squeezed economically, are casting cynical eyes at the provisions noted above and are challenging the new inequity!

Questions of Equity: Women

Questions of equity always require judgment of which group has the greatest need. Surely, when we look at the present array of financial aid for women, we discover one of the most disadvantaged groups. Though women in greater numbers than ever before have taken advantage of many of the expanding opportunities in continuing education,[11] they have done so in spite of a series of special problems. Despite Title IX, which prohibits sex discrimination in all educational programs receiving federal assistance, women face discrimination in securing financial aid, especially in the awarding of graduate student assistantships. In addition, women have a difficult time obtaining necessary funds for educational activities because they earn much less (58 percent less) than men, since occupational segregation keeps women in the lowest-paying jobs and employers send few women outside the company for training. All of these problems are magnified for minority women.

Finally, women are hurt by the requirement of many tuition aid programs which demand that the student attend at least half time. If they are self-supporting, many women either cannot afford to continue their education, or, also attempting to raise a family, they cannot afford the time to enroll half time, but can take only one or two classes at most. This prevents them from receiving any financial aid. Needs for additional counseling and for child care are compounded by the urgency of the fact that most of these women continue to contribute to their families' incomes.

Tax Allowances

Additional potential sources of public aid for the adult learner are the many tax allowance programs. There are basically five forms of tax allowances: tax deferments, tax deductions, tax credits, amortized credits, and deduction/credit options. Through the *tax deferment*, the student is allowed to defer tax liability during the postsecondary years. Repayment is amortized over a period of time at a specified rate of interest. *Tax deduction* for postsecondary education is applied against the tax base and treated like other deductions, such as taxes paid to other levels of government and charitable contributions. *Tax credits* are applied against tax liabilities. After the amount of tax is calculated, credits are subtracted to determine the net tax payment. *Amortized credit* allows the individual to accumulate credits for postsecondary education not only during the postsecondary years but also prior to them. These expenses are amortized over a much longer period of time than the standard tax credit. Finally, *deduction/credit options* permit the taxpayer to choose between tax deductions and conventional tax credits.

Tax allowance programs have a number of advantages. First, such programs enable postsecondary institutions to increase their tuition rates without at the same time deterring prospective students. In addition, by reducing costs students must pay themselves, more

[11]Joann M. Steiger and Barbara Kimball, "Financial Aid for Lifelong Learning: The Special Case of Women," *School Review*, May 1978, pp. 395–409.

students can be attracted to postsecondary institutions. Finally, as incomes grow, the indirect subsidy of the institution also grows. That is, as inflation drives up costs and wages, tuitions would simply be raised to obtain a share of the increases.

However, one of the major problems associated with any sort of tax allowance program is that the reimbursement for education is delayed; whereas in the BEOG program, for example, the reimbursement for education is provided prior to actual attendance at a given institution. From what we know about cost-benefit analysis, the BEOG payment, occurring as it does prior to attendance, is much more valuable. Aside from the psychological value, however, there is no real difference, in terms of the actual financial support, between a tax allowance program and an entitlement program such as BEOG, provided, of course, the student pays taxes.

The current tax deduction program, which allows deductions only for job-related educational expenses, is inadequate, and proposals, including the other four alternatives mentioned above, have been championed by numerous advocates. However, as Larry Leslie points out, because fewer and fewer people itemize their deductions, this form of tax allowance benefits only a small percentage of the population.[12] Leslie suggests that the most promising tax allowance program is the tax credit. The tax credit seems to be particularly suited as a vehicle for aiding the poor while being free of the administrative machinery required of entitlement programs such as the BEOG. In addition, the needs analysis, which frequently discriminates against the adult learner, is eliminated when using the tax credit plan. However, it is very likely that the greatest support will be enjoyed by the entitlement programs (BEOG), primarily because of tradition within the educational establishment and because tax legislation has been manifestly difficult to move through the Ways and Means Committee.

Voucher Proposals

Another form of federal aid is the entitlement or voucher plan. A voucher is a claim given to an individual for a certain amount of education or for a certain amount of money that may be used for educational purposes. There are no restrictions, and the choices of educational options are extremely broad.

The voucher, as defined, is designed with a number of objectives in mind. First, it attempts to create a free market situation in which suppliers offer the best programs possible in order to attract voucher holders. Second, if a supplier ignores the wishes of a customer

---

[12]Larry L. Leslie, "Tax Allowances for Nontraditional Students," *School Review*, May 1978, pp. 436–55.

(student), the customer can spend the vouchers elsewhere; that is, the suppliers will be held accountable by the students they do attract. Third, it allows the poor, particularly, to have essentially the same choices as the wealthy. Fourth, in the spirit of antitrust legislation, the public monopoly on education, which has come under severe criticism for delivering poor services, would be broken up and replaced by the free-market model. Finally, students can become actively involved in meeting their own needs.

Some claim that the voucher plan already exists. They consider the BEOG and the GI Bill to be voucherlike programs. However, the BEOG clearly discriminates against some groups, particularly part-time adult learners, and is restrictive as to the type of institution one may attend. These two conditions place the BEOG outside the bonds of the above definition. The GI Bill, although clearly benefiting adults, is also restrictive as to type of educational institutions. These restrictions drastically alter the concept of the voucher. Since it is critical to the legitimate testing of the free-market voucher model that choices be as broad as possible, covering both public and private institutions and both credit and noncredit programs, those who make this claim distort and devalue the thrust and promise of the voucher plan.

But will the voucher work? The question is empirical and can be answered through demonstration projects and related research. However, of the few voucher experiments that have been conducted to date, many have been plagued with an assortment of implementation problems. They have also been too restrictive with respect to their alternatives. Because of these flaws, Daniel Weiler feels that the voucher plan has never really been legitimately tested.[13] In addition, of those flawed experiments that have been conducted, few have been evaluated soundly. What has emerged raises at least one serious question concerning the voucher plan—that is, doubts as to whether individuals, particularly disadvantaged individuals, have the necessary consumer skills and product information to spend their vouchers wisely. Simply providing the financial resources is not sufficient to ensure rational choices.

> Vouchering tends to place overreliance on one aspect of access, ability to pay, and anticipates that this financial ability will develop within the individual an information-processing and decision-making facility to enable proper choice. It is, I believe, too heavy a burden on the consumer. The concept has not been fulfilled in other parts of our market

[13]Daniel Weiler, et al., "A Public School Voucher Demonstration: The First Year of Alum Rock—Summary and Conclusions." In Gene V. Glass (ed.), *Evaluation Studies Review Annual*, Vol. 1.

system, where consumers with flexible dollars are misled into
awkward and inappropriate purchases.[14]

Although there is little evidence supporting either side of this question, it is important that counseling and guidance and the kind of services provided by educational brokers be an integral part of any voucher plan.

Although the voucher clearly would benefit the adult learner and move us much closer to equal educational opportunity, there are numerous other barriers to its implementation. Funding is the most problematic, for a liberal voucher plan would be enormously expensive. Much more research and evaluation need to be done in this area before the evidence can even suggest whether the voucher is valuable and feasible.

The various tax plans and the voucher system speak to funding directly to the individual student. For the reasons given above, including treating the adult learner as an adult, they are indeed valuable concepts and should be implemented. But there are still questions about selection of funding plans which strengthen the capabilities of institutions. Once more we are faced with the terrible tension of institutional staff attempting to provide, on a continuous basis, high-quality educational opportunities with short turn-around time; a lack of ability to follow through on any consistent basis; and no way of long-range planning. With a system that enables the student as a free agent to move from one institution to another at will without protecting the institution, there is reasonable fear that nonprofit education—in other words, postsecondary educational institutions—will become ever more like proprietary schools.

To summarize, we know the federal government is a direct provider of continuing education through cooperative extension, the military, and so on. But there is no consensus in federal activities in continuing education; the goals are unrelated, and the definitions are unstable. The present structure favors competition among institutions for government-subsidized students and government grants. The federal government funds individuals and institutions and funnels money through the states, and the proliferation of regulations and paperwork have driven many participants and providers to the brink of despair. At the same time, national priorities, equity, and balanced development are items that can be addressed only at the federal level. The fact is, federal roles in continuing education are relatively new, increasingly funded, and evolving.

Two thirds of federal funding is directed to individuals and one

[14]Solomon Arbeiter, "Evaluating Vouchers in WIN," *School Review*, May 1978, pp. 499–503.

third is directed to institutions, again with the rationale that students should select the program they wish to attend and institutions should compete for their enrollments. There have been attempts to measure the federal investment in continuing education, but because of variations in definition the direct and indirect expenditures in continuing education have not been given a firm price tag. We *can* state with certainty that federal involvement is substantial, although still minor in comparison to amounts expended for youth, older persons, the military, and other well-organized groups.

The State Effort

The states, in concert with local agencies, are responsible for control of public education at all levels. The means for state control reside, not just in its legal authority, but also in the allocation of state and federal funds. Although there is little direct state funding of continuing education, such programs in public institutions are indirectly affected by conditions in local institutions. For example, if the subsidized portion of the institution is not fully funded, the continuing education program will also experience pressure. Richard Jonsen has identified some general conditions of continuing education:[15]

☐ Tuitions vary among on- and off-campus and credit and non-credit activities, and within these categories.

☐ Since state subsidy policies vary, the resulting charge to the participant will be as dependent upon geographic location as upon activities.

☐ The availability of subsidies to individuals for adult learning activities will depend on the type (for instance, some manpower training areas enjoy federal subsidy), economic and employment status, state of residence, employer or union membership, and so forth.

Since, in addition to distributing its own money, each state distributes federal funds, this disbursement of money from multiple sources has led states with limited resources to encourage efforts to economize at the local level. One consequence has been a number of efforts at coordination—a condition that is considered synonymous with efficiency. At neither the federal nor the institutional levels is coordination so eagerly sought! There are many styles of coordination ranging from voluntary to involuntary, formal to informal, but local institutions tend to view all coordination as control. In all states

[15]Richard W. Jonsen, "Lifelong Learning: State Policies," *School Review*, May 1978, pp. 360–81.

voluntary efforts are under way to bring together public and private providers to draft statewide plans.

The basic problem for states has been that whereas coordination is theoretically feasible in the public sector, the private sector presents different issues. Even with the state able to exercise more control over public organizations than private, the state cannot mandate binding agreements concerning the definition and scope of educational activities. In the public sector the phrase "delineation of functions" is often used with the intent to avoid duplication and overlap in educational programming. In practice state financial and legal sanctions have been unable to induce the spirit of cooperation, though the form and the effort may well be there.

How can providers be encouraged to work together when relationships seem to be getting more formal and legalistic? Both state and federal government set their own conditions for financial aid for students. Both levels enforce guidelines for employer-employee relations. Both levels are empowered to balance the conflicting interest of their respective constituencies. Both levels determine taxes to be appropriated and allocated. About 8 percent of the state dollar subsidizes individuals instead of institutions, almost the reverse of the relationship between subsidies to individuals and institutions for postsecondary education at the federal level, where about 77 percent is spent on student assistance.[16]

The most crucial financial policy question for states is: Should subsidy be made available for continuing education? Overwhelmingly, the state reply has been negative! Even in those states in which the trend over the last ten years has been increased funding—especially at the community college level—within the last two years funding has either stabilized or decreased.[17] In addition, as the spirit of California's Proposition 13 takes over in many states, there is a decrease in support for the education of adults. However, at the four-year college and university level there has been increased support for special degree programs.

Historically, continuing education has never received the amount of state funds common to other forms of public education. In the area of distributing federal funds the action is even more diffuse. States establish "local" priorities with a host of different systems. (The American urge to be unique is well demonstrated here.) And local institutions that bid for and then implement programs do so within constraints established not only by federal and state governments but also by the institutions themselves.

[16]Ibid., p. 362.

[17]Richard L. Alfred, *Coping with Reduced Resources* (San Francisco: Jossey-Bass, 1978).

One example illustrates the complexity. Federal Title IA funds of the Higher Education Act of 1965, like many others, are intended to ameliorate social problems. As with much federal legislation, the states are given room to interpret how this legislation should be implemented. In California between 1965 and 1974 there were 153 projects involving 287 institutions of higher education. The federal government supplied $3.5 million for participating colleges and universities. As in most "categorical" grants, Title IA money could be labeled "soft" dollars. (Intentionally, there is just enough seed money to get started, with the hope that institutions will adopt their temporary projects as ongoing programs.) Title IA goals include strengthening continuing education capacities in institutions to help people solve their community problems. To produce these results, what path did the dollars take in following from the federal to the local level through the state? And how did the state choose to interpret the broad terms used in the legislation?

Using one of several alternative structures, in California the existing Coordinating Council for Higher Education was designated to administer Title IA with the assistance of an advisory process. The flow of dollars was—

☐ from federal authorization

☐ to federal appropriation

☐ to responsible federal agency

☐ to designated state agency

☐ to institutions of higher education

☐ to communities

☐ to individual adult students.

Although there are various written reports cataloging the assortment of approaches taken and the results achieved, the details of how federal programs actually operate within states remains undocumented in any systematic fashion. The states exercise their discretionary rights, and the institutions strive to maintain their autonomy. Monitoring and evaluation are difficult to carry out. Charts show there are rigid procedures for grant applications, a careful review process, every dollar accounted for, and clear reporting deadlines; but there is no indication of the real costs or benefits to institutions that nurture, create, plan, administer, and make their way through the maze of policies and procedures.

Although Title IA is a single grant program among many, it shows some of the inherent problems when federal, state, and institutional policies are intertwined. Nonetheless, dollars for noncredit continuing education and community development activities flow into communities large and small, providing skills and knowledge to adults who continue to work on their own personal and local area issues. One of the smallest in federally funded programs, the investment has demonstrated the value of providing support for learning opportunities, even if a small amount.

The Private Sector

The private sector contributes to continuing education through volunteer efforts and monetary contributions. The many private organizations that directly fund or sponsor adult educational activities include, among others, philanthropic foundations, business and industry, and professional and trade associations.

Foundations

Ideas, energies, and issues may find expression through grants from nonprofit, nongovernmental institutions called *foundations*, which are empowered to spend endowed funds for "worthy" causes. Not restricted like a government agency, and not driven by the profit motive, the foundations fill gaps in society. Without the constraints of other institutions, the foundations have flexibility and use this asset to advantage. One foundation executive has underscored three of the many roles played by foundations:

> *First, it should be a perceptive* interpreter *of the social scene and of the implications for positive developments in education, health care, the arts, or any other concern that the individual foundation has selected for its area of emphasis. Second, the foundation should function as a* catalyst *for the problem solving that is at the heart of meaningful social progress. Third, located in a strategic position to monitor innovations for others seeking financial support, the foundation should serve as an* idea broker.[18]

Giving is a widespread phenomenon in our country and is indulged in by people from all socioeconomic strata. The Commission on Private Philanthropy and Public Needs has produced a useful document entitled *Giving in America*. The commission estimates the real costs of tax exemptions, volunteer efforts, and monetary donations at the staggering sum of $100 billion annually. This voluntary third sector is privately inspired and publicly oriented for educa-

[18]Robert E. Kinsinger, "The Foundation: A Stimulus for Educational Development." In B. L. Johnson (ed.), *Toward Educational Development in the Community Junior College* (Los Angeles: University of California Press, 1972), p. 41.

tional, charitable, religious, and other activities that promote the common welfare.

There are more than 10,000 foundations in the United States —foundations that administer funds in accordance with the intentions of their benefactors. A small number are directly concerned with the education of adults, and their support can be traced back to the 1920s.

It is not easy to gather information about all foundations because of their private nature and independent spirit. Fortunately, there are visible foundations with a long-standing commitment to adult education. During the developmental period from 1924 until 1961, three foundations made an investment in the education of adults totaling $77 million. While there were other active foundations, these three pioneers were precedent and standard setters.

☐ *The W. K. Kellogg Foundation* has been a prime mover in continuing education by stimulating new methods and procedures.

☐ *The Carnegie Corporation* has been identified with encouraging new ideas in adult education through publications, conferences, experimental projects, and research.

☐ *The Ford Foundation Fund for Adult Education* supported the liberal education of adults in both methods and specific subject matter.

Today, the pioneers have been joined by other foundations. One overriding criterion is inherent in the foundation mode of operation—the awarding of grants for a relatively short duration. This seed money approach permits programs to grow, but they must take root in other sources of support after a specified period of time. (The alternative would be to tie up limited foundation finances in a few projects over a longer time.) Though some experiments may have ended prematurely, the overall rate of success has validated the underlying rationale. Foundations have had profound impacts on continuing education. Books, studies, buildings, and curricula innovations have resulted from various foundations' investments in education.

Corporate and Individual Gifts

A major growth pattern of gift giving by corporations and individuals is beginning to emerge as another form of private support for both individuals and institutions, ranging from scholarships for discrete groups of students (thus far typically not adults) to program development, which mirrors to some extent support by foundations. Since many foundations and most governmental agencies no longer wish to supply bricks and mortar, increasingly the search for sources of funding for equipment and buildings is focusing on corporations and individuals. Originally corporations were the locus of support for private universities and colleges. Now not only all educational institutions but also associations, governmental organizations, and nongovernmental organizations are approaching the same corporations and individuals with similar (and frequently exact replicas of) programs and projects.

Though a growing number of corporations have established their own foundations from which contributions may be sought, it is also possible to find financial support from corporations' public relations offices. Frequently the goals of education and of corporations mesh closely enough to warrant joint support for an activity. We have seen such support for public broadcasting and find similar activities across the board when a retail store, an industrial manufacturer, or a service corporation will be interested, for purposes of community good will, in supporting certain academic activities.

The most difficult item to secure, of course, is discretionary money for the institution. It is said that no one wants to fund a custodian, and in most cases that has proven true. Loyal alumni and ardent admirers are exempted, but, in general, funding from this source tends to be programmatic as do other foundation and government sources.

Paid Educational Leave

In Europe and Canada there has been a growing movement to compensate workers for their educational time as a part of their contract of employment. Business has joined with labor to provide the cost of education for a sustained time. Such leave periods vary, but they may be as short as three months or as long as one year. In this country education, which is directly related to work, is part of some union contracts, but only in extremely few cases has it extended to the benefits of full time off to continue one's education.[19] Why this is the case has not been thoroughly analyzed, but it might be a factor of necessity in the other countries or of the American drive to be working that has kept us from moving in this direction. If paid educational leave of the European or Canadian variety were to take root in the United States, this would create another new sector in the adult learning community, a sector many adult educators have attempted to draw into programs with minimal success. One variation of this, which has been less formalized, is the practice of allowing individually selected salaried workers in business and industry, as well as in military and government, to attend classes during their

[19]Ivan Charner, Kathleen Knox, Allen E. LeBel, Herbert A. Levine, Lawrence J. Russell, and Jane E. Shore, *The Untapped Resource: Negotiated Tuition-Aid in the Private Sector* (Washington, D.C.: National Manpower Institute, 1978).

work day or to attend college for a short term on full salary. Many have achieved advanced degrees in this manner.

Conclusion

The realities of financing continuing education are extraordinarily complex and diffuse in this period of transition. The role and functions of administration of continuing education activities are being reexamined on most campuses, and many of the truisms of the past are no longer applicable. Questions regarding intrainstitution financial arrangements are laden with the specifics of definition, since each institution has its own shape and magnitude of definition. Just as the classic role of universities and colleges in this country frames the expectations and responses of administrators, so the traditional role of continuing education has established predictable expectations and responses from managers of those departments, divisions, or colleges.

Within institutions of higher education in the era of declining enrollments, when there are conflicting reports about the adults who will fill vacant classrooms left empty by traditional-age students, will financial exigency replace the university's goal of excellence in research, quality teaching, and capable students? And will the community colleges, in striving to serve all the community, be able to serve with excellence? Or will excellence in our time be limited to access?

To be reckoned with are the continuous dependencies on tuition. In private institutions, as much as 75 percent of all costs for the total budget will come from tuition. In public institutions where the tuition coverage by state tax dollars varies greatly, the base of budget allocation is still student enrollment.

With inadequate federal, state, and institutional support for the adult learner, most units of continuing education have been forced to depend upon maintaining and expanding enrollments for obtaining funds. The reality of a market economy has led to responsiveness to current (and sometimes trendy) adult needs and interests. At the same time, expensive programs have been withheld due to the lack of surplus capital or financial ability to take the risk of a sizable loss. For example, many adults want to become registered nurses, but although the demand is strong, the nonsubsidized costs are extremely high.

As a result of the requirement to be at least somewhat self-supporting, management practices of colleges of continuing education are greatly affected. Responding only to low risk and readily identifiable needs does not promote long-range planning. It is difficult enough to keep up with a volatile market driven by changing people in a changing world. In addition to the instability in curriculum, student recruitment is affected. Those who cannot afford to pay for their continuing education are usually left out of institutional plans. Some institutions have been forced to avoid government and foundation grants that could be used for underrepresented groups. Their rationale is that such money is "soft," or short-term, and creates public expectations that cannot be met for long. Consequently, many challenges go unanswered, with financing and programming capabilities inextricably linked.

Should adult students' fees contribute to the fiscal well-being of the institution? Should traditional students' fees contribute to the maintenance or growth of education for adults? These questions have not been seriously debated, and little is known about the kinds and sizes of support since they are buried in the budgets of individual institutions. We cannot answer these questions until we have answers to prior ones. Do the goals of the institution include service to the fluctuating needs of adults and of their communities? With what energy and care will the total institution consider the separate and sometimes special issues of adults? Conversely, how much does continuing education rely upon the resources, the aura, and the "connections" of the institution? Could the continuing education unit really succeed outside the institution?

Increasingly, there are multiple providers of continuing education on one campus. Especially in professional schools the urge to plan and to provide for peers who are practitioners has grown with the interaction between professionals and Town and Gown. With continuing educators in professional schools the questions regarding the propriety of adult contribution to operating costs should be raised again.

Obviously we cannot, and should not, have a single answer. There are no formulas yet devised, or enough data, to determine either the propriety or the efficiency except situation by situation. I am certain, however, that continuing education must be an integral part of the organization if judicious decisions are to be made.

Competition, which works well in business and even in education, does accelerate the reduction of available sources of funding for both adult learners and institutions. For example, the National Center for Education Statistics data show that 27 percent of adult participation in education is employer provided. However, overall, 80 percent of the $2 billion spent by large companies remains inside the companies for their own continuing education programming. Such programming is characterized by careful cost-benefit analysis, use of hardware, learning-by-doing, and the very tight connection between continuing education and actual job requirements. Today, the American Council on Education recommends academic credit be awarded by educational institutions for 1,000 courses offered by eighty organizations such as General Motors, General Electric, and TransWorld Airlines. The financial impact upon educational institutions would be substantial, for they would then be responsible for accepting these courses into their established curricula, often in lieu of their required courses, and in the process would relinquish income from student tuition.

Planners must take under consideration the impact of these various funding strategies upon traditional postsecondary institutions in general and colleges of continuing education in particular. If tuition assistance programs obtain increased revenues and at the same time set a certain amount aside for the noncredit, part-time adult learners whose numbers are increasing, universities and colleges may be forced to compete even more with the many noncredit providers.

We have seen from the data and the descriptions that most adults are disadvantaged in the competition for financial support. Except as the goals of the individual and of the donor synchronize, there is little provision for the continuing education student. Government, foundations, business, industry, labor, community groups, and private donors all seek to direct the learning opportunities available through the terms of the granting of funds. Scholarships for adults are rare because expectations (again) are that adults can and should support their own education.

The awesome reality of an ever-older population caught in the crushing embrace of inflation, technology, and pressure from youth accustomed to a giant slice of the nation's resources has not yet really penetrated the sites of decision making. The realization of necessary behavior for the continuing educators who have brought the field so far is equally difficult. One small example is the avocational need of the adult learner, which, it seems, can be justified only if the amount of leisure time for American workers increases so significantly through technological improvements that the government feels obligated to assist in the productive use of this time. Until then this need is of less concern than the educational needs that are clearly job- and career-related.

In the coming decades several economic problems will highlight the urgency of assisting adult students. The first is at the federal level, where efforts to balance the federal budget will doubtless have a deleterious effect on the various funding proposals intended to assist the adult learner. The social services, including education, have already been told that they will have to "bite the bullet." Also at the federal level are economists who argue, using cost-benefit analysis, that the economic returns of educating adults are much less than those of educating the traditional student, and that the costs exceed the benefits. This kind of false economic efficiency is deplorable, for it ignores not only the innate value of each human being, but also the reality of the social, political, and economic benefits of educating and continuing to educate adults.

DISCUSSION

"I have a sense," *Roz Loring* begins, "that you can tell much, but not everything, about any continuing education program by its funding. You could use as an example the UCLA program, which is funded—or rather not funded—in the same way that other continuing education programs are not funded; and, with a good deal of energy and imagination, it's thriving. USC, which is about the same size in budget, is funded differently, and because of our differences in funding we are proceeding to develop programs differently. Educational institutions have always followed the dollar. At the local level the community colleges have had an unfair advantage in the field of continuing education because of their local source of funding, which is denied colleges and universities. And, equally, outside or other sources have funded their own education or training programs in much the same way colleges and universities have. So it is my conviction that you can tell a good deal about the operating philosophy, about the potential of what an institution may be capable of, by its funding base, while noting that there are individual differences."

"You say," *Bill Griffith* breaks in, "that if you look at the funding you can understand the philosophy. I don't want to believe that's true. I am sufficiently idealistic to believe that in many cases the philosophy precedes funding. Prostitution has often been available as an alternative, but not everyone elects to become a prostitute!

"I think that if the philosophy expressed by this group is purely crass, then we have little claim for tax support for our activities, very little. If all we're doing is competing for funds, in a dog-eat-dog kind of arrangement; or if, in fact, our philosophy flows only from funding—which I reject out of hand here—then I think maybe we ought to fold up our tents and let General Motors run the whole show!"

"Bill, can I interrupt you and challenge your interpretation?" *Roz Loring* asks. "I think you're speaking to an issue I didn't speak to."

Competition to make money doesn't explain everything . . .

Bill Griffith shakes his head. "Throughout the symposium," he says, "Milton has insisted, 'You've got competition *because* you've got money!' It's not competition to render service. It's competition to make money. OK. You can go and find evidence that that is really the case. But the fact that it exists doesn't explain everything. We're not saying that just because you can show many instances of this there is no one who does *not* behave this way. But you could be misunderstood by people who didn't know Milton very well and who realize he sometimes overstates a bit to make a point.

"I would have to agree that one of the ways of studying an organization is to look at where its funds come from and what sort of programs it is running: what programs it chooses to subsidize, what programs it runs at a loss, what programs it makes its money on, whether it has to justify its existence to its parent institution because it is profitable in terms of the money it turns over or because it is rendering such a conspicuous service that even if it costs the university an appreciable amount of money it would stay in business. I wish, however, we heard more of an idealistic tone, some of the missionary kind of language we get from the community colleges, realizing that they had done perhaps one of the best jobs of getting funds most recently to do the things that community colleges do. But I would hope—and I don't mean to be overly critical about the point that Roz was making, but it has been reinforced yesterday and today that money is guiding the whole operation completely and that philosophy is entirely subservient to funding—that maybe that's not completely true."

"I agree with what you're saying," *Mort Gordon* says. "I'm less idealistic and I wouldn't go as far as you do, but in principle I think you're correct. You can prove, if that's the word, that it's true by looking at multicampus situations.

"You've got an institution that has four, five, six, seven campuses, at each of which is some kind of continuing education function. You discover very quickly they're funded the same way more or less. Yet on Campus A the dean does anything he pleases, and he does this and he does that, and he underwrites losses, and he squeezes the business program in order to save the social work program and so on. On Campus C—with the same funding, with the same regulations, with the same nasty and bilious vice president—he doesn't do any such thing. You know why? *They* won't let him, and he doesn't have the money! And you can see this all over the country at half a dozen multicampuses!"

"I think that the important point to be made about the cash nexus," *Milt Stern* says, "is that essentially institutions that have the devotion you speak of, and try to live up to those standards, are being chivvied and chopped up by competition that is based upon money. That is the point that I have been speaking to, and I think that, in general, it expresses my sense of alarm."

It comes back to institutional mission . . .

"I think my remarks follow along pretty well," *George Robertson* says. "Roz mentioned that community colleges have had an unfair advantage in local support. It's hard to know what the meaning of *unfair* can be. Either we're doing the job because it's needed or we're not!

"But it seems to me that when you get into the main issue of financing continuing education, it comes back again to the notion of the institutional mission, philosophy, whatever we want to call it. (It depends on which words are current in which decade.) Some institutions seem to be saying through budget restriction, as they have for many years, that they don't really accept continuing education as an important part of their mission even though they may have been permitting adult education missionary service around the bush for all these years, permitting it to do things the institution basically didn't care enough about to wipe out, nor care enough about to support properly.

"It seems to me that where institutions do accept or even claim continuing education as an important part of their mission, the budget pressures compel and permit proper funding for the kind of continuing education services that are needed rather than siphoning off funds from continuing education to support other preferred parts of the institution's mission. You make a bundle in one place, and put it in somewhere else. It's clear that the dean at Campus A is siphoning money around because he thinks the mission is important in continuing education, whereas the dean at Campus C is using the excuse that his hands are tied because he doesn't think it's important. My general feeling is that if we pay enough attention to the mission and have some toughmindedness about this, we might recognize that the real solution to the problem of financing continuing education is to tell the institutions to face up to their responsibility! If they really want to be in continuing education, they should support it. And if they do not support it, then we should assume that they don't really want to be in the business."

"I've finally found something I can agree with Bill Griffith on," *Bob Kost* says. "I think both Roz's comments and Bill's elaboration have clarified something for me that has bothered me from my consuming segment of society, and that is why it is that so many continuing education operations appear to be very short-range in nature and why it is that, in our conversations, the university was characterized as a service station. It's the practice of servicing target opportunities! From where I sit that's the absence of a philosophy of continuing education that should precede the issue of financing. You may have to look back, after the fact, and examine an institution and its funding to determine what its philosophy is, but the philosophy should precede that act. And that's what I think you're saying, and I don't think that's theoretical and I don't think it's academic."

Operating philosophy is different from basic philosophy . . .

"I would like to respond," *Roz Loring* says, "since I think some of what I was trying to say has been extended to a logical conclusion, but not *my* logical conclusion. When I speak about *operating* philosophy, which is the term I used, I mean something different from basic philosophy. At USC we have a statement of mission and goals, and we put in an inordinate amount of staff time developing it, so it isn't just *my* statement. It is the consensus of those people who are most involved in the planning and development of our unit. What is true is that within that statement the parts we implement depend on the kinds of situations we find ourselves in and on the decisions we make as a consequence. I'm free to make any number of choices because I have some basic central funding that I can rely upon and do not have to wait for the current fads and trends to bring in via students. We have enough of a fiscal lifeline to maintain us as an organization. So we can take risks. Other units without that central funding are less able to manipulate and maneuver.

"The individual differences between campuses is partly a function of the dean, or whoever is the head of that unit, and that person's philosophy, personality, aggressiveness, inventiveness, and managerial style. And it is also a function of the community in which you exist. I mean, there are many factors, but I keep coming back to how we play out whatever our resources are; and if you say that is crass, it seems to me you give that institution the alternative of nonexistence. If you were to act out your philosophy without touching base with what this will do to impact your ongoing operation, you are saying to your group, 'If we can't do it this way, we won't do anything at all!' That is often the choice: whether or not we shall continue as an organization."

"I have another question," *Milt Stern* says. "It has something to do with organizational survival. And that is the notion of internal funding. Some institutions say they fund continuing education 100 percent, but if you turn it over it's a lot of nonsense because in a review of the budget they say, 'How much are you going to produce?' And if what you produce is counted in, that's not 100 percent funding at all!

"But what I want to ask is: What is your recommendation from the point of view of the continuing education arm? Shall it be independently operated? For example, in the University of California, as you know, we have our own business office, our own front office to take care of the money that comes in and goes out, and so on. That's a very great convenience for us. We think we do better than the university generally. We also have a completely separate budget line, and we're our own masters. But in many institutions this just isn't the case. Do you have any recommendations of that kind? Are there differences between public and private institutions that have to be taken into account?"

There are differences between public and private institutions . . .

"I'm sure there are differences between public and private," *Roz Loring* replies. "I think I may have said that the whole of the University of Southern California is a continuing education institution. It is totally self-supporting. I compete with every other dean for the same kinds of resources, and I go through the whole budget procedure just as every other dean does. I am not treated differently in any of those regards. Some deans have more power than others, and I have more power than some of the other deans simply because of the independence growth provides. But I think that my view of the future is that fewer and fewer institutions will be like the University of California in the completely autonomous separate unit. I think clearly the professional schools will come in, and in my experience it isn't just the professional schools. There are separate units in the arts and sciences that are as capable as we are of developing excellent programs, and they're doing it. And I think we will see more and more decentralization. So my conviction is, I'd rather be *in* an institution and competing with everybody else in it on a more equal basis than to be on the outside and come in last."

"In a competitive situation that is a *private* institutional approach," *Milt Sterns* says.

"Yes," *Roz* agrees, "except I think more and more public institutions are acting like the private institutions. As the percentage of tax dollars decreases for the public institutions, they become more like the private institutions. The income that came from tax dollars, which used to be somewhere about 80 percent is now down to about 60 percent. So the institutions are now living with one-third outside funding, and competition for that outside funding is very keen among institutions. I think units of continuing education inside the institution would benefit by demonstrating loyalty to the institution and become members of the family in time to be in on the decision making. If you're not there when the decisions are made, I don't know how you are going to benefit!"

George Robertson nods. "Underlying most of Roz's comments," he says, "there's the ancient enmity between public and private. (Perhaps I'm a little preoccupied with that because in New York, you know, there's the situation where state assistance to the private institutions is now having a serious impact on the money available to support the public institutions.)

"Now when we go on to the notion of the public's obligation to assist in this matter, it seems to me the public may be resisting continuing education funding for some pretty realistic estimates of their own and of the institutions' various commitments to continuing education. The government's really telling us, if we want to listen to them, that they would prefer to have the traditional division of the delivery of educational services between the private and the public sectors. They don't want to fund continuing education except in institutions that are legislatively established for the purpose."

"If you look at twenty-five years of this country's decline of public support for the public institution of continuing education," *Phil Frandson* agrees, "it's a fundamental expression of the public on some pretty long-held societal views about where money should go. We don't like to spend money on adults, damn it, because they should work, they should sustain themselves, and they should be responsible! We make our exceptions only to those who are disadvantaged, etcetera, etcetera. And we do it grudgingly, very grudgingly!"

We are all competing for the same funds. . . .

"The ways in which adults have been funded have always been marginal," *Roz* says. "Even so, the competition for government financial support is as keen as in any other aspect of what we are talking about. And, again, it seems to me that those with well-funded constituencies are competing unjustly and unfairly with those who most need the help. So those institutions that have local or other sources of funding are still out there competing for even more in the way of financial support, for basically the same dollars, recognizing that on everybody's priority list there are the same sources—foundations, governmental grants and contracts, corporations that will give us money, and so on. We are all now competing together. And 'we' now means all kinds of agencies—public, private, educational, entrepreneurial. Sometimes we have a governmental agency competing for more govermental dollars!"

"With regard to governmental funding," *George Robertson* puts in, "I have a fairly technical question that refers to the cost of processing federal assistance to students. It becomes a peculiar problem when the grants themselves dwindle to the same level as the cost of processing, and I don't know if that is ever going to be solved until the government accepts the cost of administering government programs. For myself I'm not much in favor of government subsidy of tuition costs in low-tuition institutions already subsidized."

Administrative costs are a real problem . . .

"Administrative costs of handling money are a real problem," *Roz Loring* agrees. "We're already getting some part of Basic Educational Opportunity Grants and Supplementary Educational Opportunity Grants for adult students, and it costs the institution more in terms of the total number of dollars available to the institution than if they give BEOGs to full-time students. The cost of processing is so high that to process less than $400 you might as well give them the money. I mean you might as well take it out of your own pocket and hand them $200 or $90 or $75 or whatever as a gift!

"And it's not just government money that's expensive! It costs the same amount of money to process one person in one course as it does to process that person in three courses, and the institution has a good deal more money to work with with three courses than it does with one. It is not the same to have three students bringing in x number of dollars as to have one student bringing in x number of dollars. It costs us more money in processing from beginning to end of the operation, and we might as well accept that as a reality.

"We may want to subsidize adults. That's a different question. I think that there are some services adults do not use but for which they are charged. I also know from my own experience that adults demand the kind of services that traditional or typical undergraduate students do not require. So I believe adults cost an institution in many ways, in addition to costly processing, and those are costs that an institution interested in attracting more adults ought to be forewarned about.

"Then there's the notion of cooperation, which we hear all around us. It has seemed to me that the collaboration efforts are inevitably more expensive in time and personnel and real cost than simply doing things yourself. And whether or not we benefit enough to afford cooperation, or whether the benefit itself is the basis on which we should do it, seems to me to be one of the points we might well consider."

"To go back to something you just said, Roz," *Bill Griffith* says, "in terms of the identification of problems and issues, I hope that nothing that comes out will line up *adults* versus *undergraduates*. If we're talking about full-time versus part-time students, then we should be very precise about our language, because some adults are full-time students and some adults are part-time students. But so are young people part-time students and full-time students. We must be rather precise with our terms lest we set up false problems."

There are programs we can't give away . . .

"Another point—I have real difficulty dealing with the notion that 'good' programs attract people. I have difficulty with that especially when it is spoken with great conviction as if it were always true. It would also mean then, I should think, that the inability to attract people must mean it's not a 'good' program, and that, somehow, the number of people who vote with their feet is the index of quality. Now this sounds to me like pure merchandising, not like education.

And so I wonder exactly how we feel about this. We've heard on the one hand, Roz, that 'good' programs attract people, yet we're not clear about the effect of financing on participation. We know there are programs we can't give away. We know there are programs we have difficulty paying people to attend. That's a hard one to live with."

"What I should have stated more clearly," *Roz* agrees, "is that what I meant by 'good' programs are those that are clearly meeting somebody's needs. But *good* isn't a qualitative term in the sense of *excellence*, as I think I can judge excellence in a single program. Rather, it's whether or not it was needed by a given number of people."

"But given the way we use *needs*, you see," *Bill* says, "such a statement becomes tautological because how do you know there's need? We know there's need because people appeared. People appeared; therefore, there must have been need. Then what the devil does *need* mean other than a measure of attendance?"

"We could probably find a better word than either *good* or *need*," *Roz* agrees. "It's not the excellence but rather the usefulness of it."

"It's acceptability in the marketplace," *Bill* concludes.

"No," *Roz* says. "It's like a phone ringing in an empty room when there is no one there to answer."

"I like that notion," *Phil Frandson* says, "but I think what should not be lost is the judgment about whether people attend or don't attend being a criterion of good or useful, or vice versa. I think that's not as controversial as we have made it seem. I think it's an additional important point."

"There's at least one other proposal for funding adults that I think is controversial and directly related to what we've been saying," *Roz* says, "and that's vouchering, where individuals get government vouchers they can use to defray tuition where they will. I have personally been opposed to the voucher plan because I think it denies authority to the institution. I think the voucher system itself says that the marketplace is even more rigorous than it is today. Nonetheless, in a world in which there is a great deal more individualism than when I first came to this great blinding insight about vouchers, I'm beginning to see that there is some value to some form of independence or individual funding. If our programs are 'good,' or 'useful,' or what have you, we will attract people and will be able to attract people enough to build a history we can lean on so that we have a stable organization. All I can tell about federal legislation (and, by the way, these last several items have been much debated by the National Advisory Council on Extension and Continuing Education in its discussion of how it will support the Higher Education Act revisions that are coming up) is that there is a good deal of interest in supporting individual students rather than institutions."

Vouchering would open the door for conglomerates . . .

"I certainly agree with you about vouchering," *Milt Stern* says. "I'd like to ask whether you would agree, too, that a relationship to the accrediting process is involved. I anticipate that any kind of large-scale vouchering would open the door for conglomerates to move in with large capitalization to establish competitive schools very rapidly, as they tried to do with proprietary deals in the 1960s, then backed off when they discovered that vouchering wasn't going to go through. Do you anticipate anything like that? You know it's the bogey-man kind of approach. Pickwick's fat boy can make your flesh creep. I think this is a significant possibility because we're already seen it."

"I think you're quite right," *Roz* agrees, "and it does upset me. I think that the only thing that makes me less fearful, perhaps, is the fact that already people with heavy capitalization can come in and ride through several years establishing their credibility. What makes me concerned right this minute, for example, is that when I go to Washington and become aware of the number of independent consulting firms that are bidding for government contracts and grants against educational institutions, they're already there. Whether there will be more than there are right at the moment I have no way of knowing. There are clearly enough people who are using access to federal government funding right now that I just wonder how many more would really develop. This is an industry that is springing up with very little capitalization. That seems to be repeated in so many places. I think accrediting would help, but I think it is also painfully clear that even were you to warn people not to take their vouchers to those places, they would still go."

"And then there's this whole business of brokering," *Phil Frandson* says, "the relationship between money and policy issues for educational institutions that increasingly has private companies (husband-wife type particularly) knocking on the door of the university and saying, 'Here I have this very well-developed program and we will teach it; we'll take care of everything. What we'd really like is to use your name; you can collect money, do some promotion, whatever; and we'll share the profit.' The motives there may be called crass, and the amount of money is immense! I don't object to that in principle (or princip*al*), but the academic issue is, What is the relation in terms of curriculum and instruction, and how much real authority does the university have over them? Or is that really two issues?"

"Let me postulate," *Mort Gordon* says, "that a particular program is a 'good' program or whatever, and the student is happy to come, pay the money; it's a 'good' program because in this postulation the student learns all these great and wonderful things. What is the addition of the university's control, management, whatever, going to add to the program? Who needs it?"

"Don't get me wrong," *Phil Frandson* says. "The university cannot do all the good programs. Entrepreneurial Institute X does very good programs. I applaud them. But when they're offered under the name of University Y, the only thing they're really getting out of University Y is the name, and it's a prostitution because University Y is simply getting paid for the name, nothing else."

"We have been prostituting ourselves that way ever since I began and probably before that," *Roz Loring* says. "I can't tell you how many faculty members I worked with who brought me their programs, and they put on their programs, and just because they were faculty members. What's the difference?"

We are all jobbers. . . .

"I think that the point is well made," *Milt Stern* agrees. "The point really is that we are all jobbers in that sense. The extension arm must not get above themselves, because we are really coordinators of other people's skills. That's our function, and it's a legitimate function. But the classification that Phil has introduced is a much more dangerous classification, and much more complex, because it does not raise the question of quality. Quality is irrelevant. The issue we must address is the issue of turf and the issue of jurisdiction. It is much more difficult, and it has to be addressed."

"I want to say a few words in favor of poverty," *Mort Gordon* intercedes. "Many institutions do programs *with* money, and the lack of it prevents some institutions—or makes it more difficult for some institutions—to do programs. (I did not say 'good' programs; I said programs.) I have a notion, however, that the lack of money has largely prevented a number of continuing education units from doing a lot of dumb, unnecessary things. I think the fact that community colleges, for example (which someone has said have been overadvantaged), rode the crest of the financial wave wisely and were able to get funds, has resulted in many community colleges getting involved in a lot of unnecessary, dumb, and even lunatic things. These are the kinds of things that have gone on only because they have money.

"Secondly (Milt will know who said this—Sam Johnson, right?), when a man knows that he's going to be hung in fifteen minutes, it sharpens his mind wonderfully. In the California system, going back a little in history, the faculty ruled that the University of California Extension could not offer credit, real degree credit. We had the choice at that time of just going out of business on the philosophical grounds that we didn't have that right—like a lot of liberal arts colleges have gone out of business.

"My basic philosophy is, first you've got to be alive, and then you start talking about some of these things. It seems to me that the biggest problem is in having a notion of what to do next after you find out you're alive.

"There are institutions that use a lack of funds as an excuse for inaction, and there are institutions that spend so damn much time talking about philosophy that they get it so finely honed that nobody knows anything about anything.

"Finally, it seems to me that where the mistake has occurred over the years, for all kinds of good reasons, is that we are preoccupied with money. We talk about money all the time. We talk about money when it isn't necessary. And what we really need to be about is serving students, and serving constituencies, and serving society —and then the money will take care of itself—*if we go after it!*"

FINAL COMMENTARY

Continuing education programs traditionally have been self-supporting, and continuing education students have been expected to pay their own tuition and fees. Today, however, government, business and industry, and private foundations are all giving increased financial support to continuing education—primarily support to students, but also some support for programs through contracts and special grants for specific continuing education activities. This increased support has led to increased competition among providers, particularly for contracts and grants and in program areas where self-support *and* a margin of profit have become possible.

But the adult student is an expensive student, frequently requiring special counseling and extra administrative services. Contracts and grant money may also be expensive, involving extra administrative costs, as well as extensive planning, evaluation, and reporting. And offering programs at times and places accessible to adult students entails extra costs for facilities, travel, and instruction. Because of the complexities of financial matters in continuing education, program administrators seem inordinately preoccupied with money matters. Indeed, a persuasive case can be made that poverty—or at least sensible limitations on financial support—can contribute to creativity and innovation in continuing education. However, the fact is, given a sound philosophical position focused on service to students, financial matters remain the critical element in continuing education.

7 ORGANIZATION

Paper by Morton Gordon

BIOGRAPHY

MORTON GORDON is professor of adult and continuing education in the School of Education, University of Michigan. He was chair of the Department of Adult and Continuing Education from 1971–1978. Prior to joining the University of Michigan, Gordon was dean of University Extension, University of California, Berkeley, having joined the program in 1958 as administrator of its San Francisco Extension Center. He subsequently administered its liberal arts department, and was assistant director, associate director, and director of University Extension prior to being named dean in 1965.

Gordon holds a B.A. in business administration and economics from St. John's University; his M.A. and Ph.D. are in government and international relations from the University of Chicago. He started his academic career in 1951 as assistant professor of political science at Tulane University, and from 1953–1958 was a research associate at the Center for the Study of Liberal Education for Adults, funded by the Ford Foundation. From 1962–1971, in addition to his extension duties, he was director of the Peace Corps programs at the University of California, Berkeley. He is coauthor of *Theory and Practice of American Foreign Policy* (1955) and *International Political Behavior* (1956).

Gordon speaks widely throughout the country on continuing education topics and has been a frequent contributor to the NUEA *Spectator*. In addition, he has served as a consultant to Antioch College, the Toledo Art Museum, the United Nations Economic Commission for Africa, UNESCO, and the National Advisory Council on Extension and Continuing Education. He has served as member of the W. K. Kellogg Foundation Commission on Continuing Education and the University, and has lectured at the University of Edinburgh, San Francisco State College, Vassar College, Pennsylvania State University, and the University of Chicago.

INITIAL COMMENTARY

At the root of the power conflict in continuing education within universities is the question: Who's in charge? The question is germane to power and survival outside the university, but it is most crucial inside the university. As Morton Gordon points out, there are some fundamental issues of content and quality, of appropriateness and accessibility, of capability and culpability involved. On the one hand, there is the legitimate assertion that only subject-matter specialists have the resources to design and deliver courses and to develop curricula that will responsibly represent scholarship in their fields. On the other hand, there is the equally legitimate assertion that the knowledge needs of adults will not be best served by discipline-centered instructors or instruction, and may not be served at all if adults do not participate because of barriers that result from well-intentioned but ill-advised institutional policies, instructional practices, or informational procedures. Only the professional continuing educator, this suggests, can supervise the reshaping of the academy from a youth-oriented structure to one that fits the configurations of adulthood. In addition, there is the issue of whether the university itself is most likely to prosper through the independent continuing education enterprise of the several colleges and departments or by a centrally managed continuing education unit.

For both consumers and providers of continuing education outside the university, resolution of the internal dilemma has important implications. For consumers the outcome will define the nature of content and instruction available to adults, as well as prerequisites for adult participation in universities in the 1980s. For providers the effectiveness or ineffectiveness of university continuing education organizational strategies will expand or limit entrepreneurial opportunities.

Morton Gordon

The Management of Continuing Education

Centralized and Decentralized Forms and Functions

Twenty-five years ago there would have been little general interest in a symposium that focused on issues of power and conflict in continuing education. The same concerns were present at that time, but discussions on the continuing education issues of the day were likely to be held at regularly scheduled national meetings, perhaps hosted by the National University Extension Association, then one fifth of its present size; and discussants were limited to talking to each other. Few outside the continuing education fraternity were at all interested.

Continuing education did not matter. The providers, even the best and brightest, dispensed meager resources and were regarded, when they were noticed at all in the parent institutions, as second-class citizens who were not part of the educational mainstream. Continuing education was a marginal enterprise, and most faculty and administrators who worked at the core of educational institutions were certain that it would always be so.

Now, continuing education does matter, not only to the providers and their many hundreds of thousands of students, but also to the institutions within which the major providers function and, beyond, to the larger society. The fact is that continuing education is an "in" phenomenon these days, and all the signs of the present and future indicate that the successes and concomitant growth rates of the past will continue.

This paper looks at particular aspects of the management of the continuing education enterprise within institutions of higher education. It is addressed especially to the desirability of central administration support, compared with neglect, benign or otherwise, for continuing education, and to the need for more or less autonomy for the continuing education units within those institutions.

Questions about the extent of centralization and decentralization of continuing education within higher education are high on the agendas of senior administrators of those institutions—deans and directors of continuing education, central office administrators, deans of schools and colleges, and the chairs of academic departments. It is worth repeating that these questions are being asked now with particular intensity because of the importance continuing education has assumed within higher education.

It is a commonplace to observe that the current period in the United States has been, and will continue to be, characterized by cultural, social, and political change; and, further, that change will continue unabated; that "the ways things are changing is changing"; and that changes of similar quality and magnitude will be a sign of times to come as well. For centuries change occurred in small, often imperceptible, increments. There were floods, famines, and other natural and unnatural disasters. On occasion, events did get out of control, and sometimes the fabric of society was rended. In general, however, generations passed without significant attitudinal or behavioral change.

The present situation is quite different. Changes occur with great speed, and their consequences are communicated very quickly across continents and cultures. Political and social belief systems and "tried-and-true" patterns of behavior have become increasingly inappropriate, even counterproductive, to the task of learning to live in an era characterized by change. In these circumstances it is not surprising that continuing education is seen as an important vehicle for assisting citizens, parents, workers, managers—all those in our society who have assumed adult roles and responsibilities—to cope with change. We all recognize that children need to be taught how to live in society. What is new is the recognition that adults need education for many of the same reasons.

The preface to a recent general report from the Organisation for Economic Co-operation and Development (OECD), entitled "Learning Opportunities for Adults," notes:

> The education of adults is moving from a marginal position in relation to formal education systems to take a more central place in society's overall provision for education. This transition requires the public authorities to formulate comprehensive policies for it within the broad context of overall educational development strategies. Countries opting for a recurrent education strategy will seek increasingly to integrate adult education into the overall system. Other countries will wish to maintain a diversified pattern of education within which adult education will be treated as a discrete sector and coordinated with the other sectors to the extent considered appropriate.[1]

In higher education in the United States, there has never been as much recognition of the centrality of continuing education as there

---

[1]Organisation for Economic Co-operation and Development, *Learning Opportunities for Adults*, Vol. I (Paris: OECD, 1977), p. 5.

is at present. The pronouncements of leaders in government and education are consistent and clear on this point. Unfortunately, however, the rhetoric has not yet been matched by policies that establish a high priority for continuing education. "The challenge is how to expand, diversify and rationalize the present provision of learning opportunities so that adult education may operationally pursue the societal objectives today rhetorically ascribed to it."[2] My purpose here is to examine some of the reasons for the difference between rhetoric and policy.

Perhaps the best place to begin the discussion is with America's *faith* in education (an apt word to describe an attitude based on strong feelings of belief, allegiance, and loyalty, and a high degree of confidence)—all forms of education. Until the early 1960s that faith seemed unshakable for all time to come; but during the time of troubles of the middle and late 1960s (growing opposition to the war in Vietnam; loss of confidence in government; the continuing struggle for civil rights; a deteriorating economy; alienation of college and university students and the "student revolt" at Berkeley, Wisconsin, Columbia, Michigan, Jackson State, Kent State, and elsewhere in higher education, and in some secondary schools as well), America's faith in education was shaken.

The one exception to the change in American attitudes was continuing education. Enrollment in continuing education increased throughout the 1960s and into the 1970s. Even now, when enrollment in virtually all other sectors of education is stabilizing, even declining, interest in continuing education continues to increase. There seems little doubt that America's unfinished agenda for improving the quality of life (some of us would be almost ready to settle for preventing the quality from getting any worse), involves attention to the uses of education. Only adults can improve the quality of life now. If we wait for the young to grow up, take charge, and begin to work on the agenda, we have twenty or thirty years of the present to look forward to. Obviously, the adult students who are enrolling in growing numbers are not waiting.

In the United States there is an ongoing need to expand education and training opportunities. Skilled, semiskilled, and unskilled men and women need programs that will help them improve their work performance and increase their earnings and status. Those already qualified have to keep their knowledge and skill current. Others, not as well prepared, need access to programming activities that will help them become prepared. And more and better programs are needed to help Americans learn more about themselves and their society. Educational institutions have accepted the responsibility to provide such

[2]Ibid., p. 8.

opportunities for years. Living has become more difficult for most of us. Jobs have become more sophisticated and complex. New occupations are created, and old ones become obsolete. As a consequence, few educators believe any longer that individuals are educated once and for all. We hear more and more these days about the obsolescence of skill and knowledge and about society's responsibility, expressed through the action of educational institutions (and other institutions as well), to meet the needs of our people.

It is important to note that most adult and continuing education programs are offered by institutions whose primary mission is not adult education. In elementary and secondary schools the "core" consists of full-time teachers and young students (six to eighteen years of age). In "mainstream" higher education students are older (eighteen to thirty years of age, an increasing number older still), most teachers are full time, and both are typically involved with credits and degrees associated with undergraduate, graduate, professional, and vocational curricula.

Continuing education was never, and is not now, part of the mainstream. The current rhetoric of support is probably based upon simple recognition of the growing importance of continuing education, perhaps coupled with hope (pious or otherwise) that it may continue to grow on the margin without impinging upon, or competing with, the "main mission" of higher education. Problems of power and conflict have surfaced in higher education as a consequence of, and in association with, the movement of the continuing education enterprise from the far margin to the mainstream.

Continuing education has been a marginal activity in educational institutions for a long time, and in its operations it amply demonstrated the uses of marginality. Marginal people in marginal enterprises often are able to transcend "the world of everyday premises that we take for granted." Continuing education staffs were no different. They raised questions about educational holy writ: the time, place, and manner—especially the manner—of instruction; and the Ph.D., the secondary teaching credential, and other credentials as guarantors of teaching ability. They expressed doubt whether teaching was equated with learning. They transformed skill courses and travel and other recreational programs into genuine learning experiences.

In the course of their marginal existence, continuing education staffs contributed significantly to the demise of myths about education that had resulted in "time-tested" policies and practices: that youth is the best time for all forms of education; that older people cannot learn as well as their juniors; that part-time students cannot learn very much; that the best, perhaps the only, way to educate students is to bring them together in a school building; that the best place in a school to perform the act of education is in a classroom; and that a particular set of admission standards, written examinations, grades, credits, and degrees constitute a fundamentally sound system for teaching and learning. Continuing education staffs learned to live without massive financial subsidies. Some did good and useful work without any financial support except student fees.

During this period parent institutions enjoyed very high status and ever-increasing budgets. The value of education was undisputed. School and campus enrollment was up, up, up (though enrollment in continuing education often increased faster than "regular" enrollment). Then came the beginnings of disenchantment with education, and, more recently, educational institutions have begun to feel the effects of deteriorating economic conditions. Regular enrollment started to stabilize and even to decline. This is not the place to assess whether it was the war in Vietnam or the civil rights struggle, or the plight of our cities, or Watergate, or other aspects of our troubles (not ended yet) that was responsible for the decline in enrollment. A simple and more direct answer may be this: Education no longer seems to guarantee a good job, or even a job.

Meanwhile, however, in the margin, enrollment continues strongly upward. Everyone seems to have discovered continuing education. There is little doubt that these activities constitute the wave of the present and future. Continuing educators are discovering, with considerable surprise and pleasure, that their status is rising. Marginality may have helped individuals who wanted to be autonomous to be just that to a degree unknown elsewhere in education. But virtually all of them yearned, from time to time, for respectability and acceptance into the mainstream. Now that their status is rising, there may be a danger that programs will be co-opted by "regular" units of parent institutions. What price respectability? Will rising status result in a fatal embrace with the regulars?

Continuing education has been successful in large part because of marginality. In the margin the continuing education point of view came to dominate. The student, rather than the discipline, was the center. Continuing educators were disposed to adjust the curriculum and learning environment to the adult student's needs, and they were able to do so.

In the parent unit other views predominated. Subject matter experts were inclined to adjust the student to the curriculum and the learning environment. The consequences of the two views can be quite different. It will not suffice to say that both student and subject matter should be central. Can a program meet the needs and demands of both?

As continuing education moves into the mainstream, it will have to seek a middle ground. How much autonomy should there be for the continuing education unit?: The maximum possible that does not result in permanent estrangement from parent unit faculty and administration.

It would be difficult to "prove" that central administration support played a significant role in the movement of continuing education from far margin to mainstream. Historians of higher education in the 1950s through the 1970s may well conclude that the growth of continuing education was a simple consequence of the response of providers to individual and societal demand. Some programs were available prior to the great explosion of demand, and as supply became more plentiful, increases in demand kept pace.

Throughout this period boards of trustees, university and college presidents, and their senior staff were content to permit providers to respond without assisting the process. Even when central administration acted against the interests of continuing education students, reducing the already low level of state subsidy in one case, forbidding a provider to offer degree credit courses in another, insisting in a third that adult students pay for *all* instructional and noninstructional costs, including the cost of police protection provided by campus police at premises owned by the university and administered by the continuing education program—even then there was no lasting effect on the growth rate of continuing education.

There was little animus involved. These and similar actions were defended, in rare instances if a defense seemed prudent, as necessary "to maintain academic standards" or "to protect the university budget" or both. Adults were asked to pay a significantly higher percentage of the cost of their education than other students because "adults are not students."

The university defined for itself the operational meaning of standards and the status of students, and it was very clear in practice that some parts of the budget were worth fighting the legislature and other governing bodies about and others were not, and so they could be traded off for mainstream advantage. For the most part, central administration did not care one way or the other about continuing education. Presidents were fully occupied with problems of their own, especially with those that derived from growth rates in mainstream enrollment.

Later, when it became clear that full-time undergraduate and graduate enrollment was stabilizing, that is, had ceased growing, and in some institutions was beginning to decline, academic administrators began to talk about "the steady state" and "the coming depression in higher education." Much of the research on these problems was carried on in and around campuses with very large, depression-free, and steadily increasing continuing education enrollment, but researchers took no account of adult students. They were part of "the invisible university."

Most mainstream administrators and faculty still define a student as a full-time undergraduate or graduate enrollee. Few graduate departments in the so-called national research universities will admit part-time students into graduate study, not even in schools of social work or education. As for adults, there was, and still is, little central administration support, except for rhetoric.

But these are particularly perilous times for continuing education. There is some evidence that central administration is beginning to care.

Universities and colleges are having a difficult time financially. Universities have had to sell branch campuses or large blocks of real estate to help pay for current deficits and balance future budgets. The faculties of some institutions are restive, not about the diminution of academic standards, but about their own declining standards of living. Campus students are becoming increasingly resistant to continuing increases in tuition and other fees. A recent increase at one university resulted in a shortfall of several million dollars. Students did not respond as expected, and their resistance grows.

This is not the place to detail the saga of woe in mainstream education. But in some institutions long looks have been cast at continuing education. Could this be a way to help pay bills, appease faculty, buy time?

In these circumstances I advise continuing education administrators not to seek the support of central administration. Such support could result in a fatal embrace—fatal for continuing education. I confess to uneasiness about the interest of central administration in continuing education. Already some faculties are importuning their presidents: "Let us run the continuing education program. We will do it better. There will be no problem about academic standards. We will offer only the best. And we will do it cheaper." Quite possibly presidents and boards are listening. There is no ineluctable contradiction between the goals of central administration and those of continuing education. But presidents, academic vice presidents, deans of schools and colleges, and department chairs know very little about continuing education. Most of their attitudes about the university were formed during years of apprenticeship, not as administrators, but as faculty members.

The best that continuing education can hope for from central administration and faculty is a degree of sophistication about the nature, strengths, and weaknesses of continuing education. Central administration and others unfamiliar with continuing education cannot become knowledgeable without assistance and guidance from continuing education staff. The latter have demonstrated remarkable innovative flair and skill, often coupled with courage and cunning and the willingness, even eagerness, to take risks, and have produced programs that have educated and trained millions of American adults—almost everyone, it seems, except the senior academic officers of their own institutions.

It is clear that the time has come for continuing education program development staff to plan programs that will seek to educate central administration and faculty on the subject of continuing education. Certainly one of the more pressing issues involves consideration of the administrative relation of the continuing education program to the parent institution. Should continuing education be a function of academic departments or of schools and colleges? Will the university and society be served best by a centralized continuing education unit that retains considerable autonomy from other academic units on campus? What are the program content and academic standards consequences of decisions about autonomy and degree of centralization? What are the financial consequences? In considering these questions, it is well to begin with some comments on the current state of continuing education in higher education.

Continuing Education in Universities and Colleges: Some General Observations

The larger continuing education programs in the United States cater to very diverse individual and societal needs. These units offer a wide range of degree credit programs and other forms of credit and noncredit work in preprofessional, professional, and postprofessional fields, as well as in liberal arts disciplines.

A 1971 survey identified eighteen "pacesetter" and nineteen "comer" universities and colleges. The smallest of the pacesetter group enrolled 22,500 students, and the largest enrolled 213,600 students. Enrollments in the comer group clustered in the 10,000–20,000 range.

The continuing education programs of these institutions share some of the following attributes:

1. They keep relatively free of academic and administrative rules and regulations enforced throughout the rest of the university or college. They can often create, modify, and abolish courses and even curricula. They can and do move more quickly than other academic units to meet educational needs.

2. If the continuing education staff has a system of beliefs that could be called an ideology, it is based on the concept of public service. They believe that they are providing access to education for individuals who otherwise would not be able to enroll. They have a

somewhat more egalitarian attitude toward access than their colleagues in the mainstream units—they tend to believe that education should be provided for all who can benefit from it.

3. Consistent with this ideology, there are few entrance requirements for enrollment. Students do not have to prove in advance by exams or in other ways that they can do the work. Continuing education staff are not much concerned with formal academic preparation. They rely as much on practical experience, which they believe constitutes prima facie evidence that students will be able to do acceptable work. In other words, students are asked to prove, after admission, that they can keep up. If they cannot, they are dropped, or as happens more often, they decide to drop on their own.

4. Pacesetters and comers are teaching institutions primarily, not research institutions. The ideal continuing education teacher is described as a scholar with a significant record of research who is interested in teaching adults and has the ability to do so. If unable to recruit such an individual, continuing education staff would prefer a practitioner who knows the subject and can teach it to adults, rather than a scholar who is an indifferent teacher.

5. These units all seek to involve the university faculty in teaching and other programming activity but try to avoid the kind of faculty control that they fear would transform the educational program for adults into a copy, and not a good one at that, of the regular program. The staff will usually concede that the full-time daytime degree program is excellent for its purpose but will argue that it is not designed to serve adult students with different needs. Instead of replicating the regular curriculum, continuing education administrators attempt to get faculty support for a program consisting of regular courses and programs that pay some attention to the special needs of adults, and others that are "especially for adults."

6. The professional staff are not necessarily academicians, theoreticians, or research scholars. They tend to be men and women oriented toward action who believe that their primary function is to develop programs that integrate theory and practice, that bridge the gap between academic and "real" life. They take pride in doing good and useful work. These days, one hears much about job dissatisfaction in a number of fields; continuing education administrators seem to like their jobs.

Organizing the University and College for Continuing Education

The first continuing education program offered by the University of California, one of the major providers, was a short series of lectures on the plays of William Shakespeare. The impetus for the program came from university staff. This was the first example in California of "extending the resources" of the University, though the faculty sponsors would not have put it that way at the time.

This beginning was followed by additional programs. Most came about because university staff thought that particular programs should be offered. Others were developed in response to requests from individuals or groups outside the university. During this period universities in other states were also experiencing the same kind of development. In all instances, however, programs were planned and administered on an ad hoc basis. There were still only a few compared to the number of "regular" courses of study attended by full-time, degree-seeking campus students. No attempt was made to rationalize the administration of continuing education. No structure was needed, and none was established.

Today, many continuing education units have a larger enrollment than the combined enrollment in the institution's other schools, colleges, and divisions. The network of relations between continuing education and campus units and between the former and outside constituencies is very complex. The concept of extending the university's resources has been transformed from an occasional offering to many hundreds and even thousands of courses and other programs offered on a regularly scheduled basis. Obviously, some ways had to be found to organize and rationalize these vastly expanded operations.

Two main patterns of administration and program development have emerged. In the first programming responsibility is distributed among the different campus units according to the academic content of particular programs. A series of lectures on Shakespeare would be planned and presented by the campus department of English literature. A short course on the history of the United States since 1945 would be offered under the jurisdiction of the campus history department. As this type of offering grew, the administration of programs in history, literature, art, philosophy, and other liberal arts disciplines might be combined into an administrative unit under the dean and faculty of arts and letters. In this model campus departments and schools make the fundamental decisions about all aspects of program development. The continuing education function is *decentralized*.

In the other form of organization the function is *centralized*. A single unit is established to plan, administer, and staff all programs. (These units are most often called university extension, extension division, or extension service. Sometimes they are called school, college, or department.) Decision-making authority about what shall be offered, who shall teach, how the offering shall be financed, marketing, and relations with outside constituencies rests with the continuing education administration. (The senior extension officer is most often called dean or director, or sometimes vice president or vice chancellor.)

Of course, there are few pure types. The most decentralized (the

University of Michigan, for example) retains aspects of centralization; and the most centralized (the University of California, Berkeley, for example) has some decentralized flavor.

In "Diversity without Design, Continuing Education at the University of Michigan,"[3] L. S. Berlin characterizes "the nature of practice and the organizational quality" of continuing education at Michigan as follows:

> *Organized chaos; anarchy; diversity without design; institutional mindlessness; adrift in a sea of overlap, duplication and competition. Any or all of these descriptions could be fairly applied to the reality of the University's system of delivering continuing education services to the wide range of adult consumers it reaches.*

Berlin counted thirty-eight "identifiable continuing education agencies" at Ann Arbor, which included only those "activities and units which are ongoing and had some clear sense of mission or purpose."

He continues:

> *Our practice is decentralized. There is no necessary interaction and communication between the many units and finally there is no one person or administrative agency to which or through which all thirty-eight of our continuing education activities report.*

But why would a distinguished university, or any university or college, issue licenses to commit continuing education to so many? According to Berlin, such behavior is congruent with the University's value system, which places a high value on academic unit autonomy and the central role of faculty.

The deeper question for Berlin, and for many continuing education staff as well, is this:

> *Can we assume that the values of autonomy and faculty democracy which are especially appropriate and necessary for campus (residential) teaching and research are also equally appropriate and necessary for outreach activities. I think not. I would argue that a far more rational design would call for integration, consolidation and centralization of much of the University's continuing education activities.*

Is decentralization a precondition of faculty preeminence in decision making in continuing education? I think not.

[3]L. S. Berlin, "Diversity without Design, Continuing Education at the University of Michigan," *N.U.E.A. Continuum* 41, no. 4 (June 1977).

It is important to emphasize that subject matter experts on the faculty have a key role in centralized and decentralized programs alike. They alone can certify that program content is of appropriate quality and that the teaching staff is qualified. No continuing education administrator performs those functions or should; they should remain the prerogative of the campus faculty. The major differences that distinguish the two models involve other matters, such as decision-making power over finance and administration and the extent to which educational experiences are oriented toward a part-time, adult student body—all of which bears directly and strongly upon the process of decision making and program development, which, in turn, shapes the educational product (or misshapes it).

Continuing Education: Faculty Attitudes and Behavior

In universities and colleges it is typically the faculty, and administrators who think like faculty members, who make the fundamental decisions about continuing education. Most of all, of course, "the professors set the pace." As M. S. Stern observed,

> For all its departmental self-absorptions and multiplicity of schools, the faculty as a whole is the power center of the university. It is, at any rate, if we speak from the point of view of institutions rather than persons—of the relations of the evening college to the university rather than of individual relations. Sociologists have recently directed our attention to centers of power—to people in positions of power inside the social institutions. But universities, unlike business corporations, are not composed of human beings united—if that is the word—by self-interest. The university as a social institution, both for good and ill, has a history and value system that transcends money and personal power. The member of the faculty may respect these latter, but we who deal with him must remember that he is most impressively influenced by the way of thinking that permeates a university. To influence such opinion we must be prepared not merely for personal achievement or failure, but for a lifetime of effort to influence what is in many ways a priesthood to accept part of an apparently heretic faith. Whatever attention the evening college cadre may give to president, trustees or legislature, it must give conscious, continuing and creative care to its relations with the faculty.[4]

Amen to that. The faculty, too, have a history and value system that transcend money and personal power. Though they are indeed

[4]M. S. Stern, *People, Programs, and Persuasion: Some Remarks About Promoting Adult Education* (Chicago: Center for the Study of Liberal Education for Adults, 1971), p. 83.

"most impressively influenced by the way of thinking that permeates a university," we know that particular values and attitudes change when individuals move from one educational environment to another. Students of politics have noted that when liberal, urban, Democratic-leaning voters move to conservative, suburban, Republican-leaning communities, they tend to change political identifications. Faculty members carry within themselves the seeds of more or less favorable attitudes toward continuing education. In a traditional environment they are likely to behave traditionally. In a public service–oriented setting other kinds of influences can be brought to bear.

Similar issues surfaced in the Michigan State University Task Force on Lifelong Education, which could not reach consensus on the issue of organizational arrangements, evidently because the majority proposal seemed to argue a continuation of certain "academic" practices. The twenty-one-member task force met for a year before issuing its final report, *The Lifelong University*, in April 1973. The task force divided "on the issue of locus and role of the principal administrator for lifelong education. On two occasions tie votes were cast." The majority believed that the provost, the chief academic administrator of the University, should be responsible for the reorganized effort. The minority took a different view.

> *The ten dissenting members cannot accept the basic premises that lifelong education is (simply) an academic function and should be administered as such by the chief academic officer. Neither can they accept the arguments and recommendation built upon this premise. They see lifelong education as involving several major functions, only some of which are essentially academic. These members feel that the resolution of policy and strategy issues posed by the recommended new thrust in lifelong education should involve but not be confined to internal academic structures and traditional academic modes for making and implementing liaisons.*[5]

The issue was not centralization versus decentralization, but rather the extent to which academic attitudes and "academic modes for making and implementing decisions" should prevail.

There is no way to avoid, or even to minimize, the campus faculty's role in continuing education. In any case, even if continuing education could and did become autonomous from the university to a degree not presently contemplated, the inevitable result for continuing education would be the status of a "wholly disowned subsid-

---

[5]T. M. Hesburgh, P. A. Miller, and C. R. Wharton, *Patterns of Lifelong Learning* (San Francisco: Jossey-Bass, 1973), p. 101.

iary," which would serve no useful purpose. What is required is to integrate the faculty into the continuing education environment by involving them in all matters that relate to the educational mission of the continuing education program, including program planning, teaching, learning, and marketing.

But this rarely happens. The faculty's relationship to the continuing education enterprise is occasional, and, even then, peripheral. Participation in programs is almost always limited to the teaching function. Many faculty believe that continuing education administrators don't care about their problems with teaching, learning, the extension administrative structure, and the like. The reason they believe this is that administrators really don't care, or they behave as if they didn't.

The great, some believe the overriding, advantage of decentralization is that mutually supportive identifications develop between continuing education programs and the schools and colleges that assume responsibility for them. For example, the school of engineering and its faculty come to accept continuing education in engineering as one of *their own* programs. The faculty begin to take responsibility for the quality of learning and teaching. They volunteer to help plan programs. They teach in them. They assist with the recruitment and training of adjunct faculty. They sometimes take an interest in the financial problems of the continuing education enterprise. (Not often, of course; that millennium is not yet.)

However, the faculty of a school are rarely as supportive of a program administered in another part of the university, for instance, by a centralized continuing education unit. They do not identify with that program. It is not their own.

Faculty members and administrators whose academic attitudes and behaviors are sanctioned by the faculty tend to dominate in decentralized units. But the continuing education point of view is more likely to predominate in centralized units. In the centralized environment, as has been pointed out before, the student, rather than the discipline, is the primary concern. Adult student needs dominate in the development of curriculum and design of the learning environment. In decentralized units, however, subject matter is paramount, and campus schools and colleges tend to expect that adult students will adjust to the existing curriculum and to the traditional learning environment. Consequences for learning are, or may be, quite different.

A Note on Finance

The problem of financing continuing education programs is perennial. To begin with, such programs are rarely financed by public funds, or, in private institutions, by internal allocation, to the extent considered necessary for other forms of education. The belief prevails that society benefits from the education of its children from kindergarten through the Ph.D. degree, and that society should pay all, or at least most, of the costs of such education. When the student is an adult, however, society does not pay anything like the same proportion of the cost. A few programs that help adults earn secondary school diplomas or their equivalent, or that provide opportunities for adults to acquire basic literacy or mathematical skills, are fully supported or require very small tuition payments. In virtually all other forms of adult education the student is expected to pay all or a substantial part of the costs.

Sometimes this is not a problem. Immediately after the spectacular success of the first Sputnik in 1957, and for many years thereafter, there was an enrollment boom in science-related programs. Deans and directors of continuing education who had spent many lean years making do with marginal financial resources found that they could make substantial profits on such programs, and they did. Until the recent "teacher surplus" began to affect involvement in continuing education programs designed for elementary and secondary school teachers, windfall profits were made there also.

More often, however, continuing education administrators do the best they can with marginal support. Some have become so skilled at academic and financial management that their programs are the wonder and pride of higher education—or they should be. But their ability to cope should not obscure the fact that budgetary joys and sorrows are unequally shared on campus. Continuing education is typically more unequal than other units—in the joys in one direction and in the sorrows in another.

It is clear that the organizational setting of continuing education influences the way support is distributed. The Sputnik profits had a strange history. In some institutions they were used to support less than sure-fire, but otherwise worthy, continuing education programs. In other institutions profits were used to support faculty research and for financial subvention of "regular" daytime undergraduate and graduate programs.

The kinds of decisions about how basic support and profits (and deficits) are distributed obviously depend on the orientation of the decision makers. How important do they believe the continuing education function is? Which, or whose, continuing education function is worthy of support?

The management education programs of the business school of one major provider regularly earn very substantive profits over all costs. The organizational setting for these programs is decentralized, and the profits stay in the business school and are used for purposes defined, not by the university, but by the business school.

It is difficult to imagine that the dean and faculty of a school of law would cheerfully countenance charging high fees to participants in continuing legal education programs so that accumulated profits could be transferred to the department of English literature and to the school of social work to help support their continuing education programs. It is easier to believe that the dean of a centralized continuing education unit would operate by the Robin Hood principle and take from the rich (law, business administration, engineering) and give to the poor (art, religious studies, and community development). Typically, the decentralized unit looks to its own financial health, and when there are profits, these are likely to be spent for purposes defined by the school or college, not by the university. Decentralization requires, in Peter Drucker's phrase, common citizenship. It is all too easy, he observes, to go into business for oneself and lose sight of the larger enterprise. If a sense of common citizenship exists, or if it can be brought into being, all is well. Otherwise . . . ?

The chief administrative officers of centralized units can assist financially marginal continuing education programs by taxing the earnings of profitmakers. The latter are not always wild with enthusiasm about these acts of educational statesmanship, but the dean of a centralized unit can act, if he has a vision of the total enterprise, in a statesmanlike manner.

Is decentralization less efficient and does it cost more? The evidence is hard to come by, but it would seem to be simple common sense that there must be some duplication of effort. In the University of Michigan, to cite just two examples of a larger phenomenon, substantial sums are spent by the many units offering continuing education for business services and for promotion and publicity. Centralized business and marketing offices would be much less costly.

It also seems plausible that a higher degree of efficiency derives from the relative ease of intra-unit communication compared with intra-university communication. The experiences, both good and bad, of one sub-unit of a centralized organization can be shared quickly and easily with other sub-units. In a decentralized operation continuing education units are too distant from each other, psychologically as well as geographically, to be able to profit from shared experiences.

The Case for Centralization: Some Conclusions

In an imperfect world the search for perfect solutions is likely to be endless. Centralization of continuing education will not solve all the problems incident to its present and future development. On balance, however, I am persuaded that centralization of the continuing education function is the wiser course.

First of all, universities and colleges are large and complex institutions that interact with all of society and serve many different constituencies. A university is more than a collection of schools and colleges. Throughout its long history the university has changed many time-tested policies and procedures in response to changes in the larger society. I believe that centralized units could help universities and colleges, *as universities and colleges* meet the challenges posed by a growing continuing education clientele.

A continuing education program for practicing physicians will perforce rely heavily on the medical school faculty and relate its activities to the medical fraternity outside the walls. However, a decentralized unit would report to and serve the needs of the medical school, which may or may not be identical to the needs of the university. The same program will be subject to countervailing influences in a centralized continuing education unit—to the constituent demands of, among others, social work, public health, sociology, and the humanities as well. Would the result be a broader program? Perhaps. But, in any case, it would be part of a larger program that serves the continuing education needs of the university's total community.

Thus it follows that presidents of universities and colleges would do well to support the concept of centralization. Centralized continuing education units are more likely to serve the needs of the total institution than parts of it. Centralized units are best able to serve the university as a university.

Institutions should rethink their priorities. Some may opt for the best and most imaginative kinds of continuing education programs and assign a very high priority to such endeavors. It is important to add that the assignment must be made visible through actions; rhetoric alone no longer serves a useful purpose.

Other institutions may not have the same enthusiasms. The trustees, president, and faculty may decide, for good and sufficient reasons, that the continuing education unit has become too autonomous and that it must become more truly an integral part of the rest of the university, and soon; or that the university's financial problems are so acute that retrenchment is in order and public service programs, especially high-cost programs, must be curtailed; or that the needs of adults and other part-time students, who now greatly outnumber full timers, must be considered more fully than in the past; or that the university's relations with its community, which to this point have been, at best, adequate, must be improved and continuing education programs expanded because there is evidence that such programs are good for the university's image.

In a rationally managed institution overall priorities would be established, and continuing education's role within the larger design would be spelled out. If the university were exceedingly well managed, we might even expect that the president and other senior officers would adopt a mode of organization for the continuing education function that would be likely to produce the kind of program they want.

If administrators opt for high priority for continuing education, I believe they will find that the best programs are more likely to develop in a centralized unit where the continuing education influence is dominant. Some decentralized units, willing to depart from tried-and-true daytime curricula, formats, and teaching methods, can do as well, but they rarely do. Decentralized organizational patterns now in place were designed for, and have ably served, the needs of full-time undergraduate and graduate students. Continuing education students will not be as well served by units managed by schools and colleges ideologically attuned to the needs of the full-time student.

The most telling point to be made is a financial one. Decentralized forms of organization are more costly. Fifteen or twenty continuing education promotion and publicity sub-units are more costly than one department would be. The offices of ten or twelve deans and directors of continuing education located in the various schools and colleges are more costly than one dean's office would be. In centralized units these savings and profits earned in financially profitable programs can be used for purposes defined by the university or college.

Finally, it is well to recall that in an age characterized by fragmentation of learning and increasing specialization, the point of view that insures the best practices in continuing education, and which prevails in centralized units, takes its directions from all of society and its strength from the university as a whole. The continuing education generalist is less likely to take a partial view or base actions on what Alfred North Whitehead called "the imperfect categories of thought derived from one profession."

DISCUSSION

"Somewhere in my paper I said that continuing education is in great danger because presidents are starting to care," *Mort Gordon* recalls. "And I mean that. I view the interest of presidents, trustees, deans, and the like in continuing education with alarm. Members of this symposium have attended meetings over the last five to thirty years and have heard again and again that, 'Though we are lovable and need love, *they* don't love us! If only *they* appreciated us and understood us and loved us, everything would be fine!' Now, for reasons we are all familiar with, *they* are starting to love us, or so it seems, and I view that with alarm because I don't think some of us in the business have envisioned the costs of this sudden attention that we are getting. What I really fear is the fatal embrace of the mainstream."

"And that fatal embrace is right around the corner," *Grover Andrews* says. "In a Council on Postsecondary Accreditation (COPA) study that was just finished, we conducted a national survey of presidents of higher education institutions. In the survey we had about 1,500 respondents from all over the country. One section of it looked into the 1980s: What are the institutions going to do? From a long list they were to select and rank the options they thought their institutions would be choosing in the 1980s. First was off-campus programs. Second was continuing education. They have not only found continuing education, they rank it very high in their priority list for the eighties."

"Perhaps, Mort," *Bill Griffith* suggests, "you should have some degree of optimism. Try thinking like a black widow spider. As you anticipate the embrace, be so filled with seminal ideas that they, the presidents, trustees, deans, and others, will become fertile, and *they* will conceive of many pregnant ideas."

"That's what really scares me," *Mort Gordon* responds. "That could really be the end of continuing education because there is a *they*. I don't mean demons; I mean people with different points of view, which are sometimes correct and sometimes dead wrong; and many administrators and faculty members at some of the better institutions are like the Bourbons who never forgot anything and never learned anything. We had, at a school I'm familiar with, ten years of a distinguished and innovative dean, who was concerned about teaching and learning and all those good things. And we thought that the school was changed permanently! After ten years I thought—and I should have known better—well, by God, the place has really been changed! Now he has been replaced by a researcher with a capital R, and the mainstream has come through. It was there all the time! The patina of that distinguished dean, like the Missouri River, was eight and a half miles wide and an inch deep. I think we're kidding ourselves if we think the mainstream has moved very much. That's why it is the mainstream—it's main, damn it!

"On the other hand, institutions are very different from each other, and they have different histories, and admissions are different; they're located in different areas, they have different leadership, and so on. I don't have any pink pills to offer anyone that are good for everybody in every situation. I paid my dues as manager of a centralized continuing education unit at the University of California, and during that period I observed many others that were centralized. I now teach in a graduate program in an institution that is about as decentralized as it can be and can be imagined. We have counted thirty-eight different and distinct continuing education units at the University of Michigan completely autonomous from each other, including three in the business school that are also completely separate and autonomous from each other. It is not that much of an exaggeration in the University of Michigan—the decentralist institution *par excellence*—to say that it is just about decentralized to every senior professor, or at least every tenured professor.

"On balance, I come out on the side of centralization. There are good arguments to be made on the other side. The arguments for centralization are not all that perfect, either. But, on balance, I come out for centralization. Nevertheless, I think that the field of continuing education—as it has many times in the past, to its sorrow—is going to disregard my advice. The wave of the present and future is toward more and more decentralization. And I'm not so sure that's going to be all that terrible except that it will be more expensive. It will not be better done, either. It will, I suspect, be worse done, but they're telling everyone it will be better done. But there will be some good things happening as a consequence."

It is frightening to deal with thirty-eight department heads. . . .

"I'd like to comment, at this point," *Bob Kost* says. "It is rather frightening to come into an institution, especially when it is fifty miles away, and have to spend a week to get to see thirty-eight department heads to find out whether they can service you. More importantly though, I think there are a couple of items in your article that are extraordinarily meaningful for us in terms of centralization. One is the fact that students, rather than a discipline, should be the central concern in continuing education. The other is that the function of continuing education is to facilitate the development of programs that integrate theory and practice. In dealing with thirty-eight department heads from the outside, that's an impossible feat, which it isn't in dealing with a central continuing education function that is attuned to your needs."

"I suppose," *Milt Stern* agrees, "I'm also in favor of centralization. But I do have a couple of observations to make. At institutions that are actively centralized, which have given a mandate for a centralized extension arm—like the University of California, for example—the tendency is toward decentralization. But in institutions like yours, the University of Michigan, where decentralization has been in effect for thirty years at least, the tendency is toward centralization. My question, therefore, is, Isn't there more of a cyclical quality to this pattern than you have indicated?"

"My comment would be something like this," *Mort Gordon* responds. "I think that the cyclical notion—first you do it this way and then after the passing of time you do it that way, back and forth, and so on—has been operating to some extent in the past. But I think the new element is the growing importance of continuing education in this country. It is now too important to be left to continuing educators. It has become too important to institutions for survival, for philosophical reasons, for what's happening on the outside to society, and so forth. My reading of recent history, and my view of my clouded crystal ball, is that continuing education has become so important, that, as Roz has said, the whole institution can now be thought of as an adult education institution."

"Mort is right," *John Ervin* suggests. "You need to look at the whole institution. Because the range of centralization-decentralization is not as simple as you *are* or you *are not*. There's a whole range of relationships, and sometimes what is the visible symbol of the relationship obscures the fact that the power is somewhere else. That complicates the whole business. When I became dean at Washington University, what became clear to me was that even though we had a centralized unit, policy got made somewhere else. We had an administrative board composed of all the other deans, with me as chairman and my associate dean as secretary. It was very clear after the second meeting that anything that was to my interest had to run through all their computers to see what impact it would have on them. If it didn't impact on any of them, then we got support for it. So I decided I wanted to design the best of all worlds, and I started to call my colleagues around the country —started on the East Coast and came right across: New York University, George Washington, Chicago, and ended at the University of Southern California, every private university. I asked one simple question: How does policy get made in your institution vis-à-vis continuing education? Every single one was different! No two were alike, and some of those differences were substantive differences. Some had autonomy—real autonomy, with their own faculties, their own policy making, their own budget-making initiatives, and so on. Some had no autonomy; they were in a sense paper organizations; they had a continuing education unit, but they didn't grant degrees; all they were was a mechanism for funneling people from other parts of the institution into continuing education activities. Some others were a kind of a mixture; they didn't have their own faculty, but they would control who taught what kind of courses.

The real power keeps shifting. . . .

"So centralization-decentralization is not a simple either/or. It's very complex. And often it all gets more complicated by the fact that the real power keeps shifting because some of it is particular to personalities. You can get a strong guy in the least powerful part of the institution, and he can run the whole damned thing!"

Mort Gordon nods. "Administrators," he says, "are ordinary folk; what we want is freedom from above and obedience from below. And I think what happens is that the centralist-oriented administrator just wants those other people to leave him alone. But they won't. The pressures toward decentralization are there, and a lot of them come from the professional schools."

"And the reason," *Grover Andrews* points out, "is that these deans of the various professional schools are anticipating that decentralization will bring revenues or incomes to them. In fact, in the past three months I've visited several of our largest institutions at their request. They're institutions that have had a centralized form and are feeling that decentralization is the way they ought to go. (This has not come down from the administration, but up from the deans of the colleges.) In spending three or four days trying to assess their situations, I talked to each of these deans, and it was almost identical talking to each one. They have a lot of misconceptions, but two things really sifted out. One, they see continuing education as a source of income; and two, they were dissatisfied with the centralized services they were getting, and I think they were right in these cases—the continuing education dean or director had built up an empire, so to speak, and really was not service oriented. The dean of the business school in one of the institutions showed me—and I confirmed it by talking to the dean of continuing education—that it was more expensive for them to go through continuing education to plan and implement a business seminar for bankers than it would have been for them to do it themselves working directly with the bankers. He said, 'Frankly we can't afford that. We can't afford to use our own continuing education unit.' I think he was right. I think there is a problem in the administration of centralized continuing education. You lose sight of being a service unit to the institution as well as being a program development unit. In most of these cases, however, when pressed, the deans were willing to deal with the continuing education unit if the service could be profitable; they really didn't want to get in the business."

A university is not a collection of colleges . . .

"But I guess that's where I get a little hot," *Mort Gordon* breaks in. "A university is not—and if it is, it shouldn't be—a collection of colleges. In my view the dean of the school of business doesn't get to say, 'It's cheaper for me to do it myself,' *especially because it may be cheaper!* The point is that there is something called a university, which is a couple hundred years old. But what I see is that one unit—the division of executive management in the school of business, for example—if it is aggressive and has reasonably well-done programs, can hardly help but show somewhere between two and three million dollars net at the end of the year, after all costs imaginable have been deducted (and they are fairly skillful at burying profits, as some of us have learned to be). That stays in the business school! Meanwhile, other programs on the other side of the campus are running around scratching for a few bucks here and there. Now, it's too much to ask the dean of the school of business, I think, to spend a lot of time worrying about the school of social work or about the humanities department. He does well to worry about the school of business. It's the president who ought to worry about the others! But in a lot of places presidents don't. They worry about keeping the biggest barons content—as barons, not as citizens of the kingdom, but as barons!

"A decentralized mode may be ideal for a full-time student body pursuing undergraduate and graduate degrees, but the needs of the adult student will not be served that way. Everything for the adult student will be done out of the side pocket because the main mission of the school of business and its dean and its faculty is not and never will be—not in the lifetime of anybody here—the adult student! The faculty will do what comes naturally, what they've been doing for a long time. Where is it more likely that the rights and responsibility of the adult student are going to be defended? (And they need defense!) If they are not going to be defended in the centralized unit, where are they going to be defended? At too many universities, they are not defended."

We are making a raft of assumptions. . . .

"I can speak only from my own experience," *Roz Loring* says, "but I should like, nonetheless, to take an opposite point of view and speak about the value of decentralization. I believe we are making a raft of assumptions that are very difficult to support with facts. I used to make those speeches, too—that the faculty didn't understand people, as if the faculty weren't people also; or that the faculty were narrow in their perspective, as though they weren't also exposed to the changing trends of our time. In my experience of the last three years, however, that 'ain't necessarily so.' There are any number of faculty who come to us with excellent ideas for broad programs that are interdisciplinary and interdepartmental. It is possible to get faculty working together, at *their* request. (It isn't always possible to get deans to do that, but it's very possible to get faculty to do it.) They sometimes do better than program planners, generally because they know more about the subject. One of the values of decentralization is keeping close in touch with the vitality of an academic field, the whole notion that the content which people concentrate on most of the time makes them aware of changes in nuance, aware of where new literature is developed in the field, and so forth. In the very large institutions—of which we certainly have some marvelous, notable examples—there are staff people who are expert in a certain field but who view their job as management and not content. As a consequence, they generally do not know as much about specific subject matter as do the people whose major job is content—and those people can also learn management. The fact is, I think, that what we know as adult educators is not all that tough to learn! It takes only a will and some enthusiasm to do that.

"But let me go on with a few examples, because I really am concerned about this issue. It seems to me that involvement of the faculty, the core of the institution, and the ability to call upon the resources of the whole, is much greater when you have people who are intimately involved and accessible to the separate parts. I have watched far too many community agencies, which sought for all kinds of reasons—some philosophical, some economic—to centralize their activities, only to discover that they lost momentum, they lost motivation, they lost membership. And I've seen in this country far too many universities and colleges that centralized their activities and totally lost the support of their faculty. The faculty don't feel a part of it, and so they go off and do something else, maybe for another institution, but they are not available to teach in the centralized unit."

We are not the only ones who raise questions. . . .

"I'd like also to deal with another part of Mort's paper because again it's like a we-they situation, as though we adult educators are the only ones who raise questions for somebody to answer about why does it have to be that way—what Mort Gordon calls 'educational holy writ!' We are not the only ones who raise those questions these days. There are all kinds of meetings where I hear the chairman of the department of sociology raise very tough questions to other faculty members about why can't we give credit for prior learning. I'm not the one who has to raise those questions any longer. Times have changed! Wheels have turned! Our unique contribution to the enterprise, it seems to me, is changing also. I would hope we would be flexible enough to do some changing along with it.

"I also want to talk just a bit about the involvement of central administration. Maybe my situation is unusual, but I have staff people, who don't have tenure, sitting on major campus committees. They sit on the committees that approve the curriculum for the whole university. They are there to raise questions such as, 'Does the psychology department need another class in this when there is a similar course being given in the school of public administration?' We are referred to, and considered, for our knowledge of the whole campus, in a way I don't think is possible when we maintain a kind of exclusive 'We've got control over you guys' attitude. This need to control, it seems to me, is at the base of it. I think if we could educate central administration, they could do a better job of supporting us. They aren't going to support us unless we do educate them to it.

"This is my last point, or at least the next to the last one. I loved your list, Mort, of attributes of continuing education divisions. But I don't believe that anybody is free any longer to maintain such clear territory. It seems to me that whether we administer degrees or develop degrees or help other people develop them is less the point than that there *are* degrees available for adults because adults want them. And as we're prepared to move in differing patterns, it seems to me we can fulfill some very valuable aspects.

"I finally have to tell you that I really think decentralization works. (I'm sorry to be pragmatic about it.) At USC we exist—as does the extension division on the Michigan campus—along with a lot of other units that are doing continuing education—the gamut from professional schools through the arts and sciences. And we continue to grow while they're growing. It's as though we are supporting each other in providing inspiration and impetus and a sense of how the institution can serve the whole community!"

Structural change is not a cause, but an effect.

"Each coin has at least two sides," *Bill Griffith* says. "We've now been sitting here for some time watching this one being flipped, and I think what we're hearing about is the unintelligent use of structural changes to correct functional problems, and that the structural change from centralization to decentralization or from decentralization to centralization is not a cause, but an effect. It is a clear message that what you have been doing is not perceived as particularly successful from the standpoint of the entire institution. So if you find that you are being decentralized, or if you find you're being centralized, what did you do to bring this about? It would seem odd to have an effect with no cause.

"Now, obviously, when one makes such a structural change, there are subsequent other kinds of changes. But I would venture to say that, in many cases, what we are seeing is a scenario in action, and the centralization or decentralization is not a major consideration. It's a symptom of something far more important about what continuing education is from the standpoint of the university—lack of vision or distorted vision, whatever it is. Where there is no vision, the people perish. Where there is no vision, centralized extension divisions perish. If there is a vision that is kept in a closet, that's no help either. So I guess we have to say that if we look at the structural change as effect rather than cause, we might be doing something more useful than looking for what might come about after you dealt with the symptom."

These are really abstract concepts. . . .

"We, too, have to realize—and I think Mort has done an unusually good job of pointing out that these are really abstract concepts and that you don't find such things in pure form anywhere—that we don't really have perfect centralization and decentralization. We see movements, but nobody's completely decentralized or completely centralized.

"There's another very difficult thing we've got to deal with here: If you insist that it's easy to learn to be an adult educator, then you give every bloke on campus a fishing license, a hunting license, or whatever kind of license it is to be one. If you insist you have no expertise and you require no training, then that's nice—the great gifted amateurs! But don't expect to be highly regarded on the university campus as a highly creative amateur. That's not the way universities work. If you're going to insist that you don't need credentials and training and a lengthy period of professional preparation to do the job, let anybody do it! Why shouldn't it be decentralized? Where's your claim that you have some expertise? The fact that you were there six months earlier? That's not a very persuasive reason for being in charge—that you were there six months earlier, or six years, or whatever the number might be. So we have to think about it. You can't have it both ways; you can't insist that it's amateur night all the time, while at the same time saying, 'Don't let those amateurs do it! Only we, the *experienced amateurs* can do it!'

"Now, I think that the work in organization, although much of it is overblown, does have something to say about innovation. It reinforces two old saws, each of which says that creativity is found at the ends of the continuum. The most creative organizations are, first, those with the greatest amount of organizational slack, which is used for development; and, second, those that are so desperate they'll try anything to survive. I'm unhappy with the notion that marginality is a great and wonderful thing for us. I would much rather have the kind of creativity that goes with prosperity, and I would hope that none of us here would elevate the virtues of marginality unrealistically. The desperate ones do tend to be more creative than the comfortable ones, but those who are very well off also tend to be creative—the giants and the pygmies work harder!"

Flap your arms and run about . . .

"I think," *George Robertson* says, "carrying on the point that Bill raised pretty forcefully, that if you decentralize you're implying something about the competencies required in adult education; that if you simply turn it over to any old department or faculty member willing to take it on, you're perhaps not saying much about the skills required. I can get a little ironic, too; faculty, by and large, know as much about teaching adults as they know about teaching youngsters!

"I think, returning to the centralized-decentralized question, there is an old English saying that goes, When in danger, when in doubt, flap your arms and run about! It seems to me we do that. One of the ways that we flap our arms and run about is that we reorganize periodically. Having said that, there is nonetheless, nothing inherently wrong with new things—the kind of Hawthorne effect that you get by reorganizing for a momentary advantage. You could have a philosophy of organization that says, 'If it makes sense, if we can get some benefit and keep people happy by reorganizing every five or ten years, that's OK. Let's do it!' Maybe life is meant to be a continuing cycle between unacceptable alternatives."

"Roz says," *Phil Frandson* points out, "that she works in a decentralized organization, and it works. I work in a very centralized organization, and it works, and I like it.

"However, even in her decentralized system, she says, it's possible to have more and more units become part of her continuing education operation; every week another unit decides they'd rather work with her than do it alone. She's getting bigger instead of smaller without any kind of overriding pronouncement that it's got to be centralized.

"On the other hand, in our centralized operation nothing happens that does not have dual approval in writing. Every campus department, whether it is the school of medicine, engineering, arts —even a professor in adult education—has power to approve and that also means we have mutual veto power. I don't know many operations where some form of such subtle but extraordinarily powerful decentralization does not exist. For me centralization means two things: First, it's efficient. If we are not efficient, we are called to order, particularly when we're self-supporting. Secondly, we are centralized on the budget. It's a budget that permits me, in accounting, to run a Robin Hood operation. There is only one part of the operation in twenty-five years that has not had a deficit—programs with the business and industrial community. Every other section, including engineering, architecture, art, education, and so on, cyclically goes through the vagaries of deficits. What happens in a centralized operation? I am able to take, like Robin Hood, a profit here and there and keep a presence forever going in every one of these areas for which we have decided we're going to have a program. Decentralized operations come and go, because who is there to finance them unless they have pots full of money sticking out in some private account?"

It matters a very great deal . . .

"I think," *Mort Gordon* concludes, "what I tried to emphasize is a consideration of what might be called interests and requirements. There are societal interests and societal requirements; there are university interests and requirements; there are the interests and requirements of the subject matter, of the professions, of the adult student. And it's all very well to say all of these are important. But which prevail in case of ties? What are you more likely to do if there are insufficient resources? If the lights go out? If whatever? I'm persuaded, on balance, that the interests and requirements of the kinds of things I believe in—the society, the university, the adult as student—are more likely to be served by adult educators than by any others. It's as if I hear you saying (and I know you didn't) that it doesn't matter all that much! What I'm just saying is that it *does* matter a very great deal! I might be wrong in what I conclude from having said 'It matters.' However, I have said I was persuaded, on balance, that one way was better than the other, and I haven't changed my mind as a result of this conversation.

"I am reasonably well convinced that there has been some movement in the faculties and among people other than the anointed continuing educators. They are all learning a little something. I have an impression, from the places I go, the meetings I attend, and the institutions I'm most familiar with, that there's been a lot of sound and fury generated and a lot of programs started; and some are going, and some have died, and a lot of dust has been stirred up. And, academically speaking, once the dust has settled, everything will be as before—only dusty. You will find the chairman of a sociology department who will make the right noises, and not only make the right noises, but also believe in them, and upon returning to the department and trying to implement what he has sincerely proposed, he runs headlong into the way universities are organized! They are organized for the full-time, resident, undergraduate and graduate students, and it's going to be a long time before that changes very dramatically.

"Don't be surprised if you decentralize the unit down into the business school and you have a strictly business school point of view. You should have! For heaven's sake, don't be surprised if the dean of the business school acts according to character. The dean of business is supposed to be dean of business! I think that's what drives me wild—where you set up the form and are surprised to find that it doesn't perform functions that setting up the form made it practically impossible to perform! But if you really want to have form follow function, if you really want to have adequate representation of the adult point of view, then a measure of the kind of centralization I'm calling for is most likely to produce it!"

FINAL COMMENTARY

Effective management of a comprehensive university continuing education program requires satisfaction of the divergent desires of students, faculty, and administration. There are numerous successful programs managed in the decentralized manner and others in the centralized manner. Regardless of organizational form, the successful continuing education program serves the university and community alike through the active involvement of faculty, staff, and students in planning and implementing activities across the whole range of university competence and community need. To accomplish this, provision must be made for training faculty and staff in what is known about adult learning, and for insuring that there is efficient implementation of administrative tasks, fiscal support of nonlucrative content areas (usually the humanities and arts), appropriate counseling and guidance of the adult student, and active commitment of all to the total enterprise. On balance, some form of centralization appears most likely to provide for these essential elements. However, some cyclical movement from centralization to decentralization and vice versa will probably take place in most institutions as a symptom of the failure to achieve all of the essentials, rather than as an ultimate solution to the management problem.

8 THE CONTINUING EDUCATION PROFESSIONAL

Paper by William S. Griffith

BIOGRAPHY

WILLIAM S. GRIFFITH is professor and chairman of the adult education department, University of British Columbia. His B.S. is from Pennsylvania State College (1953), and his M.S. is from Louisiana State University (1955); both degrees are in dairy science. From 1953 to 1961 his teaching and research related to that discipline. In 1961 he was awarded a Carnegie fellowship in adult education at the University of Chicago, and in 1963 he received his Ph.D. in Adult Education and began teaching at the University of Chicago. From 1964 to 1977, when he went to his present position, he was chairman of the Adult Education Committee in the department of education, University of Chicago.

Griffith's primary interests in continuing education are the growth and development of adult education institutions and the organization, financing, and coordination of adult education agencies and associations. Since coming to the field, he has authored or edited more than sixty books and articles. He has served as chairman of the Commission of Professors of Adult Education, chairman of the Research Section of the National University Extension Association, chairman of the Program Committee for AEA/USA's national conference in 1966, and the same for the National Association of Public Continuing and Adult Education program in 1975. He has served as the book review editor of *Adult Education* and is senior editor of the AEA/USA Handbook Series on Adult Education. He has been a senior research fellow at the University of Sidney; an honorary visiting fellow, Australian National University, Canberra; visiting professor of adult education, North Carolina State University; and a field research associate, National Academy of Sciences, Committee on Evaluation of Education and Training Programs.

INITIAL COMMENTARY

Most persons engaged in administering educational programs for adults or teaching in those programs do so without having had any systematic academic preparation in such subjects as adult development, principles of adult learning, and teaching or administrative techniques especially for adults. Still being debated is the question of whether the practice of adult and continuing education would be improved if practitioners were required to have such specific academic preparation; still being debated is the question of whether there is or should be a continuing education profession.

What most persons who call themselves adult or continuing educators do have individually is a competency in content or process acquired from education or experience in a field other than adult education; what they have in common is a set of convictions that the desire and ability to learn is universal and continues throughout life, and that opportunity, access, support, and stimulation should be provided for everyone to continue to learn throughout life.

As William Griffith points out, there is a growing body of knowledge that reinforces those convictions, that explores the status and nature of a continuing education profession, and that details what is known about adults and how to meet their continuing learning needs. And he suggests some tasks that must be accomplished and some attitudes that must be changed if continuing educators are to be recognized as a profession rather than as that diverse group of facilitators, registrars, publicists, coordinators, administrators, teachers, scholars, philosophers, wishful thinkers, and doers we call "continuing educators."

William S. Griffith

Personnel Preparation

Is There a Continuing Education Profession?

Is there a continuing education profession? The short answer to that question is no, according to a majority of the senior spokespeople in university graduate departments of adult education. As will be demonstrated, statements by respected leaders, at best, describe adult education as an emerging profession. The literature is replete with statements insisting that adult education is well on the way to becoming a profession. On the other side, well-argued claims that adult education has already attained the status of a profession are few and unconvincing. Of equal importance is a second question: Should adult educators seek to become identified as members of a profession? And, if so, on what would such a claim rest? Might there be negative consequences associated with a move to professional status? The ultimate question in this area must address the probable effects of professionalism on adult education practice and the provision of learning opportunities for adults.

The State of the "Profession"

A. A. Liveright said that "actually, adult education cannot yet be truly classified as a profession, although it evidences many of the characteristics of an occupation moving rapidly in that direction."[1] He then described eight characteristics of the leaders of adult education that he believed were acting against the full professionalization of the field:

1. Few of them have participated in an organized program of graduate study in adult education or hold advanced degrees therein.

2. Most come from other occupations and have moved into adult education after other kinds of employment.

3. Many look upon adult education as a stepping stone rather than as a permanent career.

[1]A. A. Liveright, "The Nature and Aims of Adult Education as a Field of Graduate Education." In *Adult Education: Outline of an Emerging Field of University Study* (ed. Gale Jensen, A. A. Liveright, and Wilbur Hallenbeck) (Washington, D.C.: Adult Education Association of the U.S.A., 1964), pp. 85–102.

4. During the past ten years many have moved from adult education to other posts in the educational or community field—many to other administrative posts in education.

5. Their conceptions of the ideal adult educator and of the competencies required for the professional adult educator vary widely.

6. Many of them are action oriented rather than research oriented, and few have made major research contributions to the field of adult education.

7. Many are concerned about their status and position as adult educators and do not feel completely identified with the field, or, if they do, they feel themselves "second-rate" citizens in the academic hierarchy.

8. There is as yet no clearly defined set of values or ethics subscribed to by all of them.

Although Liveright's description of adult education leaders was written sixteen years ago, few observers of the field would say that the eight characteristics are less accurate today than they were then.

In 1965 Leonard Nadler edited a report of a federally funded workshop intended to explore ways of accelerating the preparation of adult educators. That report avoided defining what a professional adult educator might be, but it called for an enlargement of training opportunities that presumably would produce such professionals:

> We recognize the urgent needs for substantial and extensive short-range programs to provide training personnel for working with new and emerging activities of federal agencies. In addition, the established programs of adult education require increasing numbers of trained personnel. Beyond meeting the need for short-term training, we must not neglect the necessity for increasing substantially the number of professional adult educators with graduate degrees in the field.[2]

Nadler saw a need for individuals with a given set of competencies and concluded that graduate adult education programs were the most appropriate vehicles for providing individuals with such training.

Malcolm S. Knowles, historian of American adult education, executive director of the Adult Education Association for nearly a decade, and initiator of the graduate program in adult education at Boston University, also looked at the leadership in the field in 1965 and commented:

[2]Leonard Nadler, "Final Report of Workshop on Accelerating the Preparation of Adult Educators" (Washington, D.C.: George Washington University, 1965), p. 38.

Of the several thousand leaders of continuing educa-
tion—the men and women who provide staff services in
education programs for adults in colleges and universities,
public schools, business and industry, government agencies,
religious institutions and a dozen other institutional set-
tings—perhaps not more than ten percent have any formal
training in the theory and practice of adult education. They
are people, for the most part, who were on their way up in
their organizations and were available when vacancies oc-
curred; and they tend to be people who were intrigued by the
adventure and challenge of adult education. Most of them
have learned what they know about their jobs through
apprenticeship, hard knocks and independent reading.[3]

Although Knowles saw that only a small minority of the leaders had
undergone graduate education in the field of adult education, he
expressed an optimistic observation about changes he believed were
under way:

But this situation is rapidly changing. Employers are
increasingly requiring professional preparation for these
positions, and universities are increasingly making available
opportunities for graduate study. Adult education is in the
process of becoming a professional field of study and practice.

Cyril O. Houle, who epitomizes scholarly skepticism, has written
more extensively on graduate study in this field than any other
scholar. He expressed caution in discussing what effects graduate
training might have on the practice of adult education:

Most practitioners of adult education, including some of
the most eminent, received their early training for their
present positions by apprenticeship or trial and error. Can
graduate curricula (now in existence or to be developed in the
future) provide a group of leaders who are so significantly
better than those trained by apprenticeship that the cost of
such curricula can be justified? Can those who are recruited
for graduate training measure up to those who have been
chosen by the crude but effective self-selection which is now
the rule? Can the great lore of the creative but untrained
pioneers of adult education be studied so that it can be passed
on in a more systematic fashion?[4]

[3]Malcolm Knowles, "Professional Education for Leaders of Continuing Education," *Journal of Education* (Boston University) 147, no. 3 (February 1965), pp.16–20.
Used with permission.

[4]Cyril O. Houle, "The Emergence of Graduate Study in Adult Education." In
Adult Education: Outlines of an Emerging Field of University Study (Ed. Gale Jensen,
A. A. Liveright, and Wilbur Hallenbeck) (Washington, D.C.: Adult Education As-
sociation of the U.S.A., 1964), pp. 69–83.

Six years later Houle observed:

> *Some adult education specialists call themselves 'profes-*
> *sionals' but they do so with an uneasy air. . . . At present*
> *the specialist in adult education can be considered a profes-*
> *sional only in a loose and analogical fashion, such as that*
> *which distinguishes the trained from the amateur historian*
> *or the political scientist from the politician. By study and*
> *experience he has acquired a body of knowledge, a discipline*
> *and an expertise which sets him apart from other people, but*
> *he is not yet a member of a consciously defined company of*
> *men who have achieved the socially recognized and legally*
> *protected stature of a profession.*[5]

Nevertheless, Houle's optimism about the development of the field persisted, for he said:

> *Slowly, however, all too slowly, the leaders of the field of*
> *adult education are abandoning their reliance on intuition*
> *and imitation and are acquiring a body of tested knowledge*
> *on which it is possible to built expertise in attacking illiter-*
> *acy, disease, intolerance, narrowness of viewpoint, incompe-*
> *tence and other handicaps man encounters as he tries to build*
> *a better world.*

Authors seem to agree that the professions all involve a period of demanding academic preparation. The nature of such training for adult education practitioners has been scrutinized by numerous writers whose views range across a broad spectrum.

Duncan Campbell, in reviewing the development of adult educa-tion as a field of study and practice, drew upon Gordon Godbey's thoughts concerning university-based adult educators' feeling of being a part of a university:

> *University based adult educators live with an uneasy*
> *feeling about themselves, questioning their status in the in-*
> *stitution and their identity within it. They privately debate*
> *whether what they do is important or whether they function*
> *merely as hewers of intellectual woods and drawers of aca-*
> *demic water. While others of their associates seem to have*
> *secure career lines and acceptance by a peer group, support*
> *for the adult education function is meagre or lukewarm.*
> *The solution, Godbey asserts, lies in the determination of*

---

[5]Cyril O. Houle, "The Educators of Adults." In *Handbook of Adult Education* (Ed. Robert M. Smith, George F. Aker, and J. R. Kidd) (Toronto: Collier Macmillan Canada, 1970), pp. 109–19.

the adult educator to extend his competence well beyond the conventional "bag of organizational tricks" into the theory base of adult education.[6]

The development of this theory base is dependent upon acceptance of the notion that present practice can be markedly improved. According to Campbell, Britain's National Institute of Adult Education has commented that:

Training . . . is a distinguishing mark of all established professions. But, paradoxically, such a body of systemized knowledge (as adult education) can only be established by people already doing the work and interested in establishing its status and consequently their own. . . . It is a large act of self-criticism to promote, or even accept, the view that professional training which existing staff have not had, would be advantageous.[7]

Whether or not adult education is to become an established profession will be determined largely by those who have the leadership in the field today, and particularly by those who are in positions to determine the qualifications of people who are being employed to work in the field. Campbell noted that the Council for Cultural Cooperation of the Council of Europe commented in 1966 that adult education in the European setting

is not yet a profession, a recognized career, yet it seems on the point of becoming one. The speed at which it becomes a profession will depend largely upon the qualities and qualifications that employing agencies look for and the employment opportunities that they provide. The status of any profession, that is its standing in the community, is determined principally by the value of the function which the profession performs in the community, by the educational background of its members and by the monetary remuneration which they receive. By insisting on sound educational qualifications and by paying adequate salaries, employing agencies have it in their own power to establish and enhance the status of adult education in the community.[8]

Such reasoning lends support to the notion that, intentionally or

[6]Duncan D. Campbell, *Adult Education as a Field of Study and Practice: Strategies for Development* (Vancouver: The Centre for Continuing Education, the University of British Columbia, 1977), pp. 43–44. Used with permission.

[7]Ibid., p. 30.

[8]Ibid., p. 79.

unintentionally, deans of university extension divisions exert a major force in the development of the profession by the staffing practices they follow.

Adult education professors and their students have been interested in the development of the profession perhaps to a greater extent than has any other group. Inasmuch as some professors may still feel unsure of the legitimacy of their field, it would be surprising if that concern were not transmitted to their graduate students. And even some students of the most respected professors have shown such concern.

Characteristics of Professions

Lawrence A. Allen, in his doctoral dissertation completed in 1961 at the University of Chicago, studied the growth of professionalism in adult education as reflected in the literature of the field between 1928 and 1958. As a part of his research he reviewed the literature on professionalism and professions, from which he was able to identify fifteen characteristics of a fully developed profession:

A profession—

1. serves a socially valuable and highly acceptable function which deals with matters of vital importance to the client;

2. organizes its members into an association which tests competence, maintains standards, establishes training opportunities and thereby gains societal recognition and status for the profession;

3. is based upon a complex, systematic body of theoretical knowledge;

4. possesses a technique which is used in carrying out its function, and which cannot be readily understood nor practiced by the general public;

5. produces a code of ethics which protects the interests of the client, the general public, and the professional practitioner and is enforced by the professional association;

6. is composed of members who have gained expertise in the profession's body of knowledge and techniques by means of long, formal, intellectual training in a college or university;

7. exercises control over the quality of its members and their practice by means of entrance requirements and minimum standards of training, and, in return for obedience to these standards, offers colleague-group protection to the individual practitioner;

8. in collaboration with state officials sets up legal control of certification or licensing;

9. is composed of practitioners who are autonomous (self-directing) in their actions;

10. performs its functions in such a manner that the interests of the clients and society are placed above and before the personal interests of the practitioner;

11. is recognized by the general public and other professionals as an occupation of high status;

12. is made up of people who are committed to the occupation as a career;

13. tends to divide its functions into different specialities;

14. is a full-time occupation which gives sufficient remuneration for the practitioner to maintain a livelihood; and

15. adopts a common special language which can only be fully understood by the practitioner.[9]

Observers may argue over the exact number of these criteria that are satisfied by adult education, but it seems unlikely that anyone could argue successfully that all of them are now being met. Perhaps it would be useful to examine the "long, formal intellectual training in a college or university" provided for adult educators to consider how well this criterion is being satisfied.

Training Programs for the "Profession"

The characteristics of graduate programs for adult educators have been examined by several observers; their findings are represented here by a few examples.

Alan Knox, in a paper developed for the Commission of the Professors of Adult Education in 1973, described the common courses included in graduate programs in adult education:

> Many programs include some course or similar arrangement that provides an introduction, overview, or survey of the field for beginning majors and for non-majors. . . . Most graduate programs include a course on adult learning and development, which may be taught as part of the psychology department with an emphasis on theory and research in human development, or may be taught in another education department with an emphasis on working with adults as learners. Many programs include a course on group or organizational behavior. Most programs include a course on program development, which in some instances emphasizes planning, in other instances emphasizes use of methods and materials in teaching adults, and in still other instances the

[9]Lawrence H. Allen, "The Growth of Professionalism in the Adult Educational Movement, 1928–1958, A Content Analysis of the Periodical Literature." Abstract of an unpublished Ph.D. disseration, Department of Education, The University of Chicago, 1961, pp. 3–4.

preparation of administrators to provide in-service education
for teachers of adults. Another basic course deals with admin-
istrative leadership for adult education programs. [10]

Knox reported a large proportion of common elements among adult education graduate programs.

Alden A. Grosz, in a dissertation completed in 1976 at the University of Southern Mississippi, examined the program requirements for doctoral degrees in adult education. On the basis of 259 responses to 426 questionnaires, he grouped the courses into three major groups: adult and community college courses, specialized courses, and general courses. "In the adult and community college courses category, the organization and administration of adult education groups held prime position. This group was closely followed by the psychology of adult learning group of courses. Program planning and curriculum development group was third and research design courses had the fourth highest frequency." [11] Of course, the findings of the Grosz study would reflect a high degree of commonality among programs if for no other reason than the small number of categories he employed to classify the courses.

In their 1970 study of the literature dealing with the preparation of adult educators, Coolie Verner et al. concluded that

> *the graduate program in adult education has not re-*
> *ceived the attention from researchers that one might expect.*
> *Very little research has been done to assess the achievements*
> *of graduate study as a way of providing the field with skilled*
> *adult educators. Consequently there are unresolved ques-*
> *tions about the content provided in graduate programs and*
> *whether or not graduate education in adult education pro-*
> *vided the kinds of learning experiences that lead ultimately to*
> *an improvement in the field.* [12]

Nevertheless, Verner reported that the core knowledge of the discipline of adult education fell into several categories: adult learning, psychology of adults, physiology of aging, adult instruction, instructional processes, instructional devices, the client system, the

[10]Alan B. Knox, *Development of Adult Education Graduate Programs* (Washington, D.C.: Adult Education Association of the U.S.A., 1973), pp. 27–28.

[11]Alden A. Grosz, "An Analysis of Program Requirements for Doctoral Degrees in Adult Education." Unpublished Ph.D. dissertation. State College, Miss.: University of Southern Mississippi, August 1976, p. 91.

[12]Coolie Verner, Gary Dickinson, Walter Leirman, and Helen Niskala, *The Preparation of Adult Educators: A Selected Review of the Literature Produced in North America* (Syracuse, N.Y.: ERIC Clearinghouse on Adult Education and Adult Education Association of the U.S.A., 1970), p. 48.

organizational system, the social setting, the role of adult education, and historical foundations. If this is indeed the "core" of the adult education discipline, then it would be a rare graduate program that provides a thorough treatment of the lot. It might also be noted that even though the categories of knowledge have been classified logically by Verner, there is as yet no agreement among the professors of adult education regarding the core of their curricula.

Training for What Functions?

Cyril O. Houle and John Buskey, in a survey conducted in the mid-1960s, sought to determine what kind of work was being done by persons who had received doctorates in adult education. The survey reflected an overwhelming majority of respondents—64.2 percent—engaged in some kind of administration as their primary function (see Table 1).[13]

Verner identified and described what he regards as the two main roles played by the professional leadership in the field:

TABLE 1: NUMBER OF PERSONS WITH DOCTORATES IN ADULT EDUCATION REPORTING VARIOUS PRIMARY OCCUPATIONAL FUNCTIONS (n = 428)

FUNCTION	NUMBER OF DOCTORATE HOLDERS
1. General administration of a unit or organization of which adult education is a subordinate part	64
2. Specific administration of an adult educational unit or program within a unit	170
3. Administration of other units	41
4. Teaching of adult education as a field of study	55
5. Teaching in content fields other than adult education	10
6. Research in other fields of study	9
7. Advising or consulting on or stimulating adult education	38
8. Advising, consulting, or stimulating in areas of study other than adult education	11
9. Regulation	9
10. Other	11
11. Not gainfully employed	10

[13]Cyril O. Houle and John H. Buskey, "The Doctorate in Adult Education 1935–1965," *Adult Education* 16, no. 3 (Spring 1966), pp. 131–68.

Administrative Role. *In this role the leader is responsible for the use of institutional resources through determining program areas, clientele analysis, the selection of
method, the management of operations, and the appraisal of
program achievements.*

Instructional Role. *This is the basic role of leadership
and involves the design and management of specific educational activities for adults. Here the primary concern is with
the selection and ordering of the learning tasks, the use of
specific techniques and devices to facilitate learning, the
continuing management of the learning activity, and the
measurement of achievement.*[14]

Despite Verner's persistent efforts to instill a common understanding of the nature, dimensions, and terminology of the adult
education field, his fellow professors of adult education have insisted
on pursuing their separate roads to the distant destination of academic respectability and professional recognition.

Evidence of the heterogeneity of the academic degree programs
to prepare adult educators is provided by William Griffith and Gilles
Cloutier, who conducted a survey of such programs in the United
States in 1971. They found that there were

*nine programs at the undergraduate level. Twenty-six
institutions offered master of arts degree programs; 24 institutions master of science degree programs; and 17 institutions offered the equivalent of a master's degree designated
by some other name. Doctor of education programs were
offered by 26 institutions and doctor of philosophy programs
by 25. Seventeen institutions offered special degrees, awarding certificates rather than master's or doctor's degrees.*[15]

Clearly, the kind of credential conferred on those who complete
preparation programs for adult education varies widely. Even more
confusing is the extreme variety of names used to designate the
programs in which the credentials are awarded (see Table 2).

Griffith and Cloutier not only documented the diversity, but also
commented on its cost:

*A part of the price which must be paid for the privi-
lege of remaining somewhat amorphous is the limitation of*

[14]Verner et. al., *The Preparation of Adult Educators,* p. 44.

[15]William S. Griffith and Gilles H. Cloutier, *College and University Degree
Programs for the Preparation of Professional Adult Educators, 1970–71.* Sponsored Reports
Series. DHEW Publication No. (OE) 74–11423 (Washington, D.C.: U.S. Government
Printing Office, 1974), p. 21.

> *public acknowledgement of the existence of a discrete pro-*
> *fession of adult education. It is for the professors of the*
> *various programs, each one of whom is engaged in training*
> *educators of adults, to determine individually and concert-*
> *edly with his fellow professors whether maintaining and*
> *enlarging the number of terms used to describe these pro-*
> *grams are in the best long-range interests of their field, or*
> *whether greater uniformity in the use of names for these*
> *curricula would constitute undesirable restraints on the*
> *development of individual programs and their attractive-*
> *ness to potential students and to potential employers of*
> *the graduates.*[16]

Despite the lack of uniformity in the names used to identify the area of study, a steady flow of individuals has been pursuing doctoral training in it since 1935. The latest survey reported that through the calendar year 1977, 2,038 individuals had earned what they, and the institutions at which they earned their terminal degrees, believed

TABLE 2: NUMBER OF INSTITUTIONS REPORTING VARIOUS PROGRAM DESIGNATIONS FOR DOCTORAL PROGRAMS FOR INDIVIDUALS PREPARING TO WORK AS ADULT EDUCATORS (n = 67)

PROGRAM DESIGNATION	NUMBER OF INSTITUTIONS REPORTING
1. Adult education	29
2. Adult and continuing education	6
3. Extension education	6
4. Continuing education	4
5. Adult education administration	3
6. Community development	3
7. Adult and vocational education	2
8. Community education	2
9. Extension administration	2
10. Adult and community college education	1
11. Adult and community education	1
12. Adult and extension education	1
13. Adult and higher education	1
14. Adult basic and continuing education	1
15. Adult religious education	1
16. Educational services	1
17. Human resources development	1
18. No response	2

[16]Ibid., p. 32.

were doctorates in adult education. There were 157 doctorates in 1975, 169 in 1976, and 151 in 1977.[17] At least 150 individuals are emerging from graduate programs each year with the belief that they have earned doctorates in a field they recognize as adult education. Such a condition would satisfy one of the criteria commonly used to identify a profession. Nevertheless, the kaleidoscopic image of the field that is projected by the separate departments with their idiosyncratically chosen names obscures the constants among them and obscures the existence of even an emerging profession.

Associations of Adult Educators

If adult educators were members of a single national organization, that fact would satisfy one of the characteristics of a profession according to the listing proposed by Allen, so let us consider the ways adult educators have chosen to affiliate within their field.

All too often those in positions of administrative leadership in institutions providing adult education programs identify more with their employing institution that they do with adult education as a field. Consequently, their primary national organization is organized on the basis of the institutions involved (for instance, the National University Extension Association, American Library Association, American Society of Training Directors, Correctional Education Association) rather than on the basis of the common functions such adult educators perform. Similarly, individuals whose responsibility lies in providing instruction for adult learners appear to place their primary associational loyalty with organizations restricted to serving a particular clientele or dealing with a specific content (such as the American Home Economics Association, American Medical Association, American Nurses' Association, American Vocational Association, Music Educators' National Conference, National Conference on Social Welfare, National Recreation Association). Still other adult educators group together on the basis of the medium they employ (for example, the Joint Council on Educational Television, National Association of Educational Broadcasters, National Home Study Council). It is not necessary to deny the practical utility of such organizations to note that they owe their very existence to the emphasis they place on what is uncommon about their work in adult education rather than on what functions they perform in common with all other adult educators. To suggest that primary professional loyalty should be given to an association based on the common elements of a profession is not to argue for the dissolution of other associations addressing the institutional, methodological, or other

[17]Cyril O. Houle and Dolores Ford, "Doctorates in Adult Education, 1976 and 1977," *Adult Education* 26, no. 1 (Fall 1978), pp. 65–70.

particularities of segments of the field. Rather, it is to maintain that only when the adult educator's basic commitment is to the professional field as a whole, rather than to any one of its segments, can there be a profession of adult education.

Graduate programs for adult educators tend to become highly particularized, focusing on some institutional form (such as community colleges), some particular content (such as adult basic education), or some selected goal (such as community development). Such a focus in the course work prepares graduates not to view themselves as professionals in the larger field but rather to regard themselves as specialists in one sector of adult education. Courses in such programs must give considerable attention to the temporary characteristics of selected practical situations at the expense of broader theoretical foundations. If graduate study is to be the foundation of education in the profession, then premature specialization is achieved at the cost of weakening the broad profession.

Verner takes what may appear to many institutionally oriented adult educators to be an extreme view of the organization of adult educators:

> The administrative role involves essentially the same activities and responsibilities in every situation so that there is no real difference in function that is dictated by the form of the institution making it necessary to create subcategories of knowledge by institution. A professionally educated adult educator can perform the administrative functions in a school system, university, or business with equal facility. Similarly, the functions exercised in the instructional role are not distinctly different in managing instruction for adult illiterates or continuing professional education, since the principles of adult learning are common to all adults in any learning situation.[18]

Despite this and other claims of the unity of the profession, Houle and Buskey noted that 59.9 percent of those with doctorates in adult education who responded to a survey said that they were not members of the Adult Education Association of the U.S.A., which purports to be the umbrella organization for all who think of themselves primarily as adult educators.[19] Evidently, 40 percent of those who possess a doctorate in adult education are not sufficiently committed to the adult education profession to join the single national organization that is not founded on institutional, content, clientele, or methodological characteristics.

[18]Verner et. al., The Preparation of Adult Educators, pp. 45–46.
[19]Houle and Buskey, "The Doctorate in Adult Education," p. 144.

Although some adult educators regard the Adult Education Association of the U.S.A. as their professional organization, the association has also been regarded as incapable of changing sufficiently to become a true professional association. Its most glaring deficiency is that the only qualification for membership is a willingness to pay the annual membership dues. No academic preparation of any kind or level is required. Thus the association is simply a voluntary organization without a claim to professionalism. At times various individuals have considered whether one of the component groups within the AEA—the Commission of the Professors of Adult Education —should attempt to become the professional association for the field. Such a possibility is quickly ruled out for it seems apparent that an organization composed exclusively of college and university teachers of adult education is too narrow a base for the profession.[20] If there is to be a professional association, it will require an entirely new structure.

The Costs and Benefits of Professionalism

Whether adult education as a field would be helped or hindered by the formal establishment of adult education as a profession is by no means self-evident. Neither is the concern a new one. Twenty years ago Edmund Brunner, William Nicholls, and Sam Sieber, in examining the possible role of a national organization in adult education, considered the advantages and disadvantages of elevating adult education to the status of a profession.[21] They identified the following disadvantages:

1. Creation of highly visible and important prestige difference within the field may exclude and alienate many who could make valuable contributions.

2. Standardization of training prior to the existence of a substantial body of knowledge may tend to stultify and ritualize the limited knowledge, rather than encourage the exploration of new knowledge.

3. Difficulty of determining who is to be a member because founders come from other fields and lack specific training in a new profession. Including them provides a basis for others who seek admission to insist that training is not necessary.

---

[20]William S. Griffith, "Future Functional Roles of the Commission of the Professors of Adult Education as a Professional Group" (Department of Education, The University of Chicago, 1973; mimeographed).

[21]Edmund de S. Brunner, William L. Nicholls, II, and Sam Sieber, *The Role of a National Organization in Adult Education* (New York: Bureau of Applied Social Research, Columbia University, 1959), pp. 324–26.

4. In the early stages of the new profession the founders have lost their organizational and psychological ties to their former profession and yet do not have a clearly defined place and area of competence of their own in the emerging profession.

The investigators also listed seven advantages:

1. When a group of practitioners are regarded by the public and other occupational groups as holding specialized technical knowledge and as applying this knowledge ethically, the group is usually granted the prestige accorded professions generally.

2. Prestige makes it easier to acquire funds for research.

3. Prestige gives more weight to the pronouncements of the members of the occupation in areas considered within the competence of the profession.

4. Prestige helps attract able recruits to the field.

5. Professions set their own standards for training and certification and can raise them at will.

6. External groups which are not familiar with the requirements of the profession are kept from interfering.

7. By holding a monopoly of certified persons in the occupation, they can enforce their code of ethics both vis-à-vis those certified and vis-à-vis their employers or clients.

Not surprisingly, Brunner, Nicholls, and Sieber concluded that the advantages of moving toward professionalism outweighed the disadvantages.

Malcolm Brown and Jerry Miller also examined ways some professions behaved when they gained legal authority, and these authors pointed to problems that have arisen with the exercise of that power. Brown commented on ways licensing procedures established to advance the general public welfare have been misused by some professions to advance the interests of those who are already well established within the profession:

> A favorite procedure of professions is to require an excessive and increasing standard of training as time passes, for new entrants to the market. This allows practitioners to obtain an increasing amount of quasi-rent on their educational investment throughout their careers. It also reduces the possibility of new practitioners engaging in competitive practices to attract clients since they are always the highest cost producers in the market. Another procedure is to vary the pass rate on the licensing examinations according to the need (as defined by the profession) for new practitioners. A final possibility is to engage in discriminatory practices with

respect to foreign practitioners—for example, more stringent licensing requirements for foreigners than for locals.[22]

It would be naive to assume that the behavior of any professional association would be invariably unselfish and unmindful of the welfare of its members as well as its clients. But it would be cynical to assume that the members' welfare would be its only concern. Most likely, each decision would reflect both concerns. In presenting the problem of developing and maintaining standards for the protection of the client, Miller quotes from Elton Ryack's book *Professional Power and American Medicine*:

> *On the one hand, the maintenance of professionally established quality standards is generally accepted as a socially desirable function of professional organizations; this is particularly true of medical care, where the quality of services provided may mean the difference between life and death. On the other hand, the professional organization is inevitably concerned with protecting and advancing the economic interests of its members. Since it is inherently difficult to translate quality into objectively quantifiable terms, there arises the possibility of an internal contradiction in the dual role of the professional organization as protector of society's welfare through the regulation of quality and as defender of the economic interests of the members of the organization.*[23]

Reflective citizens and sophisticated legislators are well aware of the human condition and scarcely expect their fellows to behave entirely unselfishly with perfect consistency. Nevertheless, in many cases they have voted to give groups of presumably honorable professionals in certain callings the power to determine who shall have the legal authorization to practice. Such an act of faith rests upon a belief that there is a discrete body of knowledge, an assortment of skills, and a particular field of practice. Such trust is only expressed if there is a belief that the leaders in the given field are sincerely committed to maintaining and advancing the public welfare.

Whither Professionalism in Adult Education?

If there is to be a profession of adult or continuing education, it cannot be limited by arbitrary boundaries based on such distinctions

[22]Malcolm C. Brown, "Some Effects of Physician Licensing Requirements on Medical Manpower Flows in Canada," *Industrial Relations* 30, no. 3 (October 1975), pp. 436–49.

[23]Jerry W. Miller, *Organizational Structure of Nongovernmental Postsecondary Accreditation: Relationship to Uses of Accreditation* (Washington, D.C.: National Commission on Accreditation, 1973), p. 47.

as institutional sponsorship, program content, method of instruction, or characteristics of the particular adult learners who are being served. Instead, it will rest upon a common theoretical foundation that deals with the adult education institution and administration. No such profession can arise so long as those who administer adult education programs and instruct adult learners continue to give their primary loyalty to organizations and associations dedicated to advancing segments of the field. So long as deans of continuing education and others who occupy positions of personnel leadership place greater weight in hiring adult education staff and faculty on their experience in and familiarity with a given institutional form, methodology, or clientele than on their mastery of the adult education field, the profession is unlikely to emerge.

Graduate degree programs in adult education, whatever idiosyncratic designations they may bear, do not yet exhibit sufficient commonality to provide a convincing case that they are preparing individuals for a single profession. Pragmatic professors, recognizing that the majority of their students gained entrance to the field by demonstrating competence in some area other than adult education, usually refrain from presenting their programs as preservice preparation because they know all too well the predilections of potential employers. For example, in such areas as continuing medical education the program responsibility is usually vested in an individual who may be highly competent in a medical subspecialty but who has had no systematic preparation as an adult educator. Such staffing practice is all too common, but it is heartening to note that from place to place individuals holding doctorates in adult education and having no academic preparation in the content of medicine are providing leadership and earning significant recognition for their work. Undoubtedly the strongest rational justification for the adult education profession rests on the excellent performance of such individuals. However, such performance by itself would not produce the profession. Preservice graduate education can only become credible with the emergence of the profession.

The emergence of the profession requires the concerted efforts of those full-time, career adult educators who can enunciate both the theoretical basis of practice and a code of ethics. It is well known that some administrators of adult education programs have treated their temporary teaching staff with no more regard than that often associated with the management of migrant laborers. The profession of adult education could not exist without the supporting services of paraprofessionals and volunteers, and the welfare of such individuals must be of concern to the profession. Neither volunteers nor part-time staff can reasonably be expected to pursue extensive training in the field of adult education. By the same token, they are unlikely to assert claims of being professional adult educators, though the field cannot function without them. The professionals who lead such paraprofessionals and volunteers have an ethical responsibility to arrange opportunities for their systematic learning about adult education and to encourage and facilitate their participation. They must further the welfare of their staffs as well as the clientele of their institution. Without the convincing, consistent demonstration of concern and respect for the part-time and volunteer adult educators, there is no reason to expect that they would support the recognition of the academically prepared full-time workers in the field as professionals.

Professionalization of the field of adult education could have serious consequences if increased status and influence of professional adult educators were coupled with a decreased commitment to serve the learning needs of individual adults and of the society. If the desire for professionalism is motivated by a commitment to improving the quality and quantity of adult learning opportunities, then the resulting changes will be in the best long-term interest of all. Conversely, to the extent that the motivation is a veiled concern for self-aggrandizement, the tactics of exclusion and self-protection will not be in the interests of all. Nevertheless, since people singly and in groups act for a variety of motives, it seems likely that adult educators would act similarly if they seriously sought to establish a professional association.

Ideally, a professional association of adult educators would not itself conduct adult education programs other than those considered by its membership to be essential for maintaining public good will and respect for the profession. Ideally, its concern would be with maintaining the quality and the provision of learning opportunities for adults by ensuring that professional adult educators would satisfy certain requirements in terms of academic preparation and demonstrated competence. It would promote collaboration among providing agencies and encourage the in-service training of volunteers and paraprofessionals in the field. Expanding and improving the quality of learning opportunities for adults would remain its paramount concern, and no more time would be spent on exclusionary self-aggrandizing concerns than is endemic to all established professions.

Adult education could become a profession if those who are now engaged in all of the sectors and specialized institutions of the field wanted that change to occur and were willing to guide their actions accordingly. Employers of full-time adult educators could accelerate the change by hiring individuals with appropriate education in the theory and practice of adult education, broadly defined. University extension deans could nurture the emergence of the profession by seeking broadly trained adult educators, rather than narrowly prepared specialists who comprehend only a part of the field. Professors of adult education individually could control their tendency to provide overspecialized graduate programs; collectively they could address themselves to securing agreement on a disciplinary core for all graduate programs in the field.

Today the emphasis in adult education continues to be on competition rather than collaboration, and rewards and recognition flow to the aggressive leaders rather than to those who counsel collaboration and professionalism. Marketing and the ethics of the marketplace attract the middle-level leadership of the field, and the siren call is nearly irresistible. Obstacles to the attainment of professional status for adult educators abound, and prominent among these is the growing strength of the groups whose allegiance lies with a part rather than the whole of the field. Perhaps the essential catalyst is an association, such as the National University Extension Association, which, although identified with only a segment of the field, has a broad vision of the adult education profession and a willingness to work toward its realization. Such a commitment would not necessarily guarantee survival and prosperity for all, but it could lead to a redirection of focus from the welfare of the association to the interests of individual adults and of society, thereby marking yet another milestone on the road to professionalism.

DISCUSSION

"You seem to be saying that continuing education is not yet a profession but that it could be," *Phil Frandson* says. "I'd like to ask, do you think the needs of society in the 1980s will be met better if there is a profession of continuing education?"

"I think," *Bill Griffth* responds, "that the practice of adult education and its service to the public would be significantly improved if everyone working in the field had more of a common understanding of the field, possessed a certain minimal vision of what it's all about. We would be less scattered, would be able to recognize other people who are in our field, and could work together with them, despite the fact that they're paid by another institution or are in private enterprise. One of the saddest aspects of our field is our inability to organize. It's pathetic to me that we have so many specialist organizations and no effective general organization."

"It seems to me," *Roz Loring* says, "that the kind of ambiguity you're speaking about is due to the fact that we value very highly the nontraditional. It's very difficult for people who espouse nontraditional views to then go out and formalize. Would you expect us, as people who are finding ways of certifying or credentialing people in nontraditional ways, to be ourselves credentialed in traditional ways? Aren't we a collection of people who come to the mission from a variety of places because of what we believe in, a commitment to innovation, to change? And isn't it an anomaly to ask that those adventurous people who come to such a mission be certified in the same way history professors and physicians are? Won't that, perhaps, destroy what we stand for?"

"If we are creative in helping others with their continuing education or any phase of their adult education," *Bill Griffith* replies, "what would prevent us from using the same kind of ingenuity in putting together methods and systems, credentials if you wish, to get people to have a kind of common experience, a common understanding of the world of continuing education?"

"Part of the complicating facet of our work," *John Ervin* points out, "is that we are not monolithic; we are different kinds of people. There are some of us who consider ourselves policy makers and creators and innovators. But much of our work gets done by people—also considered continuing educators—who are the facilitators and who see that the chalk and the boards are out, and to many people that's continuing education. It's a difficult thing to talk about 'the continuing educator,' recognizing that we come as all kinds."

"I think that an emerging profession usually ends up with quite a collection of stray dogs and cats," *George Robertson* says, "who decide that they all have something in common and they're going to try to maximize their common field of interest. One of our problems concerns the administrative aspects of our activities. I don't know of any profession that has ever been billed as a 'profession of administration.' Teaching is a kind of certifiable profession, but I don't think a teacher-as-school-administrator is."

Continuing education is defined in terms of negatives. . . .

"There are people who argue that 'education' is not a profession," *John Ervin* says. "Yet nobody has denied that teachers need certain kinds of knowledge, even if it's only how to open and close the blinds. It seems to me, though, that—if you will permit me to digress for one moment, because I think that continuing education is, in many ways, analogous to the status of minorities in a majority-minority situation—continuing education, as were blacks, is defined in terms of negatives. When you start with 'nontraditional,' that is negative. It seems to me that much of what is in our profession comes out as negative—*not* full time, *not* for credit, *not* on campus, *not* regular, and *not* legitimate, somehow. What many of the youngsters who started out saying 'Black is beautiful!' really were doing was attempting to redefine themselves in positive terms. You start with that and build from there.

"If I identify with an entity that has within it some positives —whether they come from development of answers to some important questions that have been researched by people in the field or by the accumulation and demonstration of certain kinds of abilities and skills—that may make a difference in the way I feel about the activity I am engaged in. It also permits other people to generalize, because one of the other key things about the social environment is that everybody generalizes from something, and people's status comes not only from what they can do and not do but from the group they are associated with. So that to be positive about being an adult educator, to assert that we are a profession, may be the step toward a kind of identity for continuing education that we need."

"It seems to me that to choose to be other than a profession," *Mort Gordon* agrees, "involves, inevitably, saying in some way that there is no field of knowledge, that there is nothing that adult educators have in common. I get very nervous about credentials because they exclude people. At the same time, we ought to find some way of including the knowledge we have painfully, year after year, accumulated."

Mavericks are going to have difficulty . . .

"The history of adult education," *Milt Stern* interposes, "shows that there is a maverick impulse among the leadership to deny the desire to be a professional. The idea of marginality is a maverick idea. The idea of professionalism is a staid, belonging idea. So there is a natural hostility between the two that is distressing, and I think that Mort's close to this right now. It seems to me that we have to accept, in professionalizing the field, the value of organization and solidity to the extent of risking the fact that mavericks are going to have difficulty. My own experience is that I like the field because I classify myself as a maverick—not an extremist, naturally, but a maverick. I've had fun in the field. I've stayed in this field for thirty-odd years because it's been a wonderful time.

"Nevertheless, I feel a keen obligation to its orderly development. And I think Bill was making arguments that are modest and yet to the point. In order to get to this point, we have to do orderly, straightforward, simple things. One of the things Bill says—and I have felt for a long time—is that deans of extension should make sure they inform professors of adult education that they want people who are capable practitioners but who also have a broad-gauge view of the field. That's what I would like to get from professors of adult education. That's what I don't get right now. I don't want to hire people who come out of a narrow specialization in 'adult education.' At the same time, I do need to provide continuing professional education for some forty or fifty junior staff members who really need theory, and they don't have it. This is the opposite side of the situation to that customarily described by deans of extension who say 'These people aren't practical enough,' and so on. So far as I'm concerned, an admixture of theory would be a great advantage in the field, and I think I would go so far as to sacrifice my maverick status to attain it."

Pioneers cannot have credentials. . . .

"You mention history and you also mention a profession of adult education," *Bill Griffith* says, "and perhaps I can speak for a moment to both of those matters. Back in 1929, as I pointed out, Kenyon Butterfield tried to put together a combined extension division at Michigan State College, now known as Michigan State University. He appointed as his first director of the combined extension division a man named John Willard. Butterfield was unable to make the organization stick; it was too radical a change from the standpoint of interests both external and internal to the university. Butterfield subsequently went to Massachusetts to work, and John Willard, the first director of the combined division, went to Columbia University as the first professor of adult education. To be the first professor of anything is a pretty unusual kind of role to play. Quite obviously, he couldn't possibly have been trained for the job. The pioneers in any field cannot have credentials to work in that field. It is quite an act of faith for people to move from what is known, what is secure, from a set of credentials that establishes them within one profession, to try, because of great strength of conviction, to establish another profession.

"Since that time when Willard engaged in this act of faith with Columbia and Columbia with him, we've seen a proliferation of this kind of person. For the first generation of professors of adult education were all without any particular training in the field, without a degree in the field. (I would assume, also, that of those who are presently teaching, including those who have retired, well over half would not have had credentials in that field.) It's only in recent years that there have been people around long enough to have gone through the formal training and then to have been employed as professors of adult education.

"I can see some parallel to the kind of work that's done by practicing adult educators in a variety of institutional settings—most of whom, of course, have their credentials in some field other than adult education; most of whom could have chosen, perhaps, a more secure, less hazardous—also, perhaps, less exciting—kind of career had they chosen to stay with their original training; but all of whom elected to move into the field of adult education and to learn what they had to learn in order to survive in a very challenging kind of setting.

"Today we have over 200 professors of adult education. We have over 2,038 people with doctorates in the field of adult education, scattered all over the world. The cold, hard facts are that we don't have any empirical evidence that people who have been trained academically in the field of adult education do any better in carrying out the roles of adult educators than those who have not been professionally trained. But before you regard that as too alarming a fact, consider that we don't have any evidence for other professions either.

"I mentioned that there are some rather commonly accepted characteristics of a profession, and I guess we might also give a shorthand way of telling whether or not you are a profession. I think it's probably reasonable to say, 'If you have to ask, you aren't!'

We don't know what we are . . .

"The training provided in adult education doctoral programs is by no means uniform in terms of content or the kinds of functions that we are preparing people to serve, although it is quite clear that the number-one kind of responsibility graduates of adult education doctoral programs have is in the area of administration, not teaching or research. It's difficult for the university to figure out what we are. We insist on using a great diversity of titles as professors of adult education. I spelled out the kinds of degrees. There are seventeen different names used by programs that grant doctorates in the field of adult education; the most common one, of course, is adult education and from there the list goes in various directions. I suggest that we pay quite a price for the privilege of remaining amorphous because the public doesn't know what we are. The university doesn't know what we are. We don't know what we are.

"It seems almost foolish to say there is no professional association after having said there is no profession. But I think it's probably necessary to make the statement: 'There is no professional association in adult education!' There are some organizations made up of practitioners, and some made up of professors, but nothing, I think, would remotely resemble a professional association.

"If we look at how professions have behaved historically, we find some that behaved quite responsibly; but there is a body of literature which suggests that a profession is an artifact designed to circumvent the normal market processes. It's an irregularity in a nice, neat capitalistic system, in which one group secures power over who shall practice and a number of other things. I'd like to believe that most professions use their trust ethically, but it would be naive to assume that it's never misused.

"Similarly, if adult education or continuing education were to become a profession, we could assume the same kind of behavior would likely occur. What it would mean to those who were already in the field is not certain. If you were to take the position that there is a profession of continuing education, which requires extended academic training, you're making a statement about yourself at the same time. And if you wish to advance the field, you have to think about the cost associated with that. If, however, it would be agreed by a large, fairly prestigious group, such as the directors of the National University Extension Association, that it would be in their best interest and that of the field to become a profession, I think what would be required would be a vision of the field that goes far beyond what universities do. A definition of the field, therefore, could in no way be restricted simply to university extension. But since there is no other group prepared to take central leadership in the professional organization, about the only way I can see that we could move toward professional status, if we wanted to, would be to have a strong specialized association that says we are specialists in this area of this larger field and then to cooperate with the other people who are working in other specialized areas toward the systematic evolution of the profession. The answer to the question is not obvious to me."

"Bill," *Mort Gordon* asks, "do you care whether we are a profession?"

"I'm interested in a kind of practice of our graduates that conforms basically to the ethical standards of a profession," *Bill* responds. "The regulation of entrance to the field to the people who hold certain credentials is something I cannot get excited about at this point."

Adult education is a 'field of practice.' . . .

Milt Stern says, "Your predecessor at the University of British Columbia, Coolie Verner, allowed as how adult education is a 'field of practice,' and I take it that you also regard it as such. How do you regard the role of professors of adult education with reference to this field of practice? Are you commentators? Are you a research professional arm? What is the role of a professor of adult education?"

"I don't purport to be a spokesman for that group," *Bill Griffith* replies. "The thing that brings the professors together is that they all claim they teach. It is not necessary to claim one does any research in order to be a member of the Commission of Professors. They're not all members of the Adult Education Association, although most are. All of them are in universities that claim to give a degree which is functionally the same as adult education, regardless of its title. The professors have spent much of their time trying to identify what should be taught in the core courses in the field. That's been the major productive effect."

"Bill, to get back to Mort's question," *Milt Stern* says, "Do you care? If we consider the nature of a profession, when we deal with medicine and with law we deal with professions that have been established for approximately 700 or 800 years in Western society, and in the Western university as their study ground. But in continuing education there isn't a functional relationship between the professoriate and the field of practice represented by the bulk of that mass that is called the 'profession.' People come through, and there is no laying on of hands; there is nothing like the ritual related to the medical profession or admission to the bar. We don't have the outward lineaments of a profession. This becomes a really very important question in terms of, at least, the arguments about marginality, resisting the fatal embrace, and so on. Part of the fatal embrace would be the stratification of the field into more rigidity than it now has. At least that's the belief some people have; other people don't believe that. What's your belief?"

We're in a very early stage of development. . . .

"First, I don't equate all structure with rigidity," *Bill Griffith* says. "And second, even though it's true we go back to Italy and see law schools going in 1200 A.D., most lawyers weren't trained in universities. And most physicians weren't trained in university-related institutions, either. So I'm not sure how far we can push that comparison.

"We're in a very early stage of development when we try to draw a parallel with the old established professions. Why the link is not better between the professors of adult education and NUEA or the Association for Continuing Higher Education (ACHE) I'm not certain. I do note that the Commission of Professors continues to ally itself primarily with the Adult Education Association of the U.S.A., and although AEA/USA is a self-styled umbrella organization, nobody but AEA/USA thinks it is an umbrella, which makes it a little embarrassing. The Council of Adult Education Organizations (CAEO) is another kind of all-embracing group that doesn't quite pull us together, but it's the best thing we have right now in terms of trying to look at what might be if we are supposed to be under one tent. The Commission has no relation to that either."

"I can think of a couple reasons," *Mort Gordon* puts in. "One, we have 240 graduate students in our program at Michigan, maybe 20 of whom are associated with university programs. So tying in the professoriate to NUEA could create problems. The other might be even more compelling—and that's a spin-off from your historical sketch, Bill. That is, until very recently there weren't a lot of professors who had had very much practical experience, let alone academic credentials. Carrying this to an extreme, I can hardly imagine a department of surgery in which the professor teaching surgery had never cut up anyone. At least, if that were true, neither he nor his students would cut me up!

"Maybe the time has now come for closer cooperation between the professors and the field of practice. Maybe not with an existing organization but with a different organization (although it sounds like a lot more meetings to go to!)."

A degree does not predict ability to do the job . . .

"I'd like to just turn this around," *Roz Loring* says, "to say that some of us who have been in the field thirty years, or just a bit less, discovered that a degree in adult education did not in any way help to predict ability to do the job. There was nothing in the preparation of people by the degree process that would help you to make that determination. So a number of us went the other way and searched for people who were bright and lively and teachable. They could come from any field, and did, and there were years when, at UCLA, if you had a degree in continuing education it was almost sure you wouldn't get the job. That was, in part, because the kinds of people who went into adult education and who came for jobs as administrators, as opposed to those who went on to being professors, were typically those who didn't have, somehow, that special quality we look for—creativity, inventiveness, caring—that I think we need so much in our practitioners. We probably went overboard in the sense that we knew the kinds of personalities we needed and were willing to teach them.

"Now—and I think it is very fitting to follow Milton in this—it may be that we have reached another turn in the road and that we could, indeed, be heard by the professors in terms of the kinds of students we wish they would collect. Because partly it's such a self-selected process of who goes in to be educated that we are restricted in our choices of who comes out at the other end. We are limited by that, and, therefore, if what practitioners said was heard by the professors, we might come to a place where theory and competency would blend with caring—and that's what we need to put together! (The degree itself is a marvelous way of being credible in the institution. I can't speak for community colleges, but with colleges and universities to have a Ph.D. or an Ed.D in almost anything will do; in fact, nobody even asks what your degree is in as long as they can call you 'Doctor.' That's a great way to get immediate credibility in the system.)

Profession is the name of the game. . . .

"We are faced, I think, with trying to prove an activity in a situation where *profession* is the name of the game, and it may be that we ought not to be raising the question of whether we are a profession, but, rather, as someone else has suggested, we should *assume* we are a profession in order to get on with what we want to do."

"As I look at some of the other quasi-professions," *George Robert-son* says, "like engineering—I guess that's a profession with a little bit of doubt about itself; social work; and more recent ones, still getting out of the egg, like personnel administration, engineering technology, and others, I think there's a pattern that's pretty clear. First, there is a group of workers identified by a common interest. They form an association, and then, if they're lucky and it seems as if they can manage it, they press for some form of licensing for admission to their group. Following that, there is a period of refinement. They define training levels in which an alliance of educators begins to take shape. Some of the people in the field begin teaching in the field, and others become professors of whatever it is. After that there is a continuing stage of observing the credentials and developing admissions examinations to the profession—complete with grandfather clauses that let people in under the wire even though they do not meet the new requirements—to take care of those who have not come through the school, and also to apply to the graduates of schools that now think of themselves as professional schools.

"I think that particular pattern is typical of the emergence of a profession, or even an association of technically specialized workers. I think a movement like ours, which originates with a group of highly qualified academics, is a peculiar circumstance, and I'm not too sure it can be explained at all except that it is education we're talking about. I wouldn't give too much for the chances of forming any kind of professional group that does not first start in the field with the establishment of a group that seeks to limit admission to the club. Unless that appears first, I don't know that the rest of the steps can come."

Bill Griffith shakes his head. "There are a couple of points here that we don't want to lose sight of. The fact is, when you have a field in which people are employed yet in which specific credentials aren't required, you're going to get extreme differences in performance. You're going to get some outstanding performances by energetic, enthusiastic, open-minded people who get along well with other human beings. You're going to get some other people who are going to be very highly trained but who insult everyone they talk to after one minute. So you've got different kinds of problems."

A small group of rather cranky missionaries. . . .

"But I think the real problem is that I continue to see adult educators, continuing educators, as a small group of rather cranky missionaries," *George Robertson* says. "I think you're trying to put up a professional association of that group, and, as Groucho Marx said, 'I would refuse to join any club that would have me as a member.'"

"On the other hand," *Grover Andrews* says, "it's been appalling to me that when I go to an institution and they proudly trot out their new continuing education director, who is it? A retired minister, if it's a church-related institution; a retired military person, if it's a small regional state institution or community college; and so on. Very few trot out a Ph.D. who has been retrained. And even fewer have trotted out the trained adult educator. But overall—and I could document this—those who have brought in the trained individuals are the ones with solid development, because they have people who started off knowing what adult education is about. The other folks, some of them, can be trained; I'm not saying there's anything wrong with a retired minister or with retired air force or army personnel. But let me tell you it's a very difficult job to train them to do a very effective developmental job in continuing education."

Bob Kost nods. "Through the course of the conversation," he says, "two issues have tended to change my perception from when I arrived at this symposium. One is Bill's description of a professoriate who would offer the research and dissemination that is missing today. Unless there is research and that research is known and understood by practitioners, this field is going to continue to wander aimlessly. And also there's Mort's comment, which others have shared, that you have to start somewhere, sometime. I don't know that today is the time to start, but there's a lot of power to the notion that this is the way things begin. I don't know how to rationalize the vast number of those of us who lie outside the boundaries of academia. I suspect that if this work progressed to a true profession, it would not only discourage and clean up some of the poor performers in campus institutions, but it would also improve the practice in industry."

You must accept some responsibility. . . .

"We've raised a number of issues," *Bill Griffith* concludes, "that are like an onion; you peel them off one piece at a time. (You may cry or not as we do it, as you see fit.) We can think about a resource that is available to you, a thing called the Commission of Professors of Adult Education. To the extent that *you* advise *it*, it may become wiser. To the extent that you assume no responsibility for helping it to see the challenge more clearly, I think you must accept some responsibility for its ignorance. If you think you know—or would like to engage in a dialogue about—better ways of doing the training in industry or what have you, would it not be appropriate then to take such a step? It possibly—just possibly—might be a useful vehicle that could help you advance the field over the next fifty years.

"So maybe if we looked at the role of the university extension division, or community college, or business and industry in participating with the professors in a new and better kind of preprofessional training or in-service training, and in developing needed research, then we may make more progress than if we point fingers at what is wrong with some of the sinners in the church. We're all in this together. We all sink or we all swim together.

"Pragmatically, I am attempting to do what I can to advance the notion of an emerging profession of adult education. I believe we have an accumulating body of literature. I think we've got research. I think we've got alumni performing in a distinguished fashion in all sorts of settings. I know that our programs have a long way to go to be what we want them to be. But I have to ask, 'What is responsible behavior on *my* part with regard to the development of my profession for the next 100 years? What part can I play in it?' I think that we have many people with exceedingly narrow vision working in the field, not because there is anything wrong with these people, but because no one has made provisions for them to get even short-term training, no one has given them an opportunity to get a broader vision of what can be. I really do believe that unless some very prestigious and influential groups, such as those represented here, are willing to accept some responsibility for shaping our profession, it will be a long, long time before we ever get one. I'm committed to the notion that we ought to have one. And my attendance at this symposium is a part of *my* continuing education so that you can teach me more in the areas in which I recognize that I—like others—still have a lot to learn."

"I'm hearing you say," *George Robertson* suggests, "that you care a whole lot!"

FINAL COMMENTARY

Continuing education is not yet a *profession* according to traditional definitions of the term, yet the basic features are there waiting to be defined, developed, recognized, and acknowledged. Until recently almost all continuing educators came to the field simply because of a sense of mission or opportunity. Their preparation and experience was in other areas, and their skills and knowledge were usually related to a specific aspect of continuing education. Now, as a consequence of graduate programs in adult and continuing education, there is a tested body of knowledge about the field, extensive ongoing research, a growing number of exemplary practitioners, and increasing public awareness and acceptance of continuing education as an essential of modern life. These developments can enhance the emergence of a continuing education profession if they are coupled with other, more difficult achievements —agreement on the requisites of preservice training for continuing educators, the formation of a single professional association of continuing educators, and the endorsement of such training and such an association by those who currently call themselves continuing educators.

THREE

Continuing Education Perspective

*Where Have We Been? Where Are We Now?
And Where Do We Go from Here?*

9 CLOSING COMMENTS

Paper by John B. Ervin

BIOGRAPHY

 JOHN B. ERVIN is vice president of the Danforth Foundation, where he directs the work of the foundation in urban affairs and in minority recruitment for the Danforth Graduate Fellowship Program. A graduate of Kent State University, Ervin holds an M.A. and a Ph.D. from Columbia University Teachers College. He has had extensive teaching experience, ranging from elementary through secondary, college and university through adult education. He held positions at Stowes Teachers College and Harris Teachers College, both in St. Louis, before going to Washington University as associate dean of the School of Continuing Education and director of summer sessions in 1965. He became dean of the school in 1968, serving in that position until he joined the Danforth Foundation in 1977.

He is past president and secretary of the National University Extension Association and served on the board of the Association for Continuing Higher Education when it was the Association for University Evening Colleges. He is presently chairman of the National Advisory Council on Extension and Continuing Education, and active on the Continuing Education Board of Visitors at Harvard University. He was a consultant to the U.S. Office of Education on the Education Professions Development Act from 1969 to 1971. He received the Leadership Award of the Association for Continuing Higher Education (ACHE) in 1978, and the Distinguished Alumni Award and an Honorary L.L.D. from Kent State University in 1969.

232

INITIAL COMMENTARY

The nature of the power conflict in continuing education has been clearly established in this symposium. Whether the resolution of that conflict will result in survival and prosperity for all is not nearly so clear. To sort out the main elements of the conflict mosaic, John Ervin identifies major assumptions that underlie the actions of all the participants in the conflict, and certain myths and realities of what he terms "the dog-eat-dog world of the postsecondary continuing education providers." He points the path to a better future, if certain things are done, not just by continuing educators, but by the education establishment as a whole.

John B. Ervin

A Glorious Future—If!

It is my job to ask: Where *are* we going from here? and Where *ought* we to go from here? Being neither seer nor prophet, I have taken a second look at what we know about the relationships among organizations that provide continuing education and what they tell us about competition and cooperation. I start with a set of assumptions distilled from the presentations and discussions of the symposium.

1. *In ever-increasing numbers adults are participating in continuing education programs.* The growth rate, which is several times that of the normal population growth, is significant to educators because of decreasing numbers of college-age students and projected declines in the general population.

2. *The increased participation of adults is reflected in an increase in the number of organizations providing programs for adults.* Providers include academic institutions (public schools, community colleges, senior colleges, and universities), proprietary institutions and organizations, corporate and industrial organizations, and professional associations.

3. *There are various motivations for providing continuing education to adults.* A strong and persistent egalitarian ideology that requires an educated and enlightened citizenry leads to concern that nontraditional populations (such as minorities and women) need access to education. There is an equally strong ideology that education must help adults cope with the dramatic impact of social change on their lives; that education is not a *state*, but a lifelong *process*. There is concern among enlightened corporate providers for developing higher levels of productivity among employees. There is perception of the need for continued growth and development of professionals and for licensure in many areas. And, finally, there is the desire to make money by capitalizing on the interest in continuing education.

4. *The level of competition among continuing education providers is rapidly increasing.* Providers give increasing attention to marketing, often at the expense of program development. The competition is for students and dollars, and, for some, the stakes are institutional survival. In such an environment all providers will suffer.

5. *The problems created by increased competition can be resolved by the diverse group of continuing education providers.* Among themselves the

providers can segment the market, assign responsibility, and enforce cooperation through accreditation, to the benefit of both providers and the adults they serve.

6. *The various providers in the field of continuing education must be brought together as often as possible so that competition and conflict are not assumed to be inevitable and that greater cooperation is developed.*

In light of these conditions and developments, the future of continuing education is uncertain. This is particularly true for academic continuing education programs, whose legitimacy rests on the uniqueness of their mission and the belief that centralization of activities is the only way to ensure quality programs. From within programs are at the mercy of "power brokers" who see, for example, off-campus adult education as their key to survival. From without programs are encountering a dog-eat-dog world: unscrupulous providers, interested more in money than maintaining standards, are driving from the marketplace scrupulous providers who are determined to uphold academic standards; and private consulting firms that design and market programs to academic and nonacademic providers (some staffed by well-known scholars who are able to make excellent supplemental incomes; others attached to corporate enterprises looking for a profit center, a market-expanding gimmick, or even a tax shelter).

The optimistic assumption is that in the continuing education market there is enough to go around; if each provider mounts a vigorous marketing program, everybody will make it financially. But what is becoming increasingly clear to institutions is a kind of round-robin effect, in which the universe of continuing education students does not expand appreciably, and large segments of the adult population remain unserved by anyone. The continuing education market is, however, much more broadly based than the populations now being served. What is often not acknowledged by the contenders in the marketplace, but has been emphasized by the participants in this symposium, are two preliminary questions: (1) What are the new populations, and which continuing education providers can serve them best? and (2) How can providers assess their own strengths and weaknesses before approaching new populations, and thereby resolve problems of "turf" in cooperation with other providers?

These questions represent a considerable challenge to educational institutions in this country. If lifelong learning has become, as some suggest, almost a part of our national policy, then educators no longer have to justify its reason for being. But with this new freedom they accept new responsibilities. Continuing education must become more responsive to new clientele groups as they appear, and a central role for service to these clienteles must remain with college and university programs. Providers from all segments of society must turn to academic institutions as their most valuable resource. It would be tragic if educational institutions became unresponsive to new challenges, or if other providers failed to cooperate with them in expanding areas of education. The challenge is clearly stated by Ernest Boyer:

> A good case could be made for a more narrow definition of education, built around the academy, combining formal teaching and research. But to draw a line so sharply that one is forced to choose between the traditional and the non-traditional is a mistake. The challenge before the universities is to strengthen traditional structures while adjusting to a new clientele, recurrent education, and the new technology which is certain to shape how people learn and where education takes place. To adapt, with honor and social imagination, is the challenge that academe confronts.[1]

What can educators do to ensure that this challenge is met? Several recommendations emerge.

First, it is clear that planning for orderly retrenchment is absolutely essential if higher education is to have a viable future. The rate of college closings has been increasing since 1968; there were eighty-four closings between 1968 and 1978, and thirty-eight of those took place between 1975 and 1978.[2] However, higher education leadership is no more willing to change than their counterparts in other institutions. Harold Howe has suggested that "some colleges pin their faith on new pseudo-academic programs designed to convince students and parents of their capacity to produce both culture and a future job all rolled into one package of undergraduate happiness. A good many colleges have excessive expectations of an expanding market of nontraditional students, older persons or those who want to upgrade their earning capacity and avoid boredom. They seem to forget that several part-time students are needed to make up for the loss of one full-time undergraduate."[3] What is required? Greater administrative power to set and control goals, informed and carefully directed cost cutting rather than standard across-the-board cuts, and an end to reliance on voluntary efforts by academic departments.

Second, continuing educators must understand more clearly the power they already have and must use it more effectively. The exer-

---

[1]George Bonham, "The Federal Stake in a Learning Society. An Interview with Ernest L. Boyer," *Change* 10, no. 5 (May 1978), p. 25.

[2]Fred M. Hechinger, "Colleges Told Survival Means Some Cutbacks," *The New York Times*, Tuesday, April 17, 1979, p. C4.

[3]*The New York Times*, op. cit.

cise of power, the ability to control and to make decisions within academic institutions, will become increasingly obtrusive as the struggle for survival becomes more intense. It is critical that continuing educators become more knowledgeable about their institutions, with particular emphasis on locating the centers of power and influencing them.

Third, continuing educators must establish more effective communication with other parts of the university. The best way to do this is through quality programming. Quality program design must be seen within the total context, which includes program objectives linked to learner characteristics and delivery modes linked to environmental considerations. Only through this legitimate method of programming, which means consulting faculty about content and design, can those outside continuing education understand that excellence is just as crucial in meeting the needs of adults as in meeting the needs of traditional students. It is foolhardy educationally *and* politically to make academic policy on the basis of manpower studies and then to simply chase after markets for part-time students.

Fourth, continuing educators must resist the forces that would reduce their work to the level of facilitators and arrangers. Part of this resistance must take the shape of creative inquiry and scholarship that examine issues more fundamental than turf, marketing, and profitability. In addition, there is need for higher levels of professionalism in the field of continuing education. Organizations such as the National University Extension Association, the Adult Education Association of the U.S.A., and the Association for Continuing Higher Education have been instrumental in bringing greater visibility to the field. But numerous barriers remain that make a cohesive sense of professionalism very difficult. If continuing education is to make its greatest impact in tomorrow's world, that development must take place.

To implement these recommendations, further work is needed. Professionals in the academic world must get a clearer sense of the myths and realities of the audience so many see as its glorious future. We now accept that the character of higher education populations is changing and that there is rapid growth of continuing education; we now accept that there is a dramatic increase in numbers of nontraditional students, often referred to as the new majority. Educational planning and decision making are being based on understanding (and misunderstanding) these trends; thus a fuller articulation of what is myth and what is the reality of the "new majority" is important.

There is still misunderstanding and disagreement as to who the new majority of adult learners are, and, in many instances, of what happened to the "old majority." Some do not know, for example, that a great many of the young people formerly numbered among the old majority are no longer able to continue as full-time students because of increased costs of full-time higher education and other economic and social factors; they have become part timers, often without modifying their original educational goals. The notion that the new majority can rescue postsecondary education is misinformed at best and naive at worst. A misunderstanding of trends, data, and related information are here called myths, and they must be recognized as such if continuing education is to realize the potential of a glorious future.

Myth No. One: *The new majority can be defined explicity.*

Reality: The data we work with are often misleading and give too little information about a large, diverse group. A phenomenon like the increased number of part-time students is assumed, and we move from there to other generalizations without examining the characteristics of the individuals that compose the group. As a result, continuing educators address only a small segment of their potential market.

Myth No. Two: *Continuing education programs are designed to meet the needs of a target clientele group.*

Reality: Most continuing education programs are a response to economic stringency and are designed to make a return or at least be self-supporting. Needs assessments are too often manpower surveys and supply-and-demand studies. Most programs do little more than extrapolate from perceived trends and milk them until the next trend emerges.

Myth No. Three: *The new majority requires entirely new kinds of educational programming.*

Reality: Facts indicate that most of the programs provided for the new majority are simply extensions of already existing programming.

Myth No. Four: *The new majority wants something different from traditional educational programming*

Reality: Most of the courses chosen by the new majority relate to occupation and occupational mobility—for example, to improve job performance, to enhance promotional opportunities, or to get a new job. There is much resistance to innovative and experimental programs, and many students say, "Don't experiment on us! We want what got you to where you are."

Myth No. Five: *Continuing education has become the "open sesame" to educational opportunities for entirely new kinds of persons.*

Reality: Those participating in continuing education tend to look like those who have always been part of the educational stream. Put another way, the more education people have, the more they want; the less education people have, the less likely they are to get into continuing education, or into education of any kind.

Myth No. Six: *The new majority are seeking degrees of one kind or another.*

Reality: Growth appears to be in noncredit areas, and those enrolling in degree courses and programs are declining. Certification, or the "union card," may still be important, but it is increasingly something other than the college degree. To emphasize degree programs to the exclusion of other kinds of programming is to misunderstand a very significant trend.

Myth No. Seven: *Course programming for the new majority represents a creative new dimension in instructional delivery systems.*

Reality: There has been no instructional revolution of any great magnitude. Most continuing education takes place in classrooms with traditional lecture-style presentation. For the instructional technology that does exist, attention should be put on producing more effective software or less expensive hardware. Community colleges claim to be on the cutting edge of whatever changes are taking place.

Myth No. Eight: *Genuine interest in the new majority is limited to continuing education within postsecondary institutions.*

Reality: Schools of business, engineering, law, social work, medicine, nursing, and the arts and sciences offer programs for adults they consider to be their constituencies. Adults are not a "new" discovery, and though income considerations are important, the fundamental motivation for the programs is service through quality programs.

These myths pervade much of the continuing education scene today. What is sorely needed is research capable of securing data that will enable institutions to provide continuing education more intelligently.

These issues reveal that continuing education cannot be viewed *in vacuo*. Its future can be significant if educators develop a clear sense of connection with the rest of education. Those who assume leadership responsibilities in continuing education must define what continuing education is and how it fits into the total educational scheme. The separatist demands of some continuing educators militate against the total institution understanding and accepting responsibility for continuing education. As long as continuing education is seen as just for adult educators, it will remain marginal and receive inadequate institutional support. Continuing educators must encourage broad based discussion about the role of higher education in a changing society, and their professional organizations must provide assistance as they seek to make greater impact. The professional organizations must make possible linkages with other centers of power (government, business and industry, professional associations, accrediting agencies), must make possible professional development, and must nourish the idealism on which continuing education is based.

DISCUSSION

"I have had the impression throughout this symposium," *Mort Gordon* says, "that some quite sensible things have been said in and about each of the papers, and about other matters, too."

"Yes," agrees *Bill Griffith*, "but the tendency is always for the urgent to crowd the important out—not enough time to spend on 'why' because it is easier to talk about 'how.'"

"And not even 'how,'" *Lillian Hohmann* points out. "We talked initially about trying to develop some policy points—the 'what should be'—but I don't think, except for some of the things John Ervin has said, that we moved much beyond what 'is.' Our constant harping on the chaos of continuing education bothered me. It really isn't that much more chaotic than anything else in society."

"The context in which all this takes place," *John Ervin* says, "is influenced by the fact that the self-support mandate makes continuing education a 'business' in the economic sense of the term. The 'how' becomes a quick assembling of conferences, institutes, and so forth, and the 'who' becomes a collection of entrepreneurial hustlers."

"In my view," *Bob Kost* says, "continuing education *should be* self-supporting and, indeed, a profit center for campus institutions. It seems to me that we've described and redescribed the problems and the causes of the problems in continuing education. Let's quit rehashing them and dedicate our energies to the development of solutions. It's time for campus institutions to quit being reactive and start being proactive in their environments!"

"I certainly agree," *George Robertson* responds. "In an affluent society one can argue that education services should be able to command a share of each individual's discretionary income, without assistance from the state or anywhere else. There's some irony in the fact that many colleges are rapidly expanding their offerings in continuing education in order to generate income, while professionals in adult education press for financial support for continuing education for part-time adult students. Before we call for increased federal or state assistance, it might be sensible to insist that each institution clarify the part that continuing education plays in its mission."

"We've bandied the word *mission* about pretty thoroughly,"' *Phil Frandson* says. "And both Milt and John have peered bravely into the indistinct future. But we haven't looked much at what is being said by those who study research on institutions—all institutions, not just educational ones. They speak loudly about what has happened in society in the last ten years. One of the things that has happened is that there has been a reassessment of the mission of all those institutions, and virtually all of them have elevated the role of education in the achievement of their goals, particularly those organizations and institutions that have not seen education as an important way of achieving those goals in the past. Now they are saying that the only way to really sustain themselves and advance in the long term is to elevate the education of their constituencies, and to proselytize others, to achieve their goals. They now virtually say, 'You aren't going to get to heaven without educating your constituencies.'"

"And if we look just at educational institutions," *Roz Loring* says, "we can almost no longer speak of fields of academic study as we used to. There's beginning to be a blend of academic disciplines and traditions; and, in the process, faculty members are working more closely together in team efforts to develop curricula from which new fields have emerged. To hitchhike on your statement suggesting that institutions are creatures of the society in which they exist, they are also creatures of what is now known. And we know a little more now than we did twenty-four or thirty years ago. We in continuing education have been priding ourselves on our invention of interdisciplinary programs in response to the needs of adults. I don't think we can make use of that any longer. I think lots of other people are more interdisciplinary than we are in their thinking and in their own working out of their major tasks or functions."

"I don't want to make a pun on the word *discipline*," *Milt Stern* says, "but the fact is that there's an absence of what I'd call discipline in the university today that makes much of what we think ought to happen very difficult. The remark was made recently that the federal government has no coordinated policy on higher education. Neither does higher education have a coordinated policy on higher education! Sometimes people say, 'Well, this is the best of all possible worlds because we have variety.' We have variety, all right, but we lack discipline, and that's going to make it very difficult to get from where we are to where we'd like to be."

"What we've been doing and what we're doing now," *Grover Andrews* concludes, "is trying to look at what is and trying to look at the future. And we want what should be to be what is best. When I think about the status of adult educators, I'm reminded of the large number of small fundamentalist religious denominations in this country (and some of them are not so small). They have no educational requirements whatsoever for their ministers. Anyone who feels the call can get up and do his thing, so to speak. And we wonder why they stay as they are. The reason they stay as they are is that the light of education, in whatever form, is not brought to them!

"As I view adult education, I see a growing necessity for more specific training in the field. I think we need more specific training so that there can be more theoretical research and teaching; and I think we need more specific training for practitioners in the field."

"Just one example," *Mort Gordon* nods. "There must be more than 500,000 people teaching adults all kinds of courses in all kinds of settings, and I'm sure that no more than a few percent know anything at all about adults or about teaching adults aside from the fact that that's what they're doing."

"It seems possible," *George Robertson* agrees, "that the central continuing or adult education department in the future will be largely preoccupied with the training of staff from other departments and with evaluation of programs offered in other departments."

The field has failed itself. . . .

Lillian Hohmann nods. "The field has failed itself in the most profound way by not attempting to professionalize those who engage in adult education—especially those in association work—with the result that much of continuing education offered to professionals and paraprofessionals (our largest work force sector) is impoverished. This is a significant failure. Whence cometh the leadership within our ranks? The promoters, the marketers, are already there, selling their trick bags to the unspoiled adult educators who hope fervently that each new 'tip' will revolutionize their program!"

"The thinkers," *Mort Gordon* responds, "have yielded to the doers. Everyone has lots of graphs and charts about how to plan programs, but no one proposes a humanistic outlook. Where are the well-educated adult educators? Why should we have a profession with uneducated leadership? If the quality of our leadership declines over the low state it is in now, the difficulties will mount!"

Bob Kost has been trying to get a word in. "Milt Stern observes in his paper that perhaps by 1990 a unified policy on continuing education may be developed by the university leadership of the United States. What leadership? Where is it? Does he presume to suggest that some day, when perhaps the universities decide to enter the continuing education field in a substantive way, competitive providers will relinquish the market to them? I seriously doubt it!"

"A national policy on continuing education is not soon enough. We all agree on that," *Lillian Hohmann* says. "Hopefully, academic providers and funding providers (government) will be able to apply their artistry, as well as their knowledge, to work out relationships and develop comprehensive responses to the continuing education needs of citizens. But, like you, I'm somewhat pessimistic that there are enough professionals with the wisdom and vision to move beyond turf, and with the administrative acumen to make policy *and* viable relationships (programs) work. The issue of turf or policy among providers has become, for some professionals, a major concern to the exclusion of the central issue of continuing education for adults. Whatever lifelong learning is about has been all but forgotten as a missionary principle, and instead the zeal attends the procurement of better mailing lists and more glamorous settings!"

"The student," *Bob Kost* emphasizes, "rather than the institution or the discipline or just plain money should be the central concern of continuing education! In my view this is critical, and there can be no compromise! If we can't shift the focus in this area, continuing education will continue to wander aimlessly down the path of illegitimate education!"

"And that has to do with 'Who should do what for whom?'" *Lillian Hohmann* points out. "If adult students are merely consumers, then they can purchase a ride ticket at any booth. If they are lifelong learners, then an organized, well-defined access point to a vast resource will be more supportive of the student's needs."

"It goes without saying," *George Robertson* adds, "that the poor and certain minority groups (including women, the elderly, and the handicapped) may find themselves outside the rationale of self-support and individual decision in an affluent society that we were proposing earlier. But much of the expense of education for minorities lies not in the cost of instruction, but in special services—remedial instruction, special counseling, child care, or transportation. These ought to be funded as desirable social services, separate from 'continuing education' costs. And, incidentally, governments probably finance vocational education rather than other kinds of education because vocational education still contributes in a fairly obvious way to upward mobility, as well as to the productivity of society!"

"No matter how hard we try to get away from it, we always come back to money," *John Ervin* says. "And my view is that strategies for developing an adequate funding base for continuing education must give recognition to the fact that in today's world there isn't enough money for institutions functioning at levels to which many of these institutions have become accustomed! The impact of inflation means that costs are rising much faster than the production of real income, just when disenchantment with education as it is has resulted in a spirit of nonsupport for public, private, precollegiate, and collegiate institutions. A major task is to help institutions enlarge their vision to include programming for continuing education constituencies and to do that without demanding extra financial contribution from the continuing education unit. Perhaps—just perhaps—the time is right for that kind of campaign!"

There are opportunities for those with initiative. . . .

"There are opportunities for those who have the initiative to seek them," *Bob Kost* insists. "Empty facilities can be rented, proposals for research ventures can be made, and campus institutions can aggressively pursue proposals for replacing or supplementing the resources of industry and government. For example, I keep pointing out that community colleges are far more responsive than the university system to the continuing education needs of society. They are a most substantial source for local adult education in the United States and very significant providers for both government and industry. In the 1980s they will increase their position in the continuing education field!"

"Yet we are still waiting," *Bill Griffith* says, "for evidence to refute the claim that the open door is really a revolving door. Special treatment by short-sighted state legislatures has made it possible for community colleges to draw the adult education programs out of many public school districts with questionable benefits to society. How much longer community colleges can retain the status of favored provider remains to be seen. Good data are needed to demonstrate how well each providing institution is doing the job. Then rational choices could be made concerning how public funds might best be invested."

"Whatever faults there are within the various systems," *Lillian Hohmann* says, "we would probably agree that American industry and American higher education stand side by side in claiming credit for the achievements of this nation! If so, then our criticism should be tempered with a strong dose of introspection. There is a significant gulf in value systems between 'learn-for-profit' and 'learn-for-learning.' Collaboration that would lead to the kind of innovation in continuing education programming that would ultimately contribute to the quality of work life is aborted by divisions between industry and professional associations and academia. Industry talks about continuing education as a process but tends to act toward providers as though it were buying a product—a product with very well defined 'specs.' And there's a similar attitude, I guess, in some professional associations."

"The associations *should* deal with improving the what is," *Mort Gordon* suggests, "but shouldn't they also deal with what the profession ought to be? And here continuing education has a golden and missed opportunity. Sooner or later we will have a national health plan. Why not include a consumer education package as part of the plan? That may do more to keep prices down than anything presently contemplated."

"As providers of continuing education, associations are the sleeping giants in the field," *Bob Kost* agrees. "Members will increasingly turn to their associations for leadership in meeting constituent educational needs, and during the 1980s associations will become increasingly active providers. It's doubtful, however, that Ms. Hohmann's plea for a cooperative interface with academia will be heeded, and as a result, quite like industry, internal association staffs will grow to respond to the continuing education needs of their members."

"There's a kind of self-righteousness among university adult educators in the midst of a cheerful entrepreneurial exterior," *Lillian* points out, "that occasionally prevents them from seeing other legitimate providers and hence from developing long-term productive relationships with sweeter fiscal situations for each. If education is not a primary role for community and professional groups, what is? Perhaps the question is clearer if asked in reverse. If citizen and professional growth are not primary purposes of adult education, what is? The logical extension of those questions is that education, industry, professional groups, and community groups all serve important needs and purposes of each other, and cooperation, therefore, provides a basis for mutual support to learners as well as a force for public policy change."

Follow the lead of professional groups . . .

"When adult educators come to realize that they must use the political and regulatory machinery at state, regional, and national levels," *Bill Griffith* says, "they will begin to follow the lead of professional groups that have skillfully manipulated accreditation, licensing, relicensing, and legislation to advance the best interests of their professions. Nothing is gained and much is being lost by adult educators who do not invest the time to learn about the potential value of accrediting and other regulatory bodies to the advancement of adult education programming."

"Unfortunately," *Lillian Hohmann* says, "before the university can dress itself up in organizational adult clothes for the continuing education function, it must address the problem of entrepreneurialism among departments and within its own faculty.

"If, as Milt Stern says, faculty values transcend money and power, it certainly isn't conspicuous to outsiders. The marginality of the continuing education function may have been desirable historically, and it may be the only possible status of the future, despite the desire of both central university and continuing education administrations, if a reasonable and acceptable solution to entrepreneurialism is not found."

"It's time to bring integrity to all sources of continuing education and weed out pretenders in the field," *Bob Kost* suggests. "Consistent evaluation from a single national agency source would seem to be the most productive approach for achieving this. But, in any case, the continuing education needs of various segments of society will increasingly be filled by a variety of providers, including four-year institutions, community colleges, and private for-profit and nontraditional sources. So it seems likely that unless there's a major change in direction that I can't foresee, the university system will play a lesser role in continuing education in the 1980s."

"I can't agree with you on your final statement," *Roz Loring* says, "but I guess agreement wasn't really one of the things I thought would come out of the symposium. However, what I do think has come out of the symposium—and one of the major benefits to me —has been the opportunity to get, at this moment in time, some statements about issues of change, some suggestions about how we're going to manage that change, and some sense of where the alternatives are."

"And what I think has come out of the symposium," *George Robertson* says, "is the inescapable conclusion that adult educators must accept the penalty of their past success! No institution can now afford to neglect continuing education—and we ought to be pleased that this is so. The problem is familiar to most revolutionaries: Now that all the middle-of-the-road squares have decided we were right, how do we make sure *they* don't steal *our* revolution?"

FINAL COMMENTARY

Power in continuing education is in the hands of the entrepreneur. In the absence of national accreditation, without the internal checks and balances of a profession, and in the presence of an expanding market, opportunity abounds for the aggressive profiteer and for the innovative idealist alike. *Conflict* is perhaps too strong a word for the competition that characterizes the overt entrepreneurial efforts to attract the middle-class vocation- and profession-oriented dollar. But conflict is not too strong a word for the quieter, deeper struggle to define the field, to control the robber barons, and to establish the learning society.

Not all providers of continuing education will survive and prosper. Some worthy but inept will die; many unworthy but adept will flourish. But need and opportunity will increase, and the future has room for more, much more, continuing education. Society's demand for an informed, responsible citizenry constitutes an insatiable constituency for continuing education.

Yet, operationally, the questions posed in the symposium remain the critical issues: Who should provide what for whom? How should continuing education be evaluated, financed, managed, and staffed? And where do we go from here? The fact that a solid consensus has not emerged from the various positions on these questions underscores the complexity of the concerns and the difficulties of the decisions. But continuing education has become too important to be left to chance: the dialogue will continue, and decisions will be reached!